W9-DCC-660

ONE NAKED INDIVIDUAL

ONE NAKED INDIVIDUAL

My Fifty Years in the Theatre

Cheryl Crawford

The Bobbs-Merrill Company, Inc.

INDIANAPOLIS / NEW YORK

Excerpts from letters of Thornton Wilder. Copyright © 1977 by Union Trust Company, New Haven, Conn., Executor of the will of Thornton Wilder.

Excerpts from *Camino Real* by Tennessee Williams. Copyright 1948, 1953 by Tennessee Williams. Reprinted by permission of New Directions Publishing Corporation.

Excerpt from the poem "That Nature Is a Heraclitean Fire and of the Comfort of the Resurrection" from *Poems of Gerard Manley Hopkins*, Fourth Edition, edited by W. H. Gardiner and N. H. MacKenzie, Oxford University Press.

ISBN 0–672–52185–7
Library of Congress Catalog Card Number: 76–44666

Designed by Jacques Chazaud
Manufactured in the United States of America

First printing

To the authors whose works I produced.
To the actors who performed in them.
To those of the audience who enjoyed them.

Contents

Acknowledgments

Many people have helped me with this chronicle: Mary Martin, Agnes de Mille, S. J. Perelman, Sono Osato, Paul Bigelow, Paula Laurence, Bea Lawrence, H. William Fitelson, Ruth Norman, Michael Wager, Clinton Wilder, and Will Geer. I'm very grateful to Tennessee Williams, Isabel Wilder, George Voskovec, Robert Lewis, Elliot Norton, Lee Strasberg, Penelope Gilliatt, John Martin, Lotte Lenya, Laurence Olivier and Donald Gallup, Literary Executor for Thornton Wilder, for permission to use material that belongs to them. And I appreciate the generous assistance of Paul Myers, Curator of the Theatre Collection of the New York Public Library at Lincoln Center; the help of my brilliant editor, Stefanie Tashjian-Woodbridge; and the patience and nimble fingers of Millie Becerra and Lynne Spaulding, who typed the manuscript.

Author's Note

This book takes its title from one of my childhood experiences. In the process of skipping a grade in elementary school, I missed learning the Pledge of Allegiance. I did not want to show my ignorance, so for several weeks I rose with the rest of the children, raised my right hand and repeated what I thought they were saying: "I pledge allegiance to the flag of the United States of America and to the republic for which it stands, one naked individual, with liberty and justice for all."

Many years later, after I had become an independent producer, I found that the mistaken phrase kept running through my mind. "One naked individual" perfectly describes my sense of myself in the face of the formidable world in which I led my life: out on the barricades I was finite and vulnerable, and I had only myself to depend on. Alone against the world, one instinctively grabs for armor. What I discovered was that the reality of being one naked individual was, when I accepted it, a superior armor.

This is the story of my life as a producer. My private life is mentioned only in passing because that is how it was lived. The theatre has been my life.

I have found that writing an autobiography is like walking a tightrope: balance is the name of the game. Autobiographers must weigh the pros and cons of themselves. I have tried not to throw myself too many bouquets for success or to heap too many ashes on my head for failure.

Actually, I wanted to write about more than myself—for example, to tell the story of the Actors Studio as I see it, not just my role in it. Clustering the stories of musicals offered the chance to say something about musicals in themselves. So, instead of organizing my experiences with productions in the heel-toe order of their occurrence, I have divided some of them into separate topical chapters. The result is not one of those books that makes drama out of the fact that someone does a number of things simultaneously. True, at any one time I was engaged in several projects in different stages of development: one play might be touring, another about to open, while I was tracking down new properties and raising money. This is clear between the lines of the Appendix, in which I have fulfilled my chronological obligations by listing the shows I did and their dates. But as a theme in itself, extended over the length of a book, busyness palls. I wanted to say something more than merely that for the last fifty years I have been busy.

Cheryl Crawford
New York and Bridgehampton
September 1976

"This is the thing that I was born to do:
This is my scene; This Part must I fulfill."
Samuel Daniel

Prologue

It is almost midnight. The theatre is cold and drafty. The harsh, unshaded two-thousand-watt bulb dangling over the center of the bare stage is killing my eyes. But to have decent rehearsal lighting a producer must hire a union crew even though there is nothing for them to do.

I, the producer in question, have been staring at that stage since twelve this morning. My day began at nine A.M., when I looked over bills with my general manager to be sure we were not exceeding the budget. Then I had a session with my press agent to decide on the ads, posters and marquee billing. At noon this final run-through began. Lights and sets come in tomorrow morning at eight.

The hour off for dinner was devoted to a production meeting. Gulping coffee and chewing dry sandwiches, we rehashed the afternoon's rehearsal. Now the aisles are littered with sandwich papers. The briny smell of half-eaten pickles and the stink of cigarette butts sloshing in paper coffee cups makes me nauseated. Grubby, it is all so grubby. Who says the theatre is glamorous? I want to go home, I want to go to sleep.

My colleagues in argument and exhaustion, the director, author and choreographer, are sprawled among the orchestra seats. We sit separately so that we will not influence one another's reactions. The isolation emphasizes my responsibility. I chose this show: will an audience see what I see in it? Will audiences come at all?

Above, the composer-lyricist is lying on the floor of a box trying to take a nap. Suddenly, his haggard face appears over the railing. "The goddamned piano is lousy," he yells down at me. "How can you expect my music to sound like anything? You trying to save money?"

"Yes, I am," I yell back. "But if you pound any piano that loud all day you get tin."

"So, crucify me!" he screeches. His black head disappears behind the rail. Did I see a blond head go down beside it? One of the singers? Oh well, anything to relieve tension.

The director lopes to the back of the theatre, followed by the author. They proceed to argue *sotto voce.* I feel a dispute coming on. And guess who will be asked to take sides. But I'm caught between the two of them: the scene was too long, true—but it was also too slow. How to mediate? They're both nervous and exhausted. And eight A.M. is getting closer by the minute.

On stage the choreographer is changing some steps with her dancers. Their faces are pale and drawn in the ghostly light; their tights have long runs and smudges from the dirty floor. It's hard to believe that these boys and girls will look radiant and glamorous in a few days.

The director comes running down the aisle. "Take ten! Take ten!" he shouts. "Goddamn! Where's the stage manager?"

Someone on stage calls back, "Sorry! He's got the trots."

"Okay, okay, everyone sit for a few minutes. Cheryl, we've got to make a cut in that scene. It's not working."

The author pounds down behind him. "No more cuts! No more cuts! I've made too many already."

The moment of truth.

"Listen," I say, "everyone is worn out. A few days ago the scene went very well. I think we should leave it alone and see how it works when the actors are fresh. Besides, it's twelve o'clock. The actors can't work any more—union rules."

The director shakes his head. "I won't stop now. We're not

through. For Chrissakes, Belasco kept his actors locked in the theatre for days. They slept in the aisles. *He* didn't stop until he was finished. You don't get art by a time clock, Cheryl. You know that."

"It was Belasco's methods that made Actors Equity rule a time limit," I snap. "You won't get any more out of these people. They're dead on their feet."

"One more hour, just one more. Be a sport."

A sport? Or a tyrant?

"All right, I'll pay for it if they are willing. You ask them."

They're willing. They nearly always are. They are as desperate to be perfect as the director is. Watching them pull their tired bodies to their feet and limber up, I rise stiffly and walk around, trying to get warm. I'm coming down with a humdinger of a cold. I want to go home, I want to go to sleep. I remember the story a well-known foreign actress told me about her wedding night. Married at a certain age to a wild Russian actor, she lay in bed in a pink chiffon nightgown waiting for her new husband to leave the bathroom. Finally the door opened. Singing loudly, he jumped out naked and began dancing crazily about the room.

"Oh, God," she said to herself, watching him gyrate. "Vot I am doing here?"

Yes, I think, Vot I am doing here?

Hugging myself to keep warm, I turn to the stage. The stage manager shouts hoarsely, "Places, please. Start from the top of the next number."

The dancers take their positions facing each other. Between them the star marches forward. As her small, lithe figure moves swiftly down front, her weary face bursts into a brilliant smile. Perhaps only a star can call on so much adrenalin. The piano begins a fast one-two beat. Gershwin said a musical marches on its one-twos. As the dancers move in quick kaleidoscopic patterns, the star begins to belt out her song. It's sexy, it's stirring. How can it move me? I must have heard it a thousand times. But suddenly the chill is off. Suddenly I'm warm again. The show is going to work!

I know vot I am doing here.

So goes a day in the life of a producer. But what in the name of Shakespeare is a producer? People know that a playwright writes a play, an actor acts it, a director directs it. But a producer, they think, well, he (for they think producers must be male) . . . produces. Upon learning my profession people invariably give me a blank look. "Oh," they say. And then, "What exactly do you *do?*"

Here is a simple answer: I find a good play or musical, I find the money required to give it the best physical form on a stage, I find the people to give it life, I find a theatre and I try to fill it.

But that answer is really too simple. Sometimes I think a producer is a person who is absolutely unable to do anything else, who has a strong interest in all the arts but the talent for none of them and enough business sense to know that sometimes you must dare to go to the edge of disaster to achieve what you desire. A producer is definitely a gambler. For the education of a theatre producer, the sky is the limit, which is what makes the profession so endlessly exciting, even though you never learn all it would be helpful to know. Since the job is to bring a script and a physical production together, literature, poetry, plot construction, music (both classical and popular), architecture, painting, color, form, the ability to read blueprints of sets, history, economics, psychology (normal and abnormal), psychiatry, and even anthropology— to help us understand the audience—are all involved. Everything human and inhuman is grist. And all-important is the ability to extract money from investors. This is the least attractive part of being a producer, at least for me. I am uncomfortable at "hard sells."

Theatrical producers last longer if they lack a good memory. The disasters, blow-ups, emergencies and erroneous judgments should pass through them like a dose of salts if they are to continue. (On the other hand, one producer cut his wrists gently after a few failures, was hospitalized and succeeded in worrying a playwright enough that the playwright brought a new play to his bedside. And it was a hit.) To paraphrase Harry Truman, if you can't stand the heat, get out of the theatre. Some producers, after a failure or two, fade away from Broadway and Sardi's to continue life more calmly in parts unknown. They may be the lucky ones.

Perhaps because most of my memories have dribbled back into my subconscious, I have been able to devote fifty years to the theatre. I have produced dozens of plays and musicals independently, and have had the good fortune to be connected with many of the major theatrical enterprises of my time: the Theatre Guild, the Group Theatre, the American National Theatre and Academy, the American Repertory Theatre and the Actors Studio.

Ideally, my business or profession or art—and it is all of these—is to make it possible for people to see themselves as they are, as they wish to be, as they might be. Some playwrights have disclosed truths about human nature so profound that social scientists since Freud have used their creations to identify such classic types as Oedipus, Faust and Hamlet. To me, the function of the theatre is to clarify and influence life. The theatre is one of the oldest educational forms. Because it appeals to people largely through their emotions, it is one of the most effective. It beguiles audiences into fresh thoughts and perceptions while they laugh and cry.

It all begins with the play one chooses to do. In Herman Melville's *Mardi*, there is a rather simple test for choosing a play (and also for judging the final production).

"Tingling is the test," said Babbalanya. "Yoomy, did you tingle when that song was composing?"

"All over, Babbalanya."

Perhaps the story of my fifty years in the theatre will give the best answer to the question of what a producer does. I don't think I ever completely attained the excellence I sought, but what follows is how I tried. I'm still trying.

Childhood

How does a girl from a nice, normal Midwestern family become a Broadway producer? I'm still wondering.

Perhaps my destiny was cast when my grandmother took me to my first play, *Uncle Tom's Cabin.* After flying off to heaven on perfectly perceptible wires, Little Eva walked out into the audience hawking pictures of herself. That was the first time I criticized a performance. I stood in my seat and cried out, "Grandma, she can't do that! She's dead!" Even then I knew that the illusion must not be broken.

Akron, Ohio, where I was born and raised, had a professional stock company and traveling shows, and I got to see a lot of theatre. Seventy years ago Akron was a town of about forty thousand people, and life there was quiet and safe. We lived on a short street lined with large maple and elm trees and solid, comfortable houses. At dusk each day a man would come on his bicycle to light the gas street lamps. I made friends with him and with the truck gardener, whose visits fed my hunger for adventure. Each week in summer he arrived with a cart loaded with potatoes, corn and all the garden vegetables. I would manage to be sitting on the curb in my favorite outfit, a blue Buster Brown suit, usually eating homemade bread covered with brown sugar. The truck gardener would lift me to the high seat of the wagon and put the horse's reins in my hand while he went off to deliver supplies. What a dream of freedom! I shouted "Giddap!" shook the reins and dashed off—to the desert, to the sea, anywhere away. The stolid old horse was accustomed to standing unattended; he wouldn't have moved at any command but that of his master. But he took me everywhere. Somehow I always wanted life to be larger, more spacious, more adventurous.

I remember, too, the older girl next door, plump, with hair the color of sand, who played the tunes of the day on the piano. Singing along with her I began to learn popular American music, to "collect" songs. It became a hobby of mine, and today I can sing hundreds of them.

Storytelling was a favorite pastime then. Night after night a group of children gathered on our large porch to listen to me concoct fables. "A prince, a tin can, a pony, a rotten apple and our math teacher, Cheryl," they'd say, and instantly I would have to fashion a coherent narrative using all of these disconnected things. It challenged me to be inventive. I enjoyed it, and apparently my listeners did too. Years later, my mother told me some of the children's parents would slip into the porch swings to hear how I would manage to put everything together.

My ability to tell stories profited, I'm convinced, from my reading. I was one of those children who read voraciously, continuously, munching all the while—eyes glued to the page—on apples or cookies. I consumed all the usual children's classics and made my way through all of Scott and Dickens to two volumes of Elizabeth Barrett's and Robert Browning's love letters. These started me on poetry, which soon became a passion. I memorized dozens of poems, including many from a set of gold-stamped leather volumes containing the complete works of Keats, Shelley and Elizabeth Barrett, given to me as a birthday present by an old man of twenty-five who came to live on our street with his bride. Those books are still on my shelves, along with the seven or eight hundred more books of poetry I have collected since. I cannot explain my passion for poetry. It is simply one of the cornerstones of my life.

I was the eldest of four children and the only girl. My brother

Alden was a year and a half younger than I; the next brother, Newell, was a year and a half younger than he. Bobby, the third brother, came by happy accident when I was thirteen. He was my favorite because he became my baby, too. And he loved to listen to my tall tales. He was, and still is, like a sunflower, open, direct, always turned to the sun.

I had to do everything Alden and Newell did, and I had to do it better. I had to climb trees higher and bicycle faster around the block, which left me red-faced and panting on the grass. We even fought with three pairs of small boxing gloves in the attic, I taking on both of them until Alden bloodied my nose.

We had dogs, cats, chickens and a half-horse brought from Texas, which we ingeniously named Tex. The day he threw me, I knew I had to mount again because my brothers were watching, sibilantly whispering "chicken, chicken" as I hesitated. It wasn't easy trying to keep one step ahead of two active boys.

The three of us were very close and formed a strong phalanx in the neighborhood gang. In a large horse barn adjoining our property there was an abandoned red velvet chair, which we used as a throne. My condition for joining the play was that I would be the king or queen and sit in the throne chair and rule. Alden and Newell would kidnap the neighborhood children we didn't like and bring them before the throne, where I would decide their punishment. It usually consisted of throwing them down the hay chute into the horses' trough. But sometimes I would sentence them to be shut into an empty chicken coop, where they had to make corn tassel cigarettes for our gang to smoke.

My father, Robert Kingsley Crawford, was six feet tall, well built and handsome. His eyes were a brilliant blue I shall never forget. "King," he was called, and it was a most appropriate name. He had a quick, fiery temper, and when he lost it, those blue eyes blazed; his occasional rages scared me. He came from a farm family in Illinois which had strong religious ideas, and Father became the superintendent of our Congregational Church, where he taught a large young men's Bible class with great success. The atmosphere at our house was puritanical; there was always grace before meals and a constant admonishment to clean our plates.

Father built up his own company, Crawford Real Estate, and the evangelical style he developed in church proved very persuasive in selling lots. He became faintly rich.

Mother, Luella Elizabeth, called Lou, was five feet one and very feminine. Women were particularly proud of having tiny feet then, and Mother's were size three, which meant that she could buy sample shoes for half price; she assembled a large collection. Gentle and sentimental as she was, she was perky enough to stand up to my father when he got too kingly. "King!" she would say. "Calm down!" He calmed down.

But the one I loved most was Grandma, my maternal grandmother, Lavinia Lynn Parker, who lived with us as the unpaid babysitter. She had an ample figure and a character to match. Almost every night she rocked me to sleep, my head against her soft, warm breasts as she sang. She, too, added to my collection of songs: "Listen to the Mocking Bird," "Juanita," "The Baboon Married the Monkey's Sister." I've never discovered a pill so pleasantly sleep-producing as Grandma's rocking and singing.

Although Grandma came from Kentucky and was Southern, she had married Alden Parker, a Yankee from Ashburnham, Massachusetts, whose family had lived in New England before the Revolution. When she wasn't singing me to sleep with Civil War songs, she would tell me about her father, who had been a scout under the Lew Wallace who wrote *Ben Hur*. I still have a newspaper cutting announcing that my great-grandfather had been disinherited for joining the North. Grandma's stories about him thrilled me. He had been on guard duty at Ford's Theatre the night Lincoln was shot and had gone with the posse that searched for Booth. She was very proud that she had shaken Lincoln's hand when he passed through the town. Whenever she washed my hands, which were usually dirty, she would say, after the dirt was scrubbed off, "Now you can shake the hand that shook the hand of Lincoln." In the process I developed great feeling for Lincoln. A rare picture of him hangs in my bedroom, his face alert and lively on the left side, profoundly sad on the other. And I can say with truth that you can shake the hand that shook the hand that shook the hand of Lincoln.

To my mother's mortification, Grandma also insisted that a distant ancestor from Carolina had been a Cherokee Indian. This may have been one of her tall tales, although she and my brother Newell had strongly marked Indian profiles. I was greatly influenced by this ancestral claim and cultivated a stern, rocklike expression. It still assists me when I play poker, and it has also flummoxed some theatrical agents into believing I would not pay what they asked for their clients.

Grandma was remarkable in an unremarkable way. Stuck in a restricted life, she was able to enjoy simple things. She liked to bake bread, which was set to rise over the register in the living room, and on her baking days, a pleasant smell of dough permeated the house. And she kept an enormous cookie jar full, which was not easy to do with three continually hungry children. She also stocked candy, peppermints, rock candy and black balls that changed color as you sucked, keeping them in her dresser drawers, which she would lock to prevent us from gorging ourselves. We always located the key. She loved the movies, too, especially *The Million Dollar Mystery* and *The Perils of Pauline*. We never missed an episode, even though Father disapproved.

Grandma often complained that she needed a tonic, Lydia Pinkham's or something similar, which she kept in her closet; she had a tot before meals. I tried some one day and felt quite giddy. Now I realize it must have had a fair percentage of alcohol. Once, after the customary Sunday chicken dinner, Father put a record of Galli Curci on the new phonograph in the parlor. Grandma found it so irresistible that she rose, lifted her skirts a bit and began to dance. Father was horrified. Such activity on a Sunday! Grandma retreated to her room for the rest of the day. Retreat in the face of an argument was a characteristic I shared with my grandmother. It took me many years of self-discipline to stand up to unpleasant confrontations.

Alas, there were many confrontations over the years, since my spirits didn't conform to the conventions of virtue. For instance, I smoked and I drank. When Father was in his fifties, he was subject to canker sores in his mouth, which his doctor thought might be helped by cigar smoking. With this excuse, Father was able to enjoy cigars. So was I, graduating from corn tassel cigarettes. If I had tried to buy cigarettes—the smart brand of the day was Violet Murads—any neighborhood storekeeper would have told my parents. So Father's cigars were convenient, and they weren't bad. My stomach wouldn't stay down if I smoked a whole one, so I stored the butts under my mattress. But I ran afoul of an unexpected housecleaning. Returning from school for lunch one day, I found that Mother had turned the mattress, uncovering cigar butts *and* the new forbidden Knopf book, *Mademoiselle de Maupin.* A kind veil has been drawn to prevent me from remembering what happened after that.

I didn't reform. Later, after Father's doctor told him that a drink now and then would help his circulation, there was always a bottle of cheap sherry, occasionally something even stronger, hidden in a closet. I sampled that too.

We were constantly in and out of Father's things. What we learned about sex came from a book we found hidden under the dress shirts in his chiffonier. It seemed very dull, and we didn't think it even worth trying.

Would Father notice or not? That was always the question. My school grades were good except for conduct. When I got a red mark for conduct I would cover it with a black pen, hoping Father would not notice. Of course he noticed.

And when he noticed, he punished me with a fairly heavy hand. One of the silly punishments I received was memorizing the names of all the books of the Old Testament. It seems to me more appropriate to consider this, if anything, a reward, not a punishment. But for what it's worth I can still rattle them off if I go fast.

I had my run-ins with Mother, too. She told me that if I ate crusts my hair would turn curly. I didn't want curly hair. So I slipped crusts onto the ledge beneath the table, removing them when the coast was clear. Inevitably, I forgot to remove them one day. Mother opened up the table for a party to find a hidden treasure of stale crusts scattered on the floor. We stopped talking about curly hair after that and I ate crusts.

Considering my misadventures, I had a curious ambition. I

wanted to be a missionary. I never missed Sunday School—I had medals to prove it—in spite of the manner in which my brothers and I were taken there: Father took us at a run so that we would improve our health with "vitalic breathing" (three in, hold four, six out). After a few blocks we were usually dizzy.

I had frequent fantasies of saving the heathen; I would see myself in far-off jungles, mud villages or Arctic wastes, bravely bringing the Word of God to the benighted heathen. My heroism in these daydreams gave me great pleasure.

The desire to be a missionary led me to certain decisions. I would never ask God for anything, but would thank him instead whenever I appreciated his handiwork. This kept me fairly busy, since I liked quite a lot of things. I remember once walking through a neighbor's wood where there was a large black cherry tree. I thanked God as I ate all I could reach.

The other decision was to punish myself when I thought I had been wicked by leaving my comfortable bed and lying on the bathroom floor. This self-penance made me feel quite superior.

Religious fervor or no, I submitted to lessons in worldly accomplishments. I studied violin, piano, voice, guitar playing, swimming, and horseback riding; I also took ballroom dancing with a young couple we called "the Castles of Akron." Irene and Vernon Castle were the very tops then. They taught me both to follow and to lead, and I taught some of the neighborhood children, charging a quarter a lesson. I had a tango teacher as well, a tall Spanish gent with a gold tooth.

And of course there was acting. My parents both enjoyed dramatics. After college Mother had gone to the Emerson School of Elocution in Boston, where she learned elegant pronunciation and the Dalcroze Method of meaningful gestures. All this she used to earn pocket money by teaching Akron youth in search of culture.

Father was a powerful speaker and actor. His favorite Sunday School song was "The Little Brown Church in the Vale." On the second chorus, which began

> Oh come to the church in the wildwood
> Oh come to the church in the vale . . .

the men's voices would sing "Come, come, come" right through the chorus on one low note while the women carried the tune and words. It was quite sexy.

Father and Mother often performed in the amateur theatrical society. They also enjoyed declaiming at the dinner table all the Shakespeare they had learned in college. One of Father's most cherished performances, standing high with suitable gestures, was "The Address to the Gladiators at Capua." He made a frightening Spartacus, but when he reached the part about his childhood, which began

> But I was not always thus,
> A savage child of still more savage men . . .

his voice softened, his lips trembled, and we often sobbed until the speech became so familiar that we could do it ourselves.

I began acting in the third grade, when I played Priscilla Alden, complete with spinning wheel. I begged to play Miles Standish or John Alden instead: the roles were more dramatic and had many more lines.

But my most memorable part came later, on graduation day at high school, when I performed Lady Macbeth's sleep-walking scene. Thanks to Grandma's nightly attention with a hairbrush, my hair grew to my waist. I stood on the podium with flowing hair and a lighted candle and began the monologue. Suddenly my hair caught fire. I could hear Mother scream from the audience. I blew out the candle, grabbed my hair with both hands and put out the fire. Then I continued to the end.

By the time I was sixteen there were boys, half a dozen of them. We danced, sat in their fathers' cars while they talked endlessly about themselves, and ended the evening with a fumbling kiss. The older ones, college age, with frat pins their girls of the moment were required to wear, carried flasks of what must have been straight alcohol; in the dark outside dances we mixed it with any juice available. Later these concoctions were called Screwdrivers, Bloody Marys and such. Thanks to them I had developed a steady head by the time I reached New York's speakeasies.

It was a healthy, happy childhood. The sorrows and angers

were childish ones. There were no grave problems or tragedies. None of us went to a psychoanalyst. We hadn't heard of them. Father, Mother and Grandma were a firm, solid core around which we children revolved safely. We all ate three meals together, went on picnics, spent summers nearby at Turkeyfoot Lake or traveled by car through the Northeast and along the entire West Coast.

But the placid exterior of the street and its inhabitants was deceptive, in some cases only a facade for desperate people. Not everyone was as lucky as we were. Many years later I gave a lecture to a large group of women in a suburb of Pittsburgh. When I had finished, a woman in the audience rose and asked how I could have done four plays by Tennessee Williams, who always wrote about such sick, neurotic people. I answered by telling her briefly about our peaceful little street in Akron and what happened to some of its residents. On the corner was a family who had two children with whom I played. After I left home their father absconded with a considerable amount of money and was never found. Next to them lived a doctor with his wife and two lovely boys of whom I was very fond. The older one married and went West to live. One day he drove back to Akron, parked his car on the high bridge over the Cuyahoga River and jumped off. Just down the street lived another family whose father was found hanging from a pipe in the basement. On our side of the street another family had two sons; the younger one was my bosom friend with whom I talked poetry and listened to music. In early manhood he was placed in an asylum. The piano-playing girl next door with whom I had enjoyed singing popular songs grew up to work for the city and care for her ailing parents, which she did for the rest of her life. She was pleasingly plump with a sweet disposition and should have been a wife and mother. But the gentlemen who called didn't return after they observed what their responsibilities would be. I remember the last time I saw her, rocking on the porch in a squeaky swing in the summer twilight —alone. Are Tennessee's people so far from reality?

Smith College
and Provincetown

Escape! By eighteen I wanted the hell out of the tame Midwest, Akron social life, parental supervision, all of it. In the distance life was larger. How to get out, what to do, where to go, I didn't know. But I knew I wanted more than I could find at home.

Smith College was the answer. In 1921 Smith was the largest women's college in the country with two thousand students. They came from homes all over America, naive, virtuous and dedicated to acquiring a higher education—and a husband. I felt much more comfortable in the New England hills and valleys than I ever had in Ohio.

The first year I was a rotten student. Freedom was too heady to be wasted in study. When my senior counselor called on me, she asked what my major extracurricular activity would be. "The theatre," I answered promptly. I stopped short. I hadn't known I was going to say that. Where was the missionary of yesteryear? "The theatre" was such a ready answer—yet I hadn't thought about the matter at all.

The theatre it was, though, however my subconscious had decided on it. As a freshman I played in various one-acts. My low voice and the ability to ape men, learned from my brothers, always won me male roles.

During my second year I began to perceive that there were

interesting things to be learned, especially in drama, philosophy and English literature. This happy discovery improved my grades over the next three years to Phi Beta Kappa level. Nonetheless, my biggest achievement as a sophomore was playing the lead, Count de Candale, in *A Marriage of Convenience* at the prestigious Academy near the campus, whose boards had been trod by Ethel Barrymore and Alla Nazimova. I never guessed then that one day I would employ them. Adorned in white satin knee britches, an embroidered coat and a white wig, I became a campus star. Fame made me daring. Neither freshmen nor sophomores were permitted to have cars, so I immediately purchased a second-hand Model T touring car which I dubbed "Pooh." Pooh cost one hundred dollars—two months of my father's generous allowance meant for books, which I could borrow, and clothes, which didn't interest me. The countryside was too lovely to miss, and with the car my more daring friends and I could get to the small inns thirty or more miles away, which offered excellent steaks and baked Alaska for a dollar and a half instead of Smith's stews and bread puddings.

That was also the year I discovered Plato and Nietzsche. I liked Nietzsche particularly. I was ripe for such statements as, "One must subject oneself to one's own tests that one is destined for independence and command, and do so at the right time. One must not avoid one's tests, although they constitute perhaps the most dangerous game one can play, and are in the end tests made only before ourselves and before no other judge." I already had a taste for challenge, and this hit me hard.

But one of Nietzsche's apothegms disturbed me. "In intercourse with scholars and artists one readily makes mistakes of opposite kinds: in a remarkable artist one not infrequently finds a mediocre man, and often even in a mediocre artist one finds a very remarkable man."

I found this impossible to believe. Surely the great poets and composers who stirred me so must be altogether remarkable human beings. Not until I met a good many of them later in New York did I admit sadly that Nietzsche was right.

Professor Samuel A. Eliot, Jr., a handsome man, taught the

history of the drama and a course in playwriting. I took every course he gave. He opened entrancing horizons: Indian, Greek, Japanese drama and all the great European playwrights. Sam, as I was soon to call him, had been playreader and stage manager for the producer Winthrop Ames, and had later joined the Washington Square Players in New York. While he was at Smith, he adapted or translated several volumes of little-known foreign plays; among them was Kalidasa's Indian classic, *Shakuntala.* He upheld the dream of the ideal theatre almost as if it were a religious belief. I was his major acolyte. I spent days on end hidden in remote corners of the library, reading hundreds of plays, keeping a book on them which I still possess.

In my junior year the new student head of The Dramatic Association was to be elected by the outgoing officers. There was quite a hassle over who it should be. Of course I was discussed. Some people objected to me because of what was felt to be my eccentric, and consequently "unreliable," behavior. Was I a responsible person? I had never been part of the "all for alma mater" groups. There was gossip that I smoked and drank, that I lectured on Nietzsche and sex to innocents from Bangor, Muncie, Chattanooga and Spokane. My rival was a socially acceptable girl of solid, Protestant convictions. But despite the fact that I did all the things the gossips said, I won. And I appointed my rival head of makeup, which seemed a harmless position to indulge her in.

Fearing that I might choose something outlandish and dangerous to young ladies' morals, the outgoing officers voted to shackle me, or so they thought, by appointing a small committee of professors to approve any plays before they could be produced. What I chose was outlandish, in a way, but not dangerous, except to some of the actors. It was *Shakuntala.* This play has been accepted as the masterpiece of Oriental drama, embroidered with poetry and delightful imagery. While hunting, a young king meets a beautiful girl, Shakuntala. It is the story of their idyllic love, a separation caused by a curse on the young king and their reconciliation with the aid of a heavenly goddess. The professorial committee refused to approve it on the grounds that it was very difficult to present. It was. Yet I convinced them, and at the same time persuaded the remarkable president of Smith, William Alan Neilson, to let us use his back garden for the production. After what was done to it, his wife never forgave me.

The garden was perfect for the late spring evening performances. Below the terrace there was a large slope, where seats were placed for the audience. Beyond that was a large level grass section surrounded by trees for the stage; past that a long alley of grass and arched trees leading down to Paradise Pond.

The first problem was the curtain. The curtain! How could we have a curtain outdoors? I remembered reading in some foreign book, or perhaps Sam told me, of a water curtain. To use that we would have to dig a trough all across the front of the stage. That was not difficult, since Mrs. Neilson, who would naturally have prohibited such destructive activity, had the good fortune to be away on a trip and thus avoid a heart attack. But where would we get the water? With the promise of free seats, the Northampton fire department was conned into lending us a long fire hose to attach to a hydrant on the street about a hundred feet away. We bought a thirty-foot length of steel tubing with a three-inch opening and drilled triple holes along one side. When the fire hose was attached, a spray of water about fifteen feet high sprang up and then fell, mostly, into the dug-out trough. We played colored lights on the water between the acts. I worried about mosquitoes distracting the audience and wrote to a store in New York, which supplied substantial cones of Oriental fragrance that the ushers lit just before the performance.

We needed an impressive gold Buddha to sit in lotus position on a small platform covered with an old Oriental rug before which a nautch dancer was to perform. By the time she did this, the grass was rather wet from the water curtain, but her damp bare feet still moved gracefully. No Buddha was available, however. One plump actress with a round face volunteered, or perhaps was impressed as drunken sailors are when a ship needs extra hands. She dressed in a brief gold tunic, and we painted her face and the rest of her body in radiator gold leaf. That is what I meant by danger for the actors. Another girl who played a mysterious goddess had a silver tunic; the rest of her body and her face were painted silver, also radiator paint. She wore a silver crown which concealed, over her forehead, a small electric light controlled by a battery so that when she appeared from behind the trees, only the top of her face was lit. It was very mysterious. I am happy to say that both girls survived.

However, the most disturbing problem was the final scene between the hero and the goddess, which was supposed to take place on top of a gold mountain. A gold mountain? For days we puzzled over how to accomplish this. Finally we brought in steps of various sizes and piled them up to a height of about twenty feet. In front of them we placed thin boards cut in surrealistic shapes to resemble the sides of a mountain, reaching a pinnacle at the top. They were painted gold and then shellacked. From the railroad station we secured smoke candles. Lying on our bellies in the grass behind the mountain, the scene designer and I lit these a few minutes before the water curtain subsided. When the scene was revealed, the smoke seeping underneath the gold boards hid all but the top of the mountain, which was lit by a pale blue spot ensconced in a tall tree. Murmurs of delighted surprise came from the audience. We were s.r.o. for the two performances. This silenced the professorial committee.

After *Shakuntala,* of course, I couldn't bear the thought of spending a dull, quiet summer in Akron. It was 1924. A book I had read spoke glowingly of the Provincetown Theatre on Cape Cod, where writers like Eugene O'Neill, Edna St. Vincent Millay, Susan Glaspell, Harry Kemp and Mary Heaton Vorse lived and wrote. I had an invitation to go to a theatre in Marblehead, all expenses paid, from the woman who ran it—she had been impressed by *Shakuntala.* But Provincetown seemed more glamorous, and I had a hundred and fifty dollars saved. So, after writing my family that I intended to spend a summer working, off I went. In the center of town on Commercial Street was the home of a Portuguese fisherman where a room could be rented for five dollars a week. As soon as I had unpacked my steamer trunk, I began a tour of the town, fascinated by the shops, the informal atmosphere, the bohemian clothes, the bare feet. The euphoria of being thrown into a totally strange world lasted for several days. After walking the town end to end without locating the theatre, I went into an antique shop to ask where it was.

"Good Lord!" the owner said. "That theatre burned down several years ago."

"And there isn't another one?"

"No. Nothing this summer."

As the old popular song says, "What to do? What to do? What to do?" I wired the woman in Marblehead that I accepted her offer and packed my belongings back into the steamer trunk. A boy pushed it through the streets in a wheelbarrow to the municipal pier, where I waited for the boat from Boston to arrive. A short, bald-headed man was painting a large canvas on the pier. Since I had never seen anyone paint a picture, I asked if I could watch. We began to talk. He told me he was Auerbach Levy. I told him my misfortune.

"Why," he said, "the whole theatre group is gathering to-night at the home of a wealthy Chicago lady, Mrs. Mary Aldis, who writes plays. They are going to start a new theatre."

"Do you know if Harry Kemp is one of them?" I asked.

"Yes, I believe so."

I had directed a play of his at Smith. I quickly corralled the wheelbarrow boy and gave him a note to Kemp asking if I might attend the meeting. The answer came back as the boat from Boston arrived. "You are welcome," it said. Another quarter persuaded the boy to return my trunk to the room I had left. Thanking Mr. Levy for his welcome information, I waited impatiently for the meeting.

Mrs. Aldis's house was at the far end of Commercial Street, a charming place with a backyard containing a small pool; beyond it a large studio gave directly onto the bay. Harry Kemp, in ancient dungarees and a checked wool shirt which needed washing, greeted me cordially and introduced me around. A woman named Mary Bicknell had been elected president. Susan Glaspell was there, and so were Mary Heaton Vorse and Frank Shay, who owned a famous bookstore in Greenwich Village. The group discussed ways to raise money to build a new theatre on a wharf at the other end of town; meanwhile they planned to use Frank Shay's large barn for the summer's productions. I must have made some contribution to the discussion, because Shay and Kemp walked me home and asked me to turn up at the barn the next day to give them some advice on how to make a theatre out of it.

Since some of their ideas of construction were quite old-fashioned, they welcomed my suggestions, and finally invited me to spend the summer. I told them I had a money problem. So they called Mrs. Aldis and asked her to put me up in her studio building and feed me, which she consented to do. I located a large, powerful girl named Conway Sawyer, and the two of us, with occasional assistance, constructed a stage and a draw curtain, and began to cut and paint flats for the first production, a new play whose title I have forgotten. I was grateful to Conway, who could really hit a nail on the head, while my hammer more often hit my thumb. We found seats for about a hundred people. Furniture and props had to be begged from shops or homes, so we needed a car. For thirty-five dollars we got a two-seater Ford with a truck space in back. It ran under special circumstances. Either I had to leave it on a rise where it could roll down to start, or I had to run beside it on level ground holding onto the wheel and leaping aboard when it began to move. Since I parked it at night under an elm tree, I named it "Desire."

Our most noteworthy production was the premiere of O'Neill's one-act sea plays. I wish I could add that O'Neill was there, but by then he was involved elsewhere.

As the summer progressed, I graduated from building scenery and running the stage to some acting and directing. I didn't have much time to enjoy the ocean, but I acquired a more valuable education from my extraordinary associates than college offered me. They were older than I, and they had interests and attitudes quite foreign to anything I knew about. For instance, Mary Heaton Vorse, who became my closest friend, was a first-rate reporter, specializing in the plight of the underprivileged. When she wasn't busy on a novel, she wrote scathing articles about miners and sweat shops.

Other sorts of horizons opened, too. Mrs. Aldis gave a mid-summer garden party beside her pool for a most unlikely combination of guests. Some of them were society ladies who might be persuaded to contribute to the building of the new theatre; the rest were us vagabonds. By then, of course, I had put myself on the bohemian side. The party was ruined for Mrs. Aldis when Harry Kemp, fully clothed, walked into the pool up to his waist and ate his plate of cold cuts in the water, shocking the very people we hoped to win over. I had not seen such unrestrained behavior before, but it did not shock me as it did the proper ladies. It was my first exposure to the way creative people often alienate the very ones who have the means to help them.

One night not long after that debacle, a handsome, wealthy young man from Boston who had the house next door to Mrs. Aldis's gave an evening party to which neither she, nor I, nor her guest—the Chicago playwright of the period, Alice Gerstenberg —was invited. As more and more liquor was consumed, it became very noisy. I lay in my studio bed unable to sleep, listening to sexual cries and exclamations coming from under the pilings of the studio. About three A.M. all hell broke loose. I got up to see what was happening. On the second floor porch of Mrs. Aldis's house I saw Alice Gerstenberg in an ample, virginal nightdress with her golden hair in two long braids reaching to her waist. She shouted across to the next house, "We've called the police. The police are coming." There was a wild scramble as the guests fled. The police arrived to find only two survivors. A fist fight had taken place between Shay and Kemp. Mary Vorse had tried to intervene and been flung to the floor with a black eye. Kemp had knocked Shay out and had fled. The cops took Mary home and Shay to a cell in the police station.

The next morning a meeting was held in my studio of all the proper members of the scandalized theatre committee. They decided to separate from the disreputable delinquents and finish the season in a a theatre they would make in the studio. I was elected to take Desire to Shay's barn and remove the curtain, props and anything else that was movable. I protested. I thought it most unfair to take advantage of a man when he was behind bars and couldn't protect himself. But I was deeply indebted to Mrs. Aldis for bed and board, so I hopped in Desire and went. First I looked for Mrs. Shay, who was in her kitchen cooking breakfast for her little golden-haired daughter. Her husband's incarceration had so disturbed her that she had taken to drink. An almost empty gin bottle was on the stove beside her as she attempted to cook. She was breaking eggs, shells and all, into a frying pan, stirring them about and saying in a slurred voice, "Breakfast in just a minute, darling." It was the only life I ever saved. I grabbed the pan and threw the whole mess into the garbage, persuaded Mrs. Shay to lie down, and got a glass of milk for the little girl. After that I piled all the movables in the barn into Desire and returned to the studio. The rest of the summer was not much fun. It was the "disreputable delinquents" who had the talent.

On the night before I left to go home for a brief visit before returning to Smith, some of the younger group decided to have an evening on the beach. Desire, packed with guests, chugged slowly because the headlights were giving out. Other cars brought people too. We stopped at Race Point, where I carefully left Desire at the top of the rise, and assembled on the wreck of a boat which had been thrown up in a storm to lodge at a sharp angle in the sand. We all had some cold food; then the drinking began. My partner, Howard Rubien, was a somewhat older man who worked at writing. His face looked like some Italian painter's soft and gentle face of Jesus. His most successful parlor game was hypnosis. But it was alcohol that hypnotized me that evening. Whatever poison was served completely paralyzed both of us, and we spent the night immobilized, gazing at the spinning stars. When the sun rose, we found that all the others had gone. Staggering, wanting to retch, we reached Desire, pushed it off, and drove back to town. The car stopped, I believe forever, in the center of Commercial Street. I was too wretched to feel bad about abandoning it. Saying goodby to Howard, I proceeded cautiously until I reached Susan Glaspell's house. She was in the yard and saw me.

"Why you poor dear, you look dreadful. What's the matter?"

I explained in a voiceless whisper that the matter was murderous alcohol.

"Come on, I'll give you something that'll help," she said. I don't know what it was but it induced the vomit which made me feel weak but willing to live.

When I got to Mrs. A's house, she looked so respectable and scrubbed in white dimity with her ubiquitous dog collar of small pearls that I felt ashamed. She didn't ask where I had been all night. I don't think she wanted to know. When I left that afternoon, I'm sure she was pleased to see me go.

I reached Akron with long, straggly, salt-encrusted hair, sloppy clothes and stubby nails still blackened by misplaced hammers. My family sensed the change in me and couldn't seem to decide whether to accept or reprimand. After two weeks at home, I returned for my senior year cleaned, trimmed and properly dressed. College life was tamer than ever after Provincetown. I rented a room in the basement of the old Plymouth Inn so that I could smoke and drink red Italian wine in private. And I concentrated on The Dramatic Association.

For the major production I chose Masefield's *The Faithful*, a story of the forty-nine Ronin of Japan, a classic in its Japanese version. The Theatre Guild had produced it in 1919. Again the guardian committee protested, but again they didn't stop us. We produced *The Faithful* in an old, inadequate theatre in a building we called Studes. On the dilapidated asbestos front curtain we painted a lovely monochrome outdoor scene of misty Japanese mountains and valleys. The Guild rented us the costumes, which were refitted from their male measurements to our female ones. I directed and gave myself the leading role—Kurano, who led the Ronin warriors. Sam Eliot directed the scenes I played in. The part appealed to me because it had a great drunk scene. I evidently played it convincingly: from the first row I could hear, "Oh goodness! She's really drunk!" Some of the students would have believed anything of me. The role also required me to kill myself with a dagger. I insisted on using a real one and got so carried away that I drew blood on my breast. Again we were a sell-out.

But with the spring my troubles began. My hideout was discovered. Students said that I was impossible, that I told exaggerated tales of sex exploits, that I boasted of low life among real bohemians, that I incited wide-eyed innocents to follow the teachings of Nietzsche and that, in general, I was obnoxious.

When some professors happened to come to an inn in the country where I had driven some girls for lunch and found us smoking, the lid blew off. Laura W. L. Scales, the warden of the College and protector of female morals, called me to her office and expelled me.

I didn't know what to do. I couldn't go home and shock my family and I didn't know where else to go, so I drove to the Whale Inn high in the hills in Goshen and settled down to write the play I was supposed to do for Professor Eliot's class. I couldn't look beyond each day. I didn't know where to turn. I sat in my room staring out the window, wondering if there was any point in trying to write the play. What the hell, I decided, I had said I would write it and I would, even if it ended up in the wastebasket. I finished it in two weeks.

Then God in the person of President Neilson intervened. My friends had told him where I was and he sent for me. The year 1925 was the fiftieth anniversary of the College. There had to be some first-rate entertainment for the hundreds of old "grads" who would convene to dress up in old costumes, shout their class songs and inspect what the young were up to.

I entered President Neilson's office with the most chastened face I could muster and his see-through-you eyes softened.

"You are a very foolish girl," he told me. "Your grades would have won you the honor of Phi Beta Kappa. But that distinction also rests on moral excellence, as you know, so we can't give it to you. I hope you have learned a lesson."

"Yes, sir," I answered. He was more regretful than I was.

"Because your scholastic record is exceptional, we will let you graduate. You will also be allowed to produce the fiftieth anniversary play at the Academy. You're a bright girl. Behave and don't be foolish."

"I will try, sir," I said, but I didn't mean it.

Yet the experience must have subdued me, because the play I chose was not very impressive. Gordon Bottomley's *Gruach* was the tale of a young lady who was to be the future Lady Macbeth. It was very literary and full of windy verse. But the old grads liked it enough.

Finally the day came for giving out the sheepskins. When I

went up to receive mine, I swear that President Neilson winked at me. Some of my classmates were certain I had received a blank diploma, so I displayed it publicly to assure them that I was their equal. In fact, it was "cum laude." And though I may not have had moral excellence, I did have the satisfaction of leaving The Dramatic Association more money than it had ever made.

So I left, brighter, I think, than I am now, with no "agen bite of inwit," which is the only Anglo-Saxon I ever learned.

By MDCCCCLXII my purple past had been forgotten, and Smith awarded me the honor of Artium elegantium exquisitarumque Doctor.

The Theatre Guild

Just before Commencement I had heard exciting news. The prestigious Theatre Guild whose progress I followed in *Theatre Arts Monthly* was starting an acting school. By this time it was a foregone conclusion that I would go into the theatre. Moreover, I knew that what I really wanted to do in the theatre was to produce—not act, write, or even direct.

I had gained something important from *Shakuntala* and *The Faithful,* for with them I began to develop a sense of what a production is: a rendering of a play, a translation of words on a page into physical form and live action. Just as pianists could argue over the correct interpretation of a Beethoven sonata, so, I perceived, various productions of the same play—one by Shakespeare, for instance—could be more or less effective, more or less successful in embodying the meaning on the page. Besides, the producer had the boss spot, and I enjoyed being the boss. I was dimly aware that most producers were men, but Theresa Helburn was a producer, wasn't she? And anyway, I wasn't going to let something like that stop me. I was much more concerned that because I didn't want to be an actress, the school might not accept me.

In June I went down to New York to be interviewed. A wealthy undergraduate friend had found a new dress shop on

Madison Avenue run by Valentina, who later became one of the most successful couturières. There she bought me, as a graduation gift, a black, pure silk shift. Attached at the back was a long scarf with panels of white at the ends, which could be tossed about nonchalantly. I wore this for my interview, complete with a black turban and a black walking stick with a white enamel top. It was 1925, and sophistication was everything. I debated wearing a monocle to look even more worldly, having heard that the daughter of the designer Aline Bernstein wore one, but I decided that that would be overemphasizing my cosmopolitan appearance. My interview was with Miss Helburn, the executive director, who proved to be a short, rather stocky woman with bobbed salt and pepper hair and keen twinkling blue eyes. She seemed impervious to my appearance.

Since Theresa Helburn was one of the very few women, and certainly the most important one, in an executive position in the theatre, I hoped that she would look on my ambition favorably, woman to woman. Her tiny office at the rear of a whole string of offices was most unimpressive. It seemed odd to me that since the Guild's new theatre on West Fifty-second Street had just been built, the architect had not made the executive offices more imposing. I told Miss Helburn that I had just graduated from Smith. I threw in the cum laude, the success of The Dramatic Association under my leadership, especially the success of the Guild's play *The Faithful.* "Here," I said, proffering my resume, "I've written my qualifications and experience."

She pushed it aside. "No, no," she said, "just tell me." That was a lesson I learned. Get people you interview to talk. You can tell much more about them from their faces, their gestures, their voices than you can from reading their dossiers.

"Well," I confided, "I really want to produce, like you. I'm not so interested in acting."

She frowned. "But this is an acting school, you know."

"Yes, I know." I nodded. "I've acted, and I will if I have to, but I really must learn about the professional theatre and I know the Theatre Guild is the best group."

"Do you know what the training costs? Of course, we do plan

to take a few who can't afford to pay, but they would have to be actors."

Hadn't she noticed my elegant costume? "Oh, I have the five hundred dollars," I answered airily. "I don't need any charity."

She laughed. "All right, you can enroll, but I should warn you that by mid-season we will weed out the students who we feel should not be in the theatre."

She could warn me all she liked. I was in.

"It's up to you," she continued. "We start with over one hundred applicants. Be here by September 15. Give my secretary your address on the way out—and your check."

I got up. "Thank you. I will."

"And when you get to be a producer, come see me. I'll give you some pointers."

"If I could only be like you someday," I blurted.

"Oh, go on with you," she said, beaming and turning away.

I went off on a cloud. Outside, I crossed the street to look up at the impressive new theatre where Helen Hayes was playing in Shaw's *Caesar and Cleopatra*. "I'll be here," I thought. "My God! I'll be here."

I returned to Akron for the summer to educate my parents to accept my decision. Bombs bursting in air! My father's eyes flashed, my mother's were full of tears. The response couldn't have been greater if I had told them I was going to enter a brothel or a nunnery.

"I can't let you go to that wicked city," Father shouted. "Besides, you can't be an actress."

"I don't want to act."

"Then what do you propose to do?"

"I want to produce plays."

"Nonsense! Who ever heard of such a thing?"

Then his tone softened. "Look," he cajoled, "I'll send you and Mother abroad—England, France, Italy, Greece. Now, won't that be exciting?"

"Yes, but I'd rather go to New York and be in the theatre."

"Damnation! I forbid it. I'd sooner—yes, I'd sooner lock you up until you come to your senses. I certainly won't pay for such a crazy notion."

"Father! You forget I'm of age. Besides, I have Grandma's money." My beloved Grandma had died while I was in college and had left me twenty-five hundred dollars. This salvo stunned him, but the arguments raged on until Mother recalled that an older girl whose father she knew was working in New York. She suggested we take an apartment together. Luckily the girl agreed, and my parents calmed down.

So off I went in early September, stuffed with good advice. Liberty! I remembered my favorite line from *Shakuntala:* "There are doors to the inevitable everywhere."

Of course after Provincetown I wanted to live in Greenwich Village among the bohemians. The apartment we found was the second floor at 66 Bedford Street, catty-cornered from the famous slender house where Edna St. Vincent Millay no longer lived. We subleased it for one hundred dollars a month. It was a strange apartment; it had a large living room with a black marble fireplace and huge portraits, all of men in the somber, picturesque dress of cavaliers. Underneath each picture were crossed rapiers. Unlikely as this decor was for two young women, I was thrilled to have a place of my own.

School started in September and was to last for one year. Winifred Lenihan, who had recently played Shaw's St. Joan for the Guild, was in charge. Various Guild actors taught us: Alfred Lunt, Albert Bruning, Philip Loeb. We had voice lessons, dance classes and acting lessons. The teaching wasn't remarkable, since there was no method of any kind, but the contact with real professionals was inspiring. We worked mostly in a large room called "sixty-four" on the top floor. At one end was a platform supported uneasily at the sides and center only, which made it necessary to walk with some delicacy. Sylvia Sidney, a luscious-looking young girl, was in the class, and I recall her entering the platform as Peas-blossom in a scene from *Midsummer Night's Dream.* As she tripped across the uneasy platform speaking the verse beginning, "You spotted snakes with double tongue," her feet made sounds like a galloping herd. We laughed at the incongruity, and Sylvia burst into tears, rushed from the platform and did not return. She overcame this with a delightful performance of *Prunella or Love in a Garden* for our graduation play at the Garrick Theatre, which the Guild still operated; it has since been demolished. We gave three matinee performances of *Prunella* directed by Winthrop Ames, who had done the play on Broadway previously. I was the stage manager, and Mr. Ames was sufficiently impressed by my work and my prompt book to promise that I could be the stage manager of his next Broadway show. Unfortunately, he never did another play.

As Theresa Helburn had warned, people were weeded out. The graduating class was reduced to twenty-one. The Guild decided to use us as a stock company for four weeks starting July 21, 1926 on the donated Vanderlip estate in Scarborough, New York, which had a theatre as well as guest cottages. Each week would feature a different play.

I was appointed a director, assistant to Miss Lenihan. This meant that I directed the four plays up until three days before their public presentation, when Miss Lenihan took over, changing performances and stage business as she chose. I tried to invent unusual business and fresh interpretations for the old plays we did, but Miss Lenihan did not approve. It was frustrating to have all my exciting ideas destroyed, and my ego suffered. I managed to control my resentment, but the experience wasn't fun.

In August, the stock company finished its program and my misery ended, only to take a new form. I had been trained and given a little experience. Now it was time to find a job. In the heat, when shoes made indentations in the scorching macadam, I made the rounds from office to office looking for work as a stage manager. I was told that there had been only one woman stage manager in the professional theatre. No producer seemed interested in a female stage manager. Or even an assistant stage manager. Or even a water girl. Females were actresses or nothing, it seemed.

I became accustomed to sitting for hours in the outer Siberia of producers' offices waiting for an appointment. There was not much talk among the crowding hopefuls. We were all after the same thing, a job. Usually I didn't have the opportunity to impress anyone. A secretary would finally appear only to say, "Nothing today." Once as Arthur Hopkins, a round, stubby man and one of the top producers, hurried through an outer office, he looked bleakly at all of us, muttering as he passed, "Sorry, sorry." Years later I sometimes saw him waiting in a theatre lobby hoping to be passed in free. He had lost all his money doing distinguished plays.

My situation began to look desperate. My roommate had gone, leaving me responsible for the total rent. Grandma's money was nearly used up. My electricity and gas were turned off for nonpayment. But I believed strongly in a Quaker proverb, "When you pray, move your feet." I kept making the rounds. Then one morning a card arrived from Philip Loeb, who had directed me as Hedda, to tell me I had an appointment to see Miss Helburn. Full of excitement, I went to her office.

"Sit down," she said. "You are in luck. Philip Loeb has recommended you to take over his job as casting secretary. He doesn't want to do anything but act."

"But I can't type or take dictation," I wailed. God! What a disappointment.

"Oh, you only have to interview the hundreds of actors who pour in here, and catalogue them as to types and experience for future reference. You can keep a card index. You don't have to type."

"Is it a full-time job?"

"No, only about four hours a day. You'll get thirty-five dollars a week."

I had no choice. I wanted to eat. But I hesitated.

"I don't want a half-time job," I said. "I want to work back-stage."

"My child!" she exclaimed. "Take what you can get."

"Well," I bargained, "if I can be third assistant stage manager on your first fall production, I will be glad to work in the daytime and at night."

I looked at her, holding my breath. She smiled. I suppose my nerve had amused her. But instead of answering, she stared out the window. I began to wonder if I had gone too far. Then she slammed her hand on her desk. "Okay! I'll give you a try. Go to it!" What persuaded her, I do not know. But she had made her way as a woman in a man's profession, and perhaps she wanted to give another woman a break. Whatever the reason, I now had a job—two jobs!

The first fall production of 1926 was Franz Werfel's *Juarez and Maximilian,* starring Edward G. Robinson as Diaz, representative of Juarez, Alfred Lunt as Maximilian, Clare Eames as Charlotte, and Arnold Daly as Bazaine, Marshal of France. As well as working backstage, I had two roles: that of a lady-in-waiting (with one line introducing the entrance of Mr. Lunt to Miss Eames in her boudoir) and, at the end of the play, that of a Mexican peasant woman with a baby. Now I received an additional thirty-five dollars a week and felt like a pro among pros.

Early in the rehearsals Miss Helburn asked me how it was going. I told her I was very worried about Arnold Daly, who sat beneath his straw hat muttering incomprehensible lines. She told me not to fret, that he was a distinguished actor, which I knew. Thus I learned something that stood me in good stead later: when an actor gives a superior reading at the beginning, watch out. That is usually as far as he can go. He has not explored all the various possibilities of his actions or feelings or adjustments to the other players. Clare Eames put it very well for me once. She said, "A good actor makes clear the meaning of the words, a better actor gives also the emotion of the part, the best actor adds emotion of which the character is unconscious."

Dear Arnold Daly. He would try to tempt me to go out with him, saying, "My dear girl, I know how to say I love you in over twenty ways." I never discovered them. On opening night I was standing offstage left where he made his final exit, after a threat to Maximilian in which his voice changed tone in a way so extraordinary that you felt as though a sharp dagger were aimed at Maximilian's heart. When he came offstage, he paused in the wings. "Is there something wrong, Mr. Daly?" I asked.

"Yes, my dear, there is. This is the first time in thirty years I have made an exit to no applause." To a star, I realized, the lack of response was an insult. My eyes filled with tears, and I turned away. Bazaine was Daly's last role. Asleep in his hotel room, he burned to death from a careless cigarette.

In those days stage managers had much more freedom than they have today, when everything is compartmentalized and unionized. Now they are not permitted to place a prop or a piece of furniture or to do any of the things I did. In *Juarez and Maximilian* I never had a dull moment. Under a blue smock, one pocket of which held a revolver that I shot off at some point, I wore a green and black hoop skirt and a heavy black wig decorated with green grapes. In this outfit (minus the smock), I said my single line; then I cued in and beat time for a seven-piece orchestra, ran down to the basement where I shot off a cannon, saw to it that the actors got on stage at the proper time, and changed into the peasant costume. I had no time to get to a dressing room, so I changed behind the light board while Mike O'Connor, the Irish electrician, turned his bashful head away. Then, reaching down to the dusty floor, I spread the dust over my face, picked up my baby, cued in the orchestra, and appeared for the final funeral scene to the music of a death march by Beethoven.

Meanwhile, during the day I was seeing actors and actresses, a very depressing experience since unemployment was severe, as it is today. They came flowing in from all over the country with dreams in their heads and nothing in their pockets. In a year or so I had an exhaustive file, well documented. But I had few jobs to give.

One afternoon a stout lady entered my office, awkwardly dressed and wearing an impressive hat decorated with a bird's green wing and a half veil, which failed to conceal the erosion of time.

"I would like to see Miss Helburn," she said in a firm, throaty voice.

"Do you have an appointment?"

"No, but I'm certain she will see me."

"May I have your name?"

"Mrs. Patrick Campbell."

Mrs. Patrick Campbell! My God! George Bernard Shaw's

admired one, the first Eliza Doolittle in *Pygmalion!*

I pressed the intercom to speak to Miss Helburn. "Mrs. Patrick Campbell is here to see you." The answer came back, fortunately heard only by me.

"Ask her to wait."

I couldn't repeat that. "She will be free in a few moments."

Mrs. Campbell sat on the couch with a stately grace. I kept stealing glances at her, incredulous that this heavy, ravaged woman was once the beauty of the London stage. Five minutes passed, ten, fifteen. I became embarrassed, but she kept looking into some unfathomable distance which did not include me. After twenty minutes the intercom buzzed. "Send her in," Miss Helburn's voice squawked. I escorted Mrs. Campbell to the inner office, curious as to what brought her. She was there briefly, then sailed back through my office without a word. I ran back to Miss Helburn. "What did she want?" I asked.

"A job," Miss Helburn answered. "Did you have a good look at her? What could she play now?"

Who cares, I thought, who cares? How do you live when the pink star spot will never illuminate you any more?

When *Juarez and Maximilian* closed, I went to work again as assistant stage manager on *Pygmalion,* starring Lynn Fontanne. It was fascinating to watch her skill and imperturbable spirit.

Lynn had a game with me in *Pygmalion.* When she drew off a ring and threw it away, she would throw it in difficult places, like the fire, where I was supposed to go to retrieve it. After a few such experiences, I bought a number of rings at the five-and-ten, keeping them in my smock so it got to be no more fun for her.

In December 1926, the Board brought over Jacques Copeau, the famous French director, to stage Dostoevski's *The Brothers Karamazov,* which he had done with great success in Paris in his own version. It was a distinguished cast, with Dudley Digges as the father, Alfred Lunt, George Gaul and Morris Carnovsky playing his three sons, Edward G. Robinson as Smerdiakov, Lynn Fontanne as Grouchenka and Clare Eames as Katerina. Again I was assistant stage manager. It was thrilling to work with such a distinguished director. Copeau was an ascetic-looking man with a very high forehead on which two enormous blue veins stood out like antlers when he became annoyed. Since the language barrier was severe, he was annoyed rather frequently. He spoke little English and it was difficult for him to re-create, in a limited time with American actors, the vision of his French production. I was happy to be his "go-fer," a theatre expression meaning go for coffee, tea, sandwiches, pencils, note pads or anything else required. I spoke no French, but we managed to communicate well through a kind of osmosis; he gave and I received, eager to grow.

The play did not turn out to be an audience favorite, but one incident I will never forget. At the end of Act Two, Robinson as Smerdiakov climbed a long flight of stairs at the top of which he went through a door to hang himself. Since the act ended in a few minutes, he stayed behind the door; no ladder was provided for him to climb down offstage. During one performance I was standing on the side where Robinson made his exit. Hearing a groan, I looked up to see him there at least twenty feet in the air, blood pouring down from his left hand, which had been caught by a sharp nail on the stair rail. I whispered up that I would drop the curtain. He shook his head no and stood there, bleeding, until the end of the scene.

That's what is meant by the old saying, "The show must go on." He was in great pain. Fortunately, Smerdiakov was dead, so Eddie did not have to appear again for that performance. But many years later, I saw him at a party and said, "Eddie, let me see your left hand." He showed me a heavy scar.

In the spring of 1927 the Guild decided to open a repertory of two plays at the Garrick Theatre. They were Pirandello's *Right You Are If You Think You Are,* with Edward G. Robinson, Laura Hope Crews, Helen Westley and Morris Carnovsky, among others, and a revival of Milne's *Mr. Pim Passes By,* with Laura Hope Crews, Dudley Digges and Helen Westley. For these plays I w:s promoted to full stage manager. I also continued to work in the casting office five days a week. The Guild Board raised my salary for day and night employment from seventy to one hundred dollars a week.

At the Guild Theatre, Sam Behrman's comedy *The Second*

Man opened in April with Lunt and Fontanne. Lunt played the part of a charming man kept in funds by Fontanne. At his first entrance she hands him a check. It's a tricky moment: the way he accepts it makes the difference between a gentleman down on his luck and an unattractive gigolo. Lunt accepted the folded check casually and put it carelessly into his pocket. When Earle Larimore replaced him, he opened the check, looked at the amount and placed it away carefully with a satisfied smile. This piece of business made a totally different character.

Lunt and Fontanne were famous for working on their performances right up to the final night. When they played together I saw how adept she was at keeping his more volatile temper controlled. The only time I ever observed a lapse of their discipline was at a matinee performance of *Caprice* in 1928. Toward the end of Act Two Lynn (as I could call her by then) was required to slap Alfred on the face with her gloves. The slap was harder than usual, and Alfred said something pungent under his breath to which Lynn whispered something like, "I'll fix you for that." When she went offstage she was supposed to return after a moment—during which Alfred was on stage taking bicarbonate of soda—for a brief scene before the curtain dropped. I was watching from the mezzanine. She did not return. Alfred kept drinking the bicarb, growing paler and paler. Finally the curtain was pulled. I ran down to the stage and got hold of the stage manager. "Stay out of it, for God's sake!" he said. "They're furious. Give them time to get over it."

I was working hard and learning a lot, but, as I confessed in a letter to Sam Eliot back at Smith, I was frequently troubled by the complex make-believe world of the theatre. I wrote,

It is so difficult to keep clear of the clouds in order to remember just why I am here and for what. The disconcerting pressure of more experienced lives and a more sophisticated environment frequently leaves me wobbly and uneasy. It is only by the sheerest bravado that I can fight them, for at times I even forget the inner certainty that assures me I should go on as I began. What mental and physical force it takes to stand inside and outside of this monster New York. And yet I would feel a very second-rate person if I once contemplated leaving. Rather the danger

is in losing focus and perspective and your memory of me serves inesti-
mably in recalling me to myself. I am grateful.

I was twenty-five years old. Sitting at a desk most of the day
interviewing desperate actors to whom I could give no hope and
working at night among high-strung egos was not a healthy way
to live. I decided I must give some attention to my physical and
psychic well-being. So I became very susceptible to various ideas
for self-improvement. One assurance of perfectibility was diet. I
became a vegetarian, chewing away at raw vegetables, fruit and
rice. Several weeks of this fodder and my stomach began a continuous rumble. Going to the doctor, I discovered I had diverticulo-
sis, which still bothers me when I eat raw food. I returned to meat
and potatoes.

Another inspiration was yoga—not just the exercises, but the
whole philosophy of self-abnegation and asceticism. In some ways
I was still the zealot I had been as a child. During this period I
met someone to whom I was greatly attracted, and the attraction
was reciprocated. But no, I had to be firm: physical attraction was
deplorable to the sages I was reading. Principle, principle! What
an idiot!

The next enthusiasm was exercise, and, as usual, I went over-
board. I exhausted myself doing backbends and pushups, lifting
dumbbells, and swimming lap after lap. This phase was short-
lived. It occupied too much time and it was boring. A fast walk
was sufficient.

(I am still addicted to books and articles on self-improvement,
the "how to's." But now, having developed an interior dialogue,
I simply hoard them and ignore them. One part of me asks,
"Don't you want to be healthier?" The response is, "No." "Don't
you want to be irresistible?" "No." And every time I read about
all the superior advantages afforded by some new scheme, the
"no's" have it.)

But all my various regimes were secondary to the theatre. In
1927 the Guild decided to produce the play *Porgy*, directed by
Rouben Mamoulian. *Porgy* became one of its most successful
productions. (Their subsequent production of the musical *Porgy
and Bess* was not equally successful at first.) I was still assistant

stage manager, and I enjoyed the work with Mamoulian, whose own assistant I later became. For the famous shadow scene, Mamoulian asked to have a lamp placed in front of the group of mourners. By accident, the main lights were brought down, and suddenly we saw the gigantic shadows of the mourners outlined against the back of the room. Everyone gasped at the effect, and of course Mamoulian kept it. For this fortuitous incident he received great credit. Such happy accidents often occur in the theatre.

The company and I had a long love affair. Their uninhibited exuberance, their sense of fun and their ability to live "for the day thereof" entranced me. Once a week a bunch of us went to Harlem, to Small's Paradise or the Lennox Club or a rent party or one of their apartments, to sing and dance as if there were no tomorrow. Actually, we weren't sure there would be a tomorrow.

Besides the income from my jobs, I had three other means for living well. One was playing poker, at which I was unusually successful because of what my partners called my "Indian face." Another was a "sugar daddy," as they were known in those days. He was a well-to-do stockbroker, a lonely bachelor who enjoyed bringing champagne and excellent bourbon in cobweb-decorated bottles to my apartment, which was by then a floor-through three flights up in an old brownstone on Forty-ninth Street between Fifth and Sixth. I always managed to have some indigent friends around to drink his liquor and be taken for a fine dinner at one of the nearby speakeasies. He asked for nothing more than to enjoy our high spirits, which grew higher as we polished off his libations.

My third means of support was making gin from good alcohol procured by the stockbroker. This I put in the bathtub with distilled water and juniper berries, bottling it in Gordon gin bottles, which could be bought for twenty-five cents each. I would load five or six cases of the stuff into a secondhand, four-gear Mercer touring car and drive to Amherst and Northampton, where I could sell a bottle for two dollars and fifty cents. A young man lugged the cases around for a fee. I did this "business" on Sundays, usually my only free day.

The first play by Eugene O'Neill to be produced by the Guild

was *Marco Millions*. I was transferred to that for a January opening, and, having missed O'Neill in Provincetown, now got to meet
him. He was a very handsome, laconic man who always seemed
to be under great pressure. When he sat far back in the auditorium during rehearsals I noticed that he couldn't stay still for long.
He would wander out to the back or disappear. It was obvious that
his nerves couldn't take the trial and error, the fumbles, the actors
protesting a line they insisted they could not speak.

Although the play was not very successful, it was swiftly followed by another O'Neill work, *Strange Interlude*. I read it lying
in bed. When I put the script, in three parts, on the floor, I
couldn't see how it could possibly work and I had no great admiration for the writing. Then I wondered why my bed seemed to be
moving. It was my heart beating wildly. Obviously, my heart was
smarter than my head. The play set a Guild record of four hundred and thirty-two performances in New York alone and later
had two companies on tour.

My next involvement was with Stefan Zweig's *Volpone*,
which alternated with *Marco* at the Guild, using most of the same
actors. Alfred had a field day as Mosca, Volpone's scheming
servant. At one matinee performance he exceeded himself for the
entertainment of Noel Coward, who was in the audience, by
playing some sexy games with a basket of oranges and bananas.
At the curtain of Act Two, he has thrown out the scavengers who
are after Volpone's money and stands against the door saying,
"They have gone, Master," and looking across the stage at Dudley
Digges (Volpone), who is lying in a large bed. At this point the
curtain is supposed to come down, but Alfred leaped across the
stage, pulled down the covers and got into bed with Dudley.
When I came on stage after the curtain fell, Dudley was blue in
the face with fury; he wouldn't speak to Alfred for some time.

While *Marco* and *Volpone* were running, I was helping to
cast productions of *Faust, Major Barbara, Wings over Europe*,
and *Caprice*, which followed each other swiftly in the fall of 1928.
Caprice was a light play. Philip Moeller told me that directing it
was like putting girders in a cream puff.

I learned a lot about casting in my Guild years, and my

experiences stood me in good stead. As a professional tea-taster does not find it easy to explain why one tea tastes better to him than another, so a casting director has difficulty explaining how he knows just the right actors to select for certain parts. Some casting directors say they do it by "intuition"; one of the best of them claims that she knows by a peculiar sensation she gets "right in the middle" (presumably the middle of her stomach), but even she cannot describe exactly what the sensation is. A great deal of the process of casting a play stems from the subconscious.

There are many problems in casting, depending upon the type of play, the interpretation that is intended, and the available material (for often casting a role is a matter of compromise). The moot point, however, is so-called type casting. I found a middle ground to be the most tenable one in practice. I didn't always believe in casting to type—but then, I didn't always believe in casting against type either.

Sometimes one cannot get any expression in a part by casting an actor who is the exact counterpart of the character as the author has him in mind, because then the actor can't contribute anything except the quality he and the character already possess; this quality is so perfectly "right" that it is impossible for the actor to "grow" beyond it. This is particularly true in the case of a rather flat or dull part. When I had to cast a dull businessman part, for instance, I immediately put out of mind all of the actors who were perfect examples. I racked my brains for someone with some personal eccentricity in voice, appearance or general style of acting, who would give an extra touch to the part and keep it from being dull.

For *Roar China* the Theatre Guild started out selecting Equity actors for the bit parts and extras, but the results were unsatisfactory. So I spent ten or twelve nights wandering through Chinatown picking out types. I found one man addressing a political meeting; he turned out to be the best actor in this anti-imperialistic play. Some of the best bits in *Porgy*, too, were played by people who had never been on stage before, and they added a great deal of authenticity to this folk drama. Some of them couldn't read, and we had to train them to remember their lines by speaking them over and over. One woman whom we found scrubbing a floor—she was seventy-two years old at that time—never did learn to say her lines consistently; but whatever she said was always so apt that no one ever minded. We nicknamed her Addaline.

Early in 1929 I was asked to take charge of the *Porgy* company on a trip to London. Charles Cochran, the most important producer there, had made arrangements to present our show at what was then His Majesty's Theatre in the Haymarket. I was twenty-seven years old. My sugar daddy had won fifteen hundred dollars for me in the stockmarket, and I planned to spend it on myself in London. The eleven-day trip on the S.S. *Columbus* was a ball. The company would take over the second-class lounge by noon each day. There was a continuous dice game, a poker game and music.

In London I rehearsed the actors to reduce the tempo of their gullah speech indigenous to Charleston so that English audiences might possibly understand it. Mr. Cochran came in occasionally. He was very amiable, inviting me to what he promised would be a celebrity party after the opening. On the night of the final dress rehearsal I noticed programs stacked in the back of the theatre; picking one up, I was shocked to see that it read "Charles Cochran presents *Porgy.*" No mention of the Theatre Guild. As soon as Cochran arrived, I showed him the program. He promised it would be corrected for the opening.

The next evening I arrived early to pick up the program. It still did not acknowledge the Theatre Guild production. I could not return to New York with such an error, not just because the Theatre Guild wouldn't like it, but because Cochran had not produced *Porgy.* I went backstage and ordered the company to stay in their dressing rooms until they heard from me.

Curtain time arrived. The house was packed with men in black tie and women in evening clothes. Jewels flashed as I peeked through the opening. Ten minutes passed. Then fifteen. The audience became restless. Finally Mr. Cochran appeared backstage to inquire what was wrong. I told him I could not permit the show to go on unless he went before the curtain and explained that there was an error in the program: the Theatre Guild had produced *Porgy.* He said he had never appeared before a curtain and wasn't going to do it. I just stood where I was, saying nothing. I was scared, but I couldn't let Cochran take all the credit. Finally, after pacing the stage in anger, listening to the audience noises, Cochran said, "All right!" I opened the curtain for him and placed my arm against his back. He made the acknowledgment and I ordered the curtain up, almost twenty minutes late. He never spoke to me again.

The English audience didn't really understand the play, but I had a grand time, returning with four handsome tailored suits and four sets of Irish linen handmade underclothes. But best of all, thank God, I brought a program that said

Charles Cochran

presents

The Theatre Guild Production

of

Porgy

For the fall season of 1929 I became full stage manager of Romain Rolland's *The Game of Love and Death,* starring Alice Brady and Claude Rains. The play, laid in a handsome drawing room at the time of the French Revolution, was directed by Rouben Mamoulian. Among the extras I cast to represent the rag-tag revolutionaries was Henry Fonda. At that time the Guild paid extras ten dollars a week, which I thought pitifully small. I debated how to present my case to the Board. Finally I decided to try a joke. When they assembled, I said, "I'm sorry, but I can only hire fairies at ten dollars a week." They laughed and raised the salaries five dollars.

There was quite an important part in the play for a young woman. I had seen a performance of *The Earth Between* at the Provincetown Playhouse on MacDougal Street in which there was a young girl I thought very talented. I cast her in the part, but after a few days Rouben said he didn't want her. So I had to fire Bette Davis, who hasn't held it against me. As far as I know, her replacement was never heard of after that show.

I had meanwhile become friendly with a young man named Herbert Biberman, who had studied theatre in Russia, particularly with the talented and innovative director Meyerhold. And there was another interesting young man around. His name was Harold Clurman; he read plays for the Guild and did various odd jobs.

I first met Harold Clurman in 1926 during *Juarez and Maximilian*, in which he played a Mexican Indian. He spent his scene squatting on the stage floor against a white adobe wall. He had one line: "Ugh!" or perhaps "Ugh! Ugh!" He still claims he got a laugh on it. Harold was full of ideas of what the ideal theatre should be, and after performances we would talk. Rather, he would talk. Embellishing his views with quotations, sources and philosophy (he had just returned from doctoral studies at the Sorbonne), he would hold forth. "If the theatre is to be an art," he insisted, "one must have a permanent company trained in a unified method of work to which all elements—sets, costumes, music—contribute. And the plays one does should reflect our social and cultural life."

Harold also introduced me to a friend of his named Lee Strasberg. Strasberg liked to talk about the Stanislavsky method of acting, which he had studied with Madame Ouspenskaya and Richard Boleslavsky, both of whom had been members of the Moscow Art Theatre and had left that company to establish a school in New York. Strasberg claimed that there was a clear and definite technique by which the actor could be trained to use himself truly and effectively without tricks and clichés. This, too, was a new and heady idea for me. I thought a lot about Harold's and Lee's ideas, and we discussed them with Herbert Biberman. The Guild Board got wind of this and decided to let us try putting on a play. Herbert, Harold and I were umbrellaed under the name Theatre Guild Studio, and we had high hopes.

For our first production we chose *Red Rust*, a Soviet play. Harold and Lee had been trying out their ideas by working uptown with a group of actors, and we cast some of them in *Red Rust*. The Board considered *Red Rust* good enough to present, and it was performed in December 1929. To our delight, the public received it warmly. It looked as if our Studio had a future. I began to direct a second play, *Dead or Alive* by Philip Barber. For the lead I tried to get a young man named Clark Gable, who then had a prominent gold tooth, large protruding ears and an infectious smile. He was bright to refuse the part, because the play got no farther than the Board's first viewing. Autocratically, they ruled against it. The Theatre Guild Studio died aborning.

Early in 1930 the Guild decided to do Turgenev's play *A Month in the Country* with Alla Nazimova, and I began to search for suitable actors. The year before I had spoken to drama students at Bryn Mawr. Among them was a beautiful young girl with startling blue eyes and bronze-red hair. After the talk she sat at my feet, wearing me out with endless questions. She said she wanted to leave college and come to New York to act. I urged her to finish, telling her I would audition her after graduation as soon as something suitable turned up. She appeared at my office, having graduated, as I was casting *A Month in the Country,* and there happened to be a part that she auditioned for successfully. Her name was Katharine Hepburn. After some days of rehearsal, Nazimova came to me. "I don't want that girl in the company," she said. "She's never on time for rehearsals. Her excuses are that she has been fencing or taking lessons or playing tennis. Fire her." So I did. The only two people I ever recall firing were Davis and Hepburn, a sorry record.

But Alla Nazimova was a most enchanting person with sex appeal galore and a mischievous sense of humor. The heights and depths of her career were staggering. When she came from Russia, Lee Shubert was so impressed by her that he supplied her with an English teacher. After she had learned the language, which she always spoke with a delicate, attractive accent, he starred her in a number of Ibsen plays. Then she went to Hollywood and made a fortune, building herself the famous Garden of Allah, which long afterwards was turned into a hotel. But when the studios became interested mostly in American stories, her career declined to a pitiful nadir. It was Eva Le Galliene who saved her, bringing her to New York for her famous performance as Madame Ranevskaya in *The Cherry Orchard,* after which she appeared in other plays. After *A Month in the Country* she starred again for the Guild in *Mourning Becomes Electra.* After that she played in Ibsen's *Ghosts* and in *The Mother.*

She and I got on famously. Once after a performance of *A Month in the Country* we drove with two others to her home in Westchester, which was really a large apartment attached to her sister's house. She looked old and tired that night, dressed in an ancient gray sweater and baggy skirt, with black-rimmed glasses and her hair pulled back. After a few drinks we all decided to play the game "Who Am I?" She excused herself, went up a few steps to her bedroom quarters and returned in about fifteen minutes totally transformed. She had made up, with blue around her eyes, shocking red lips, hair brushed in a halo around her head, a long cigarette holder with a brown cigarette alight and a large colorful Spanish shawl draped around her. She slithered sexily down the steps saying, "Well, who am I?" All of us were stunned. After a few minutes I went to her and whispered, "I know. You are Alla Nazimova twenty years ago." I was right. It was an incredible impersonation.

One afternoon I attended the first and perhaps the only performance of the *Sacre du Printemps* ballet at the old Metropolitan Opera House. The leading role was danced by Martha Graham; the direction was by Leonid Massine. I was sitting in an aisle seat where, during intermission, Lee Simonson, one of the Guild directors, passed me. "Well, what do you think of it?" I asked.

"Too much messing (Massine), not enough fucking (Fokine)," he answered.

Then Alla passed. "Well, Alla?" I questioned.

Her reply was brief and succinct. *"Coitus interruptus."*

My friendship with Nazimova taught me that great stars could be lonely people. I once received this letter from her:

Cheryl, dear, I am leaving tomorrow for Columbus, Ohio. Did you really want to see me? Four weeks at the Longacre I've been waiting, so *hoping* for a kindred soul. Why are we all so small-circled? Surely we know that others are just as lonely, and yet—No, of course I can't see you now—too late. I am terribly tired, terribly discouraged and can't see farther than my nose. Perhaps someday we shall be able to have a talk, sans holidays, sans whiskey, and until dawn. Who knows? Alla.

She died on the West Coast, without money, her great career forgotten.

Nazimova wasn't the only one who needed friendship. I also spent evenings with Pauline Lord, Fanny Brice, Alice Brady and Laurette Taylor.

I would be faithless to my feelings about the theatre if I didn't mention Pauline Lord's work. So little has been written about her. Yet I can say that more than almost any other actress she lifted veils—that is, she revealed the unconscious feelings and motives that Clare Eames mentioned as the sign of the best actor. She had incredible sensitivity. Her most fleeting and unexpected reactions made me aware that I knew more about Amy, her character in *They Knew What They Wanted,* than Amy knew about herself. This was also true of the way she played *Strange Interlude* when she toured it—and every other part I saw her do. In one of her last failures she had a very difficult scene. Alone on the stage she was required to show that she was going mad. This is damn hard to do, especially when there is no one to react to. There was a large couch center front, the wall on stage left and a big piece of furniture behind the sofa on its right side. She trapped herself between these to play the scene, prowling like an animal in a cage. It was very moving. I asked what made her do this. Was it the director's choice? "No," she said. "No one told me. It just seemed right." She didn't know why. I realized that her instincts were so sensitive that she didn't need to have reasons. After four successive flops, I think she wanted to die. So she did.

There was one strange star at the Guild who, having lurked backstage so long, was eager to have the spotlight. This was Guildy, the house cat, who protected us from mice. No one was very certain about its sex. Sometimes it seemed aggressively male, sometimes purringly female—a very modern cat. Guildy appeared unannounced when Ina Claire was starring in *Biography.* The scene was in her large studio; a red fire glowed behind the glass window of a Franklin stove in the corner. Ina was on stage when her lover, played by Earle Larimore, entered, and they went into a long embrace. The audience began to titter. Ina thought her underwear might have dropped and began to feel around her body. No, it hadn't. Since the tittering continued, Ina broke the embrace and glanced around. Guildy was encircling the couple, looking up appealingly for attention. Ina bent down, seized the cat, trying to decide how to get rid of it; then she crossed to the stove, opened the door and threw the cat in. It of course landed safely offstage past the light that simulated the fire, but the audience screamed. Then, realizing that no harm had been done, it burst into laughter which stopped the show for some time.

One day a young actor, tall, well built, with a shock of curly hair and very penetrating eyes, came to see me. His talk was fluent and interminable but interesting. He spoke mostly of Mozart, Beethoven and how much he wanted to write. And he confessed he needed a job badly. His vitality and enthusiasm were so overwhelming that I wanted to give him one. I was able to use him in a small part in *Midnight*, which the Guild produced in the spring of 1929, and after that I sent him for a long tour in the repertory company of *Marco Millions* and *R.U.R.* From the road he frequently wrote me typed letters of eight or ten pages, chaotic confessions of his beliefs and his life in a sort of diarrhea of the typewriter. Often I couldn't understand what he was talking about. I threw the letters away. Now I wish I had kept them. I feel like Lincoln's secretary, who, when he was asked for reminiscences said, "If I had known he was going to be a great man, I would have kept notes." The young actor was Clifford Odets, who became one of the original members of the Group Theatre and its most talented dramatist.

By 1929 the Guild had 30,500 subscribers in New York and 30,000 in six cities on the road, with the problem of finding six plays each season worth doing for them. With this New York subscription, each play could run five weeks regardless of its reception. That was remarkable, because the best efforts can often result in a one-night stand. Other producers had to close a show at once if the reviews were unfavorable.

The swift and autocratic demise of the Theatre Guild Studio

had only served to inflame Harold and me. Nonetheless, when it came time to renew my contract with the Guild, I signed. Ideals or no, it was a good job. For the 1931–1932 season I received one hundred and fifty dollars a week with three weeks' paid vacation —a handsome salary for the time—and I became assistant to the Board. "You may say what you think," Terry Helburn told me, "but you are not allowed to vote."

As assistant to the Board of Managers, I had the opportunity to appraise their work more closely. It was an interesting combination of people, encompassing a female executive, Theresa Helburn; a lawyer, Lawrence Langner; an investment banker, Maurice Wertheim; a scene designer, Lee Simonson; a director, Philip Moeller; and an actress, Helen Westley. Langner, Moeller and Helburn also wrote plays. Their weekly meetings were a nightmare for me; everyone argued constantly, and every argument was delivered at top voice and top speed. Later I was to become accustomed to people yelling, but at that time it was a new experience and I always left with a headache. Entitled to express my opinions, I couldn't find an opening in the continuous, deafening uproar. Also, I couldn't seem to talk loud enough. Finally, I hit on a solution. I moved my mouth silently as though speaking, using expressive gestures. After a while they looked at me and stopped, wondering what I could be talking about. This gave me a few minutes' interval to speak my piece in a normal tone.

What do I think now of this extraordinary and diverse group? They put on many unusual plays which no other producer in his right mind would have done, if any producer *has* a right mind. There is no question that they made an enormous contribution to the theatre of that period. They were cultivated and dedicated people; in a way they were amateurs in the best sense, quite unlike many of the casting-couch, cigar-smoking producers operating then. Their impulses were highminded. I think they believed with George Bernard Shaw, many of whose plays they produced, that "The theatre should make people feel, make them think and make them suffer." But commercial producers had taken the hint. There was gold in them thar foreign and special plays. Competition, and the dereliction of some of their playwrights to the films or to other managements, made it more and more difficult for the Guild to find exciting plays to satisfy their elite audiences. In time the subscription list became an albatross.

The Theatre Guild Company, which finally consisted of twenty actors employed by the season, was never a group that played all together as a company under a single purposeful idea or directive. So to my mind, it was not a true company, though it was considered one at the time.

Someone, I forget who, said that it is not the nature of an enterprise but its duration that makes it great. The extra activities the Guild undertook never lasted. The Theatre Guild School existed for only three years and was then abandoned, although at that time I think it was the only really professional school operated by people who were engaged in the theatre. The Theatre Guild Studio, an interesting forum for developing younger talents who might eventually have contributed something fresh to the older group, lasted for only one production, *Red Rust.* In other words, the Guild's fuse was too short. The fires they lit burned out too quickly.

In my last two years there I took over some of the executive duties when Terry Helburn temporarily resigned to work in Hollywood. The bonds that had tied the directors together had begun to disintegrate. Only *Reunion in Vienna, Biography* and *Elizabeth the Queen* were successful. Alfred Lunt and Lynn Fontanne refused to sign for another season.

One of the last plays I helped to cast was later used to make one of the most splendid musicals in our history. The play was *Green Grow the Lilacs,* which, as any theatre buff knows, later became *Oklahoma.* Herbert Biberman was directing it and objected to the extras I offered as cowboys. Well, of course they weren't bowlegged or horseriders. No "ippy i yea" about them. But at Madison Square Garden, then only a few blocks away, there was a cowboy exhibition which was about to close. I went there, got hold of the impresario and said I thought I had employment for a number of the boys. Would he please tell anyone interested to be at the stage door at noon the next day to be auditioned? Promptly at noon those of us who were sitting on stage heard the thunder of heavy boots and the jangle of spurs. About thirty genuine cowboys strode in. We picked those who seemed most suitable. It did make a difference to the show. It made a difference to me, too, because occasionally I was hurriedly called to the basement where some of them were quarreling, open knives in hand. I never felt they really meant to kill each other. I think they just wanted attention.

In *Green Grow the Lilacs,* Lee Strasberg played the peddler. So our opportunities for long talks increased. He and Harold were as fervent in their ideas as ever. And Harold kept picking on my job and the Guild. "This isn't what you really want, is it?" he kept saying. He was very persuasive. Lee was often silent, completely nonverbal unless his passion for the theatre was aroused. They had continued to work on plays at an uptown studio with a few actors, but they confessed that their efforts seemed aborted. They needed an executive, someone to spearhead their work. "Someone like you," Harold said. "Someone who believes in our approach and who knows how to get things done."

So in 1930 I suggested that we gather a group of actors for informal meetings to see if it was possible to enthuse them about the ideal of a true theatre. The Guild soon heard of this and requested an explanation. I wrote a report on what we were up to, explaining that we might become a real studio aligned to the Guild. I also told the Board that I wanted to leave, if that was necessary, to become a part of this new organization. In response they offered me full membership on the Board and an increased salary. But I refused. It had taken four years, but Harold and Lee had seduced my mind. The Theatre Guild wasn't what I really wanted in a theatre after all. Not for nothing had I daydreamed as a child of being a missionary. All that had changed was the religion.

The Board was very understanding, even offering to help us. Lawrence Langner doodled a drawing of me on top of a blanket supported by six figures (the Board), being born to the Group. And so I took an irreversible step, dangerous to security but in its way inevitable.

The Group Theatre

We were a bizarre trio, two Old Testament prophets and a WASP *shiksa*. In the fall, we began the weekly meetings I had suggested, inviting promising actors to whom Harold and Lee could set forth their dream. As more actors heard about these meetings, they grew larger and larger.

Harold did most of the talking. He exhorted his listeners with an unlikely synthesis of Jeremiah and Walt Whitman. In "Democratic Vistas" Whitman had indicted his age, writing, "The official services of America—national, state and municipal—are saturated with corruption, bribery, falsehood, maladministration, and the judiciary is tainted—it is as if we were somehow endowed with a vast and more thoroughly appointed body, and then left with little or no soul." Yet he prophesied optimistically that wider vistas would open when democracy was truly practiced. Similarly, Harold's jeremiads deplored the state of the theatre, and his Whitmanesque moods painted the ideal, what it could be. Some of the listeners were bored or baffled and never returned. Others were exalted by Harold's vision and eager to commit themselves.

By early spring of 1931 we felt we had the makings of the kind of theatre we wanted. The Group Theatre was ready to be born. Harold, Lee and I appointed ourselves directors. Lee and Harold were immoderate men, as the saying goes, full of piss and vinegar, or to use more theatrical terminology, full of pride and passion. In the early days it was never any use to stem the heat generated by either of them. It would have been like trying to stop a forest fire with a teardrop. And sometimes my tears fell, when I was confronted by their furious conflagrations. I don't know whether I cried because I was carried away by their exaltation or jealous that I could not verbalize my beliefs with anything approaching their vehemence and endurance.

We chose a group of twenty-eight actors, or perhaps I should say they chose us. Some of the original members were people who had acted in *Red Rust:* Franchot Tone, Luther Adler, Eunice Stoddard, Ruth Nelson and William Challee. Others were Robert Lewis, Stella Adler, J. Edward Bromberg, Morris Carnovsky, Sanford Meisner, Phoebe Brand, Mary Morris and Clifford Odets. But what to do with them? We needed at least one play, we needed a place in the country where we could spend an uninterrupted summer of work, and we needed money.

Still under contract to the Guild, I asked them if we could prepare Paul Green's play *The House of Connelly,* which they had held under option for some time. They agreed to let us have it. It was a very American play about the post-Civil War adjustments facing plantation owners, their freed slaves and the "white trash." One version was over two hundred pages; another was under one hundred. By stretching these out on a long table, I attempted to combine them into a workable script. Working on scripts became one of my jobs. The money for the summer came from various sources: the Guild contributed one thousand dollars; the playwright Maxwell Anderson, who had attended some of our meetings and fallen in love with one of our actresses, fifteen hundred; Dorothy Norman and Edna Ferber, five hundred each. It wasn't enough; but a benefit arranged by Robert Lewis, one of our actors, made up the difference.

To form ourselves into a true company and to prepare our first production, we planned to go away for the summer. In Brookfield Center, Connecticut, I found sufficient space in a country enclave with a large barn and numerous houses, including one that contained a big kitchen and dining room. There we spent twelve weeks. Besides the twenty-eight fanatics, "we" comprised some wives and children, twenty-one victrolas, three radios and assorted cars and dogs. It was a stimulating but battering summer. I was unused to living in such close quarters, especially with extraordinarily volatile actors; it was like living in a goldfish bowl. It frayed my temper.

The directors soon evolved their roles. Lee directed the play. Harold worked with individual actors and passionately kept our aims before us. My responsibilities were more mundane: reading scripts, working on finance and calming tempers.

There were two black field hands in the play who had several scenes: Rose MacClendon, a splendid actress who looked a bit like pictures of Duse, and Georgette Harvey, an ample woman who had played in Russia, where she was called the "Queen of Spades," a name she cherished. I knew both of them well from the *Porgy* production, so I was elected to direct their scenes. They were experienced professionals, and if I had tried to work with them in the Stanislavsky method which Lee used in his personal interpretation, they would have turned white. What I knew about that method at the time was gleaned mainly from books, from every book I could find on the subject. I learned more when Lee permitted me to observe some of his work with the actors. As rehearsals progressed and the actors discovered they were being trained and extended in a way they had never known before, Lee became their father figure—to some of them, their God figure. He relished this, naturally; his frustrations in the past had been acute.

I was troubled about the future, because I realized during the summer that my main responsibilities would be finance and the business problems for which I felt ill equipped. The Depression had begun in 1929 and was deepening. Where was I going to find the money? I didn't know any millionaires. No foundations, governmental or private, were subsidizing the theatre then. So I worried. Also we had no second play to follow the first. What would happen if the play didn't succeed—or even if it did? My Indian mask concealed a very nervous interior.

During rehearsals of *The House of Connelly*, we three directors became concerned about the way the play ended. As it stood, the black field hands got rid of the tenant farmer's young daughter, who was taking over the plantation by marrying the weak son who owned it. She was determined to make it work. The blacks wanted no part of her ideas of progress and ended by smothering the girl in a sack. In effect, then, the play said that the South had no future. But we didn't believe that. I knew Paul Green best, and I didn't think this conclusion was true to his belief or temperament. We asked him to come North and talk with us. First we approached him in general terms. What hope did he have for the South? "A lot. Of course. Certainly." Then we pointed out that by having the only hope, personified in the young girl, murdered, he was symbolically saying the opposite. He was convinced, perhaps reluctantly, and wrote a new ending in which the field hands were put down by the son so that the audience was left with the feeling that the young man might, just *might,* make a go of it with the girl's strength and vitality.

When we returned to New York in the fall, we gave a run-through for the Guild board. They were impressed by our work, but they were horrified that we had changed the tragic ending. Unless we went back to the original, they said, they would put up only five thousand dollars, only half the money they had been prepared to put up to back our production.

I was sitting at my desk in the Guild office wondering where another five thousand could be found when Eugene O'Neill walked in. "Is something wrong?" he asked, looking at my gloomy face.

"The Group needs five thousand dollars," I told him. Although he knew nothing about the play, he promptly wrote out a check for a thousand. I persuaded an executive at Samuel French, the agents for the author, to risk the rest.

The opening night was torture. So much depended on the play's reception. Paul Green and I sat in the mezzanine lobby of the Martin Beck Theatre pretending to converse. We were both listening for response from the audience. Paul's fawnlike face was masked, his usual eager, questing look gone. When the final curtain fell, I began counting the calls. When they reached six-

teen and the audience began shouting "Author, author," I pulled
Paul to his feet. "For God's sake, get up on that stage!" I said.
He did. The curtain rose and fell twenty-two times.

We were all euphoric. But I had been through enough openings to know that the reactions of the audience and those of the
critics did not always coincide. So I returned to my apartment to
wait for our press agent to phone me the reviews, at least the
morning ones; there were then about eight newspapers in print.
The rest of the company went a few doors down my street to the
walk-up apartment of Walter Coy, one of our actors. I could hear
them making noise as I waited. At two A.M. I got the call. The
reviews read to me were raves, the kind we had dreamed of,
singing the praises of our company. We couldn't have written
better ones ourselves. I called and relayed the news, then dressed
and joined the party. By the time I got there someone had gone
to Times Square to bring the papers back. Lee read them aloud
to cheers and yells. Paul, a very tall man, pushed up the ceiling
with one hand and quoted something appropriate from the Bible.

In spite of the fine notices, *The House of Connelly* ran for
only ninety-one performances in New York. The Guild turned
over another play to us, one by Claire and Paul Sifton, entitled
1931. Written in a pedestrian style, it was a series of vignettes
describing the life of the unemployed and of two young lovers
desperately seeking a way to exist in a crumbling society.

But the people who still had money for theatre tickets did not
want to be reminded of the hopeless economic conditions; they
wanted to be entertained with happy endings. They preferred to
avert their eyes from the huts of wood and corrugated iron
crowded with desperate men under the Fifty-ninth Street Bridge
on the fashionable East Side; from the men selling apples on
street corners; from the long lines waiting for soup in Times
Square. Men in tattered clothes paraded Broadway carrying signs:

> Work is what I want and not charity.
> Who will help me get a job?
> 7 years in Detroit
> No money
> Best of references.

And of course a popular song of the period was "Brother, Can You Spare a Dime?"

A stage relief fund established a dinner club to keep actors from starving. A dinner was either free or one dollar. Over one hundred thousand people were served free. Another hundred and fifty thousand paid one dollar.

Tin and tar shacks grew up around cities all over the country to house the unemployed. They were called Hooverville in honor of the President.

Those who wanted to face what was happening in our country occupied the balcony of the theatre. For the last few of the play's twelve performances it was full. The orchestra was almost empty.

In spite of the failure of *1931*, the faith of our company remained firm and held us together; we certainly didn't have contracts to bind us legally. Maxwell Anderson brought us *Night over Taos*, a play about a family of Spanish grandees in New Mexico fighting to hold their land against American invasion. We opened it on March 9, 1932 at the Forty-eighth Street Theatre, now demolished. It had some of the social significance we always searched for, but it was written in a turgid, florid style and lasted only one more performance than *1931*.

All through my time with the Group our offices were pillar to post, any place we could beg that cost no money. The first season we used my office at the Guild since I was still fulfilling my contract. Then we had a free office on the top floor of the Forty-eighth Street Theatre. It was almost one hundred steps up; I seldom went out to lunch. One very rainy spring day I was sitting there alone, wondering where to get the money for us to go away again for the summer so that we could continue to develop as a company, where to go, and what to work on if we went, when my secretary announced two young men. They had been recommended to me by Philip Barber, whose play *Dead or Alive* I had directed up to its one calamitous run-through for the Guild "Death Watch." They came in and announced they were graduating from Yale, where they had studied with Barber and other theatre professors. Now they wanted to join the Group. That was rather naive of them, I thought. Didn't they realize what a tremendous honor it was? I explained, "We take only experienced actors, not amateurs. We are a professional company."

This didn't seem to faze them. "We'll do anything," they said in concert. One was Alan Baxter, a tall, good-looking leading juvenile type who seemed placid and shy. The other, with burning eyes and a compact body full of fidgety energy which probably accounted for his college nickname Gadg (short for Gadget), was Elia Kazan.

The more they talked, the more impressed I became. I told them that if we managed to go away for the summer they might be able to come along as apprentices. I arranged for Lee and Harold to meet them. They too responded to the young men's earnestness and enthusiasm. And so they joined us.

Summer came. Harold and I had somehow scraped together enough money to go to a place I had found near Dover Furnace, not far from New York. It had a main house, a number of cottages and a large barn for rehearsals. More actors were added and a number of apprentices who paid twenty dollars a week for room and board. We had found two plays to work on, *Success Story* by John Howard Lawson and *Big Night*, a first play by Dawn Powell, who was quite well known as a novelist. Again, both of these plays had something true and important to say about the society we lived in. At that point there was no backing for either production. Lee rehearsed *Success Story*. I cut my professional directing teeth on *Big Night*. "Cut" is not quite accurate as it eventually turned out. It was more like an extraction.

We were most enthusiastic about *Success Story*, and as it developed to the run-through stage, I returned to New York to seek backing for the production. The man I thought most likely to help with finance and a theatre was Lee Shubert who, with his brother, owned most of the theatres in New York as well as a large group in other cities. He had a simian face, not unattractive, with obsidian, impenetrable brown eyes and a small, dapperly dressed figure. He was feared and disliked by many theatre people because of his business acumen, but to me he was invariably kind. His constant companion was a sharp silver letter opener with which he scratched his head or an ear as he pondered your pleas. I persuaded him to come to Dover Furnace to see a rehearsal.

When he arrived we sat him in a thronelike red velvet chair, sometimes enjoyed by mice, and the actors played close to and around him. This was a new, exciting experience for a man who usually sat removed from performers far off in an aisle seat where he could get out when he was bored. Here there was no escape; he became part of the scene. I think he was particularly taken with Luther Adler, who played one of the leading roles, that of an ambitious young Jew on the make—a character whose story was not unlike Shubert's. Shubert was impressed to the extent of promising to put up all the financing and to install us in his Maxine Elliot Theatre. *Success Story* opened on September 26, 1932.

During the Act Two intermission on opening night I was pacing the downstairs lobby when the *New York Times* theatre columnist Sam Zolotow—an alert bloodhound who reported what you were going to produce before you knew you were going to do it—came rushing to the telephone. I heard him say, "They've got it. It's going to be a hit." I damn near fainted. But he spoke too soon. After two tough realistic acts, the third act became rather mystical, leaving the audience confused and indifferent. However, the play ran for one hundred and twenty-eight performances, longer than any of its predecessors, which wasn't bad when you consider that few people had money for theatre tickets. The ranks of the unemployed had grown to fourteen million. Few plays were able to run for long.

Success Story survived only because, for the last five weeks, after Mr. Shubert took "first money" for operating expenses, the three directors gave up their weekly fifty-dollar salaries and the actors went on half salary, although their full salary was little enough. The production cost was only sixty-five hundred dollars, so Mr. Lee, as he was called, was still solvent.

Noel Coward saw *Success Story* seven times. I never learned what hooked him so, unless it was the acting.

Big Night, which followed, was a disaster, playing only nine performances. The play was a bitter comedy about a husband in the clothing business who offered his wife to a prospective customer in order to make a sale. Stella Adler played the wife.

Franchot Tone, who had rehearsed a leading role, got a film job and left for Hollywood, which did not help the production. My direction was indifferent. It seemed impossible to transfer the vision in my mind to the actors. I became as impatient as Toscanini had when he was once rehearsing a very tall, very busty opera singer. Time after time they repeated a section of the opera; she failed to sing it to his satisfaction. Finally, in anger, he broke his baton, rushed to the stage and reached up to grab her breasts in his hands. "Aaaah!" he screamed. "If these were only brains!"

I knew how he felt. My diary entries, though sketchy and sporadic, tell my troubles:

Dec. 27, '32, Tues.
   At office at one. Lee has flu. Sent Doc Weischel over. Rehearsal two to five. Had doctor come to see Stella [Adler, who played the lead in *Big Night*]. Studied Max's [Gorelik] set until six thirty. Worried about finances for play. Hard to work with that pressing on me all the time. Don't think I'm a really good businesswoman. Must get the money or we're washed up. Nerves jangly. We're trying to run a business like a philanthropy.

New Year's Eve, Dec. 31, '32, Sat.
   Eleven A.M. at Banks Tailors choosing clothes for men for *Big Night*. At noon having pictures taken. One to three at Russeks picking women's clothes. At theatre at four to get Lee Shubert to cut down on house expense so I can give actors some salary.

Jan. 17, '33
   Big Night opens tonight, my first directorial job. People won't like it. No matter how tired I am, I've got to stick. I don't know what to do. Work, another year, another time, we must go on.

Work. Work. Work. At this time I had little or no private life. Anxiety for the future of the Group absorbed most of my energy. There is a spurious belief that theatre people enjoy a hot bed of sexual experience. It ain't true. The "casting couch" is mainly a myth.

I did have three experiences with what is called indecent exposure. The first was with the owner of a theatre I was attempting to engage for one of our productions. The man—I can hardly call him a gentleman (besides being ancient, he was at least fifty) —came into the office from his bathroom with trousers open and penis erect.

"Oh, Mr. X," I said, thinking quickly, "how funny you look!" This remark persuaded his ardor and his instrument to subside. He returned to the bathroom for a few minutes to replace himself. I got an exceptionally favorable contract.

The next occasion was a visit to the apartment of a well-known public jokester, also an ancient fiftyish, whom I wanted to host a Group Theatre benefit. As we were talking, he suddenly unzipped. My reply to such activity had worked so well the first time, I tried it again. Yes, it seemed the heaven-sent response, but he was not persuaded to do the benefit. No matter. I got Heywood Broun, a sweet bear of a man who was most entertaining, partially due to a hip flask of gin.

The only other time I received an unrequested advance was during an evening visit from a very attractive man. Since the visit took place at my apartment and at my request, I'm sure he thought he was doing the obligatory thing. Actually, I wanted to discuss a role. (Are you sure of that, Cheryl?) Anyway, when I saw the equipment I was struck with awe. The usual response was certainly unfitting. "Good God!" I cried. "Put it back. It isn't possible."

The major part of what little private life I had did include some intermittent love life but centered mostly on books, records and dinners with friends, whom I usually asked to bring something to read. "Come to dinner and bring a book," I'd say. I had so little time to see my friends or to read, and this arrangement enabled me to do both. I was fortunate in having friends who liked to read as much as I did.

After *Big Night* the critics began to write the Group's obituary. We were overdrawn at the bank. None of us knew how we were going to continue, but we were determined not to give up; in spite of our hazardous condition we had acquired a loyal following. Some of the company collectively rented a large, decayed floor-through on West Fifty-seventh Street, past Eighth Avenue.

They named it "Groupstroy," and there they lived in uncomfortable abrasion, sometimes getting odd jobs, sometimes eating from
"CARE" baskets brought by the more fortunate members. All of
them were waiting for the word that would revive them like the
phoenix from the ashes. Lee stayed there in a tiny room with his
new wife, Paula Miller, a Group actress. He read and studied in
silent endurance. Clifford Odets had an even smaller room where
he banged away at his typewriter day and night, hoping that what
he was writing was a play the Group would produce.

As for me, I could no longer afford my hundred-dollar-a-
month apartment at 100 West Fifty-fifth Street. I rented it furnished to Aaron Copeland at a small profit and moved in with
Dorothy Patten, another Group actress, whose wealthy father
enabled her to live in a pleasant townhouse on East Fifty-first
Street near the river, where I occupied the maid's room and ate
healthily at her father's expense.

My chief concern was to find a play for us. I had maintained
good relations with Lee Shubert, who was still somewhat enamoured of what seemed to him our crazy fanaticism, and at one
meeting he pointed to an enormous pile of scripts on the floor of
his office, suggesting I read them to find something suitable. I
called this collection the woodpile; every week I picked up half
a dozen indiscriminately, took them back to Dorothy's place and
read them. Weeks passed as I ruined my eyes on dull plays. Then
I came across one called *Crisis*. I had just finished it when Helen
Thompson, who was doing some audience promotional planning
for us, came in. (Helen later invented and ran the successful Play
of the Month Club.)

"Have you found anything at all?" she asked anxiously.

"Yes," I said. "I just finished a play called *Crisis*. The script,
as usual, needs work, but it's a hell of a subject, and it hasn't been
treated in the theatre. I think we could make a fascinating production of it. I'm going to give it to Harold and Lee right away."

But Harold and Lee were not very enthusiastic. I took it to
Theresa Helburn, who also liked it and offered to produce it with
me. When I returned to my co-directors with this news, they
refused my request to work outside the Group. This was a great

disappointment, but since I had committed myself, I accepted it. The search for a play continued.

In any event, the Group members were determined to spend the summer together. I spoke to Lena Barish, who, with her husband, owned a large and famous summer camp named Green Mansions. In the name of the Group I offered weekend entertainment for her guests if she would feed and house us, including wives and children. Since our reputation by now was considerable, she bought this idea. We may have been broke, but we were famous.

The time grew close for us to leave for the country, and we were still without a play. Finally Harold told me that since nothing better than *Crisis* had appeared I should negotiate for it. I was pleased. *Crisis* had been around for some time, so I didn't expect trouble. But on investigating I discovered that it had been optioned by two young men, Sidney Harmon and James Ullman. This meant that if we had a success we would receive only half as much as if we had owned the play ourselves. I was able to work out a co-production deal with them: we would do the play with our company and be responsible for half the financing, which we figured at six thousand each, or a total of twelve thousand dollars. When this was settled, we drove to Green Mansions. On Monday, June 26, 1933, I noted in my diary:

We all arrived at Green Mansions a week ago today. I feared there would be a lot of temperament and dissatisfaction, but the place and the food are excellent and the spirit of the company calm and sure and quiet. Better than ever. I was in a bad temper all day—rain, problems of financing, housing difficulties, sex—Mae West picture at the lodge. I saw part of it and then dropped in to see Lee. He was copying some words of Lenin in German into a notebook. I was touched by the quietness and scholarly atmosphere and felt ashamed.

Sometimes during the week there were more actors and their families on the Green Mansions grounds than there were guests. Yet I think the guests got more than adequate entertainment with scenes from plays we had done, revues with scenes taken from various sources, Chekhov, O'Neill, solos by actors who could sing or do comic turns, and—most interesting of all—the second act of a new play called *I've Got the Blues* by Clifford Odets. The guests responded strongly to it; its milieu was familiar to many of them, and the sparkling colloquial dialogue engrossed them. Their enthusiasm encouraged Clifford to rework the first and third acts. It was the first incarnation of *Awake and Sing.*

Meanwhile I worried about where our six thousand dollars for *Crisis* was going to come from. It occurred to me that a film company might be interested in putting up the money on a preproduction deal. It wasn't. I was introduced to Doris Warner, the daughter of Harry Warner, who, with his brother, owned the film company. She was in the East learning the business in the story department. After reading the play, she agreed to put up the money.

My big problem solved, I relaxed for the summer and enjoyed the actors' improvisations as doctors and nurses. They were instructed in professional behavior by doctor friends imported for the purpose and by medical guests. *Crisis* was a multi-scened play laid in various parts of a hospital; the story primarily concerned a young doctor, played by Alexander Kirkland, who had recently joined the Group after a successful career on Broadway and in films. We didn't care for the title, and during the summer the author, Sidney Kingsley, suggested *Men in White. Men in White* it was.

Toward the end of the summer we arranged for a run-through for the author, our co-producers, and our backer, Doris Warner. The roof of the theatre must have been made of tin, because a heavy downfall of rain kept drowning the actors' voices. The performance did not go well; nerves and the water plummeting like buckshot didn't improve matters. At the end the small audience dispersed glumly. I didn't feel like facing anyone so I returned to my room; I lay in bed thinking desperate thoughts most of the night.

But, as time showed, there was only one thing wrong with the production: the actors playing doctors and nurses had brought their own sensitivity to the sufferings of the patients instead of the professional objectivity with which real doctors and nurses perform their tasks. When this change of attitude was incorporated it made a great difference. Now the play demanded an audience's concern.

Lee Shubert put us in the Broadhurst Theatre, where there was sufficient side room to roll the platforms of the set beautifully designed by Mordecai Gorelik off and on. When we got to the key scene of the operation at the curtain of Act Two, a nurse, who had been made pregnant by a young doctor who was engaged to a wealthy society girl, was wheeled into the operating section. The surgeon and his assistants, all in white, were scrubbing up in a finely orchestrated rhythm. They would attempt to save her life. Strasberg wanted to have great white lights focused on the operating table to increase the tension. Eddie Kook, the head of Century Lighting, arranged four spots of exceptional strength with no gels in them to hang out of sight on a high pipe, all of them concentrating on the white sheet covering the girl and the doctors' uniforms. The power of the unrelieved whiteness was breathtaking. The last word of the scene was "scalpel," as the surgeon lifted his hand and his assistant handed the steel instrument to him. But Lee wanted a further shock at that point. "More light!" he demanded. No addition seemed to work. I remembered seeing a tall gooseneck lamp at the corner drugstore at Eighth Avenue and Forty-fourth Street. I ran down the street and bought it. We put a strong bulb in it and placed it next to the surgeon's assistant. As he handed the surgeon the scalpel, he turned on this lamp. The sudden excess of light did the trick, creating an effect as painful as the scalpel making the incision.

We had only two previews. After the first one Lee Shubert came up to me in the lobby. "Well," he said, "it's a wonderful production, but I'm afraid people don't want to see such a play."

"Mr. Lee," I answered cockily, although trembling inside, "after we open, you will thank me on your knees that we are in your theatre." He was thankful. But he never knelt.

The first preview taught us that the ending fizzled. It was a scene in the young doctor's room. His fiancée, who has learned about his sexual relations with the nurse, who had died during the operation, comes to tell him she is breaking their engagement and going to Europe. As the curtain falls, he is left alone, miserably unhappy.

The directors and author met to discuss what might be done. Something upbeat was needed. There was only one more performance before the opening.

In an earlier scene an Italian woman had brought her injured son to the hospital. It was decided that after the fiancée's exit, the doctor would be alone on the stage for a few seconds. Then the phone would ring. The doctor would answer it to hear the boy's mother, distraught, asking about her son. Despite his own pain, the doctor would comfort her, telling her not to cry, not to cry, her son would live. Curtain.

It worked. You knew that the young doctor was going to go on, that he would do his job no matter what. Most of the critics were full of praise. *Men in White* was the first medical drama. Who knew then that the world of medicine and hospitals would one day be exploited ad nauseam on TV? It was the Group's first big commercial hit. It won the Pulitzer Prize and played in New York for three hundred and eleven performances.

The winter of 1933–1934 gave us the respite we needed after the strain of the previous years. Everyone received a salary whether performing or not. "Groupstroy" was abandoned. The company had places to live their individual lives and knew where their next meal was coming from. Hamburger at twenty to twenty-five cents a pound was regularly consumed. Most of us became involved as teachers with other socially concerned theatres or organizations. I taught acting and playwriting to the Theatre Collective, a group of young aspirants who occupied a once-elegant house on the northwest side of Washington Square.

At a party in the Village, I met a writer, Melvin Levy, who had studied American history under Vernon L. Parrington, the author of the classic three-volume socio-literary work *Main Currents of American Thought.* Melvin was eager to write a play on an American theme, and we discussed various ideas. Finally we settled on the story of a power-hungry robber baron in San Francisco. (Most of our plays seemed to be about the obsession with power and money, perhaps because they were such a basic part of the American dream and so much on everyone's mind during the Depression.) The title was *Gold Eagle Guy*. Melvin wrote, and I met him frequently to discuss and criticize.

During *Men in White* our office was a cubicle off the balcony in the Broadhurst Theatre; you reached it by entering the orchestra and going up the inside stairs. For several weeks I found an attractive young man with an appealing smile sitting on the steps whenever I entered. "I'd like to talk with you," he would say.

"What about?"

"I want to be in the Group."

"I'm sorry; we're not taking any more members at present." Undaunted, he kept turning up. He wore me down until I finally said, "Come on up to the office. What's your name?"

"Jules Garfield," he said.

Lee Strasberg was in the office at the time. He often came to sit, hiding behind a newspaper, listening to what was said on the phone or in an interview. When I could hear the paper rustle, I knew he was displeased.

This time the paper didn't rustle.

All of us were pleased with Jules and decided to accept him as an apprentice for the following summer. And that is how the famous movie star John Garfield began.

While we were working on *Gold Eagle Guy,* John Howard Lawson brought us another play, *Gentlewoman.* John Wildberg, who had become our attorney-for-no-fee, found a new backer, D. A. Doran; he had come from Hollywood with funds to produce plays. He put up the total financing for *Gentlewoman.* In it, Lawson was trying to straddle the conflict and attraction between the wealthy middle class, personified in a beautiful woman searching for contact with what was going on in the world, and a young radical, who is also searching for some meaningful involvement. The audience was mystified by the dichotomy between what appeared to be both a drawing room drama and a poetic, social document. The play ran for twelve performances.

In the spring, Lee, Harold and Stella took a brief trip to the Soviet Union to see the theatre in Moscow. To us, the most exciting innovations in the theatre were taking place there. I stayed in New York working with Melvin Levy, reading plays (finding none for us to do) and looking for a place where we could spend the summer inexpensively without entertaining guests, which had become tiresome. The place I found was an abandoned summer camp on a high hill near Ellenville, New York.

I hated that summer. We lived in a kind of barracks behind the decaying Victorian main house overlooking the valley—damp, full of mists and, I'm sure, ghosts. There was no swimming, which has always been my favorite type of exercise. To make matters worse, many of our actors had been radicalized in a jejune sort of way through their contacts as teachers, writers and directors with the radical theatre organizations which were then developing rapidly. There were wearying arguments in which the directors were accused of exploiting the actors, the designers, the kitchen help—in fact, everyone except the animals. It was ironic that Mordecai Gorelik, our talented stage designer, who was an insurgent constant complainer, always received his union salary when the directors frequently received nothing.

I never have been able to stand up well to criticism, deserved or undeserved, and of course I usually felt it was undeserved. I had worked so hard. I shared their desire for more money, better plays —but where from? I didn't know and neither did they. I was hurt and I was fed up. One day I simply walked out—for a week. Someone asked, "Won't you be lonesome?"

My answer was, "I hope so."

Harold was astonishingly able to roll with the punch of their brickbats. Lee responded with a Gotterdammerung violence that left the members speechless—temporarily.

At some point that summer Clifford presented us with *Awake and Sing*, greatly rewritten after the Green Mansions period. The milieu was completely foreign to me, but I liked the vivid dialogue and, to me, unusual characters. But when Lee and Harold didn't strongly insist that we produce it, I sat the fence. As work on *Gold Eagle Guy* proceeded, we decided to try a six-week fall season in Boston, where we would repeat *Men in White* and *Success Story* and open *Gold Eagle Guy*. I went there to set it up with Helen Thompson, who had come from Boston. She introduced me to a redoubtable lady, Mrs. Roland Hopkins, who became our chairman and netted a group of important Boston Brahmins who guaranteed the season. Pulling rank with my Revolutionary ancestor buried on Bunker Hill, I spoke at select clubs and lovely old homes, whose lavender window panes faced Boston Common. Things looked promising.

Then we discovered that due to some booking skulduggery, we were forced to play in a huge, ancient and musty theatre, the Majestic, totally unsuitable for our productions. *Men in White* suffered at the box office from competition with the film that had been made of it. *Success Story* had good notices but not good audiences. *Gold Eagle Guy* was impressively set and acted, but it lacked dramatic tension.

My best times in Boston were spent at Goodspeed's Bookshop, where I bought some rare books by Thoreau, Whitman and Emerson and photographs of all three which still hang together in my bedroom. Facing my bed I placed a copy of Thoreau's survey of Walden Pond. Nowadays, when so many nervous people seek solace in various methods of spiritual regeneration, I find that looking at these pictures in the morning suffices.

But the most exciting event occurred when I was standing beside the electric light board after a matinee. Clifford walked in clutching pages of yellow paper. "Where have you been?" I asked. "I haven't seen you for three days."

"I've just finished a long one-act, and I want you to read it right away," he said. The "long one-act" was *Waiting for Lefty*, and I may have been the first to read it. Although I thought it was dynamite, I still didn't anticipate the enormous effect it would have, not only on our theatre but on the whole country.

As the Group actors became more socially aware, largely because of their reaction to the Depression, so did I. I met a remarkable woman, Mother Bloor, through my acquaintance with her son-in-law, the actor Will Geer. She was a tiny, gray-haired bundle of energy who worked to radicalize the dispossessed farmers in the "dust bowl" region. Her activities put her in constant trouble with the law, and she was often jailed. When she came East for a brief stay before being sent to jail again, I put her up in my apartment so that she might have a respite before the incarceration. Her stories of poverty and injustice were a revelation to me. Before she left I accompanied her to the office of Robert Minor, who was the head of the Communist Party in the United States.

"Mother," he said, "I want you to listen to me. They are really going to give it to you this time. They'll tell you to scrub the floors, empty the slops and any other indignity they can think of. And you do it. Don't argue, don't fight back or you'll be in bad trouble. They're just waiting for a reason to knock you around. You hear me?"

Mother Bloor nodded her head amicably in agreement, but I saw her blue eyes flash and knew that her mild manner was deceptive.

Women radicals of that day were often called "Mother." Mother Jones (after whom a magazine was recently named) preceded Mother Bloor. Her mass meetings were famous. She would open her speeches with the salutation "Friends, Comrades and Stoolpigeons." She was usually arrested.

Back in New York, *Gold Eagle Guy* opened at the Belasco in 1935 to some excellent reviews. Evidently they did not impress theatregoers. We lasted only sixty-eight performances.

So there we were, stuck in midwinter at the height of the Depression with zero prospects. Our office, although you could hardly dignify it by that name, was a dressing room in the Belasco. I vowed some day I would have a real office. I was bone tired as much from frustration as from work. Many of our company had been offered excellent acting opportunities. It was unfair to deny them the freedom to accept when we had nothing to offer. Finally, we called a meeting of the entire company in the cellar of the theatre. Harold laid it on the line. "We can't go on," he said. A blast of protest began: we must not disband. We *must* find a play. What was the matter, were we chicken after all we had gone through? The members determined to search for plays.

They read many plays—to no avail. By the closing night of *Gold Eagle Guy,* nothing had been found. Harold decided that we would do *Awake and Sing* and that he would direct it. Clifford

read the play to the company, and their enthusiasm was conta-
gious. The phoenix struggled from the ashes once again. Harold
persuaded Franchot Tone to put up the five thousand dollars for
the production before reading the script. Somewhere I found
fifteen hundred to send *Gold Eagle* to Cain's, the dead-end
warehouse. Between rehearsals of *Awake and Sing,* Clifford and
Sanford Meisner directed other members of the company in
Waiting for Lefty, which they showed the directors one afternoon
at the Belasco. The three of us were standing in the back when
they came up for comments. Harold and I praised their work. Lee
said nothing. But none of us guessed what would happen before
an audience. Clifford and Sanford wanted to find out.

So one Sunday night in January *Waiting for Lefty* was shown
as a benefit at the Old Civic Repertory which Eva Le Gallienne
had run for so long. Never before or since have I heard such a
tumultuous reaction from an audience. The response was wild,
fantastic. It raised the roof. More Sunday benefits were given with
similar response. The play was taken up by groups all over the
country. In some cities it was suppressed as being too radical.

In February we opened *Awake and Sing.* Although the reviews were favorable, they were not as enthusiastic as they were
when it was revived some years later. However, the audience
response was quite good, and with the small weekly expense the
play was able to run for over two hundred performances.

We decided that *Lefty* could be done for a regular Broadway
run at the same time; Clifford wrote another to go with it, an
anti-Nazi play, *Till the Day I Die.* By sort of an eenie-meenie-
minie-mo game, I was elected to direct it. Lee and Kazan played
small parts. We charged a dollar and a half top. With *Awake and
Sing* and these two plays running, Clifford became the white-
haired boy, the hope of a new theatre. And the Group Theatre,
after its tortured existence, became the talk of the town.

Maxwell Anderson then offered us his new play, *Winterset.*
When it was read to the company the response was negative. I
thought we should do it. Although the dialogue was pseudo-
Shakespearian, rather windy verse, it dealt with the Sacco-Van-
zetti case in an indirect way and was a lot more promising than

many plays we had done. However, we accepted the company's reaction. Produced by another management, the play was a great success. I began to wonder if the vote of a group was the way to decide on a production. I knew that Lee, too, had been for doing it but hadn't been in the mood to insist against the company's reaction. Harold later told the company that we had made an error.

But spring was coming, we were doing well and could coast a bit on our laurels, and I was jealous of my co-directors' earlier visit to the Soviet Union. I, too, wanted to see the productions they had praised so highly. As Harold's previous trip had been a brief ten days, I persuaded him that we should take a five-week trip together and see everything. With the success of *Awake and Sing,* it looked as though the directors would receive their fifty dollars a week for some time. We might never feel that secure again.

The Russian Theatre, 1935

Harold and I left for the Soviet Union in April 1935 on the *Ile de France.* Our trip had been booked by an organization called The Open Road, which took care of everything at a cost of five hundred dollars each. I decided to take one very long book that might last the trip and chose *War and Peace* as the most suitable. It so enthralled me that in Paris, for instance, after a swift look from my hotel window at a full moon glowing over the romantic Tuileries gardens, I would return to bed to pore over the remarkable story of the land I was soon to see. As a result, *War and Peace* did not last the trip.

Enroute to Moscow by train we carried a large basket of food and wine; we were determined to buy nothing as we passed through Germany. We had also packed a lot of splendid large pictures of Group productions taken by the photographer Paul Strand. And we had some scenes from the play by Clifford Odets that I had directed, *Till the Day I Die,* the story of a young Communist who was caught and tortured by Nazi soldiers. One of the photographs graphically showed a Nazi officer in full regalia starting to bring his gun butt down on the outstretched hand of the young hero. Another one showed a Nazi swastika being torn from a soldier's uniform. These were in my suitcase and as we neared the German border, I became alarmed. I didn't want to destroy the photos, which we planned to show Stanislavsky, Eisenstein and others; I wanted even less to have them found in my possession if we were searched, which, the porter assured me, was likely. We would reach the German border about midnight. I told the porter I was very tired and gave him five dollars to be sure I was undisturbed. I had fallen asleep when suddenly the overhead lights in my compartment flashed on. "Heil Hitler!" I heard, and opened my eyes to see two Nazi soldiers entering. In preparation for directing the Odets play I had read a number of pamphlets from a worker's bookstore in the Village describing the Berlin Brown House and the tortures that went on there. I was truly scared. I pictured myself being carted off the train, bravely refusing to recognize a pale Harold wringing his hands, a frequent gesture of his expressing muddle. Then, I knew, I would be thrown into a cell to be tortured, and of course raped. But behind the frightening figures I saw the porter's head with one eye slowly winking. I don't know what he did or said, but the search was very perfunctory, and with another "Heil Hitler!" the soldiers withdrew, leaving me trembling.

In Moscow we stayed at the Hotel Metropole, which was on one end of a great square; the impressive Bolshoi Theatre was at the other end, decked out with many large, red, billowing flags. Looking from my window, I could count over one hundred brilliant red flags smacking in the wind. "Red" in Russian means beautiful, and that they were. We were eager to explore. On one long street, Petrovka, packed with people, every window had a theatre display of models, photos and costumes; it gave us a sense of the enormous vitality of the theatre in Russia. I wondered what Broadway would look like with a similar display and if people would stop to observe and discuss as they did on Petrovka. Later we were told that about two hundred thousand people attended the theatre in Moscow every night and that most citizens went at least three or four times a week.

The displays were part of the upcoming May Day celebration. At night the city was dazzling with lights, waving flags, lovely singing over radio speakers and gay throngs. It was very moving, and I turned away from Harold as tears came to my eyes. Before

I turned I noticed that Harold was affected too. Does that mean we were Communists? No, we never were. Ever. But we were stirred by a people celebrating their hard-fought freedom from bitterly oppressive tyranny. We had no knowledge then of the labor camps or the vicious trampling of human rights.

The next day we had an appointment with Gordon Craig, the famous theatre innovator whose ideas influenced many directors. Craig was a large, aristocratic-looking man with long silvery hair and piercing blue eyes. I could imagine women falling hard for him and, according to gossip, many did. He talked for an hour and a half. He had recently returned from Italy and told us that Italy's theatre was debilitated. He couldn't understand it. Mussolini was a nice man. Craig reported that he had asked the German ambassador why they didn't let Piscator—the German director who was in Russia, having become a Communist—return to Berlin. He couldn't understand why they wouldn't. Rhetorically he asked, "Can't a man wash himself clean? I believe an artist should not be concerned with politics. They are beneath him and meddling will only get him into trouble." After these words of wisdom, we bowed our way out and walked in the snow, discussing how a man who was such a brilliant theoretician, who had expressed such innovative thoughts about the theatre, could be so unaware politically—in fact, so ignorant.

We had been promised good standing room for the May Day celebration in the enormous Red Square, and the night before May Day we were too excited to sleep. We were roused at six A.M. to be driven to a new hotel to wait with an English and French delegation until nine A.M. The French Communists were husky, intelligent-looking fellows, built like Percheron horses. There was an American farmer in our small delegation who told me, "I only begrudge the time between home and here. Now I want to get back in the wrastle."

By nine-thirty we were in place on the great square close to Lenin's tomb. It was cold, but I had provided myself with a thermos of hot tea. Stretched across the square were about five thousand soldiers from selected regiments. At ten the Cathedral bells started pealing as General Voroshilov, a huge man who had distinguished himself in the Revolution, galloped into the square on a magnificent white horse. Simultaneously my thermos bottle crashed to the cobblestones with a noise like a shot. All eyes turned instantly in my direction, fearing an assassination attempt. How could I convince them it was only an innocent accident? I wildly waved the bottom of the bottle aloft, grinning idiotically. The searching eyes left me. I was lucky.

As Voroshilov passed each regiment, a great cheer rose. Then the bands started playing the "Internationale" as Stalin and other officials took their places above the tomb. The parade began; regiment after regiment passed in perfect order, then party members, not in uniform but carrying rifles, then navy, air force, cavalry, bicyclists, young Pioneers, multitudes, until the eye was bewildered. There were numerous women among them, and among the Pioneers a girl always led with a boy. Then came the light artillery, heavy artillery, tanks. Overhead roared a fleet of what seemed to be a thousand planes. The tanks below and the planes above made a powerful display.

It was reported that a million people passed through the square that day. But by two o'clock we had had it. By shrewd tactics our guide got us out, stiff and sneezing. We were too tired to do anything for the rest of the day.

Our days, except for matinees, were devoted to interviews with important theatre and film people. Sergei Eisenstein, the famous film director, lived in one messy room with hundreds of books scattered about and several cockroaches, which he pointed out, smiling. No swank estate, no pool, no tennis court, no Mercedes. He was highly educated but seemed to like to complicate the simplest things with profound reasonings. His conversation was more egocentric than that of any of the other men we met. I had read an article in which he said he was greatly influenced in composing his frames by the Japanese haiku, where a linking of simple images produces an unexpressed emotional reaction. He acknowledged that this form of poetry did indeed have value for him.

When we visited Madame Tumonsova, an official at the Moscow Art Theatre, we were delighted to learn that Stanislavsky was in Moscow after all; we had been told he was in Paris. She promised to arrange an appointment for us. She told us that the Moscow Art employed one thousand and eighty-six people, two hundred and forty of them actors. We were jealous and almost unbelieving.

"What would the Group be like," I asked Harold, "if we had two hundred and forty actors?" No answer, but his sigh was sad.

At that time, all actors in the Soviet Union got six weeks' vacation with pay while other workers got four. Actors were given the extra time because they worked six days a week instead of five. The therapeutic rather than the pleasurable aspect of vacations was emphasized: a doctor examined a prospective vacationer to determine whether a visit to the sea or to the mountains would be preferable. Theatre students got free board and lodging with some pocket money. They rehearsed five hours a day in all branches of theatre training, physical exercises, acrobatics, voice, singing, and they studied the history of the theatre. After four years of this, the heads of the theatre decided whether or not they should continue and where. I turned to Harold with the only adequate remark I could think of. "Wow!" I said.

At three the next afternoon we were told we could see Stanislavsky at four-thirty. Moscow was so overcrowded in those days that scarcely anyone had a private house. But Stanislavsky had been given one. He was, after all, the first person to devise a complete method of training actors, and he had an international reputation. Even the government respected him. The house had servants; the rooms were comfortably furnished but in no way elegant; and there was a large, bare rehearsal room where the great man worked with his actors and students. Stanislavsky had not left the house for five months because he was recovering from a heart attack. He greeted us warmly and asked about Stella Adler, who had worked with him in Paris. He was a most impressive figure, very tall, with a handsome face now lined with signs of pain; the full, red lips suggested a sensual nature. I felt it was an actor's face, capable of instant emotional reactions. We asked him about a new device we had heard he was using as an exercise for students: it consisted of one red and one blue disk attached to a metronome which set the tempo of a scene for an actor. When the actor played the scene to Stanislavsky's satisfaction, the rhythm of it was set by this instrument and recorded in the script. When the tempo of the scene varied, the device was used to correct it. He said he would illustrate how it worked, but when he tried, he couldn't untangle the wires.

I asked, "Do you set the problem for an actor or do you make him set it for himself?"

"I would like the actor to set it for himself, but the actor is lazy so I do it for him," Stanislavsky replied.

"Your actors are lazy?" Harold asked with surprise.

"Oh, they know how to work, but they don't unless you push them."

It is well known, of course, that Stanislavsky's theatre concentrated all its attention on the inner life of the characters, on the subjective, psychological side of their behavior. Stanislavsky wished to draw the audience into a sympathetic experience with the characters on stage—as if it were invited into their homes— so that it might find among them friends and relatives who shared the hopes and sorrows of the Russian intelligentsia.

Stanislavsky was convinced that feeling does not come of itself, that the more an actor orders or pleads with himself to cry, the less chance there is of his doing it. "Feeling has to be enticed," he said. "Don't wait for feeling—act at once." The technique involves re-creating an emotion by recalling not the feeling itself, but all the circumstances surrounding it: visualizing concretely the place, conversation, clothes, smells, sounds until the specific emotion is aroused from all these sensory recollections. Everyone has had the experience of becoming aware of a sound or an odor that brings an old emotional event alive. That is a simple example of affective memory.

I asked Stanislavsky about voice exercises. "While on tour," he answered, "I had to rehearse all day, play at night, make speeches at parties, banquets, five o'clock teas. I realized that soon I would lose my voice and be unable to play. So I began doing voice exercises and I did them every day. But you have to have great patience." He demonstrated the exercises briefly. In spite of his illness, his voice was resonant and almost mesmerizing in its tonal variety.

We also asked about body work. "Acrobatics are very useful. But even more for the soul than the body." We smiled. "Yes, acrobatics train you not to be afraid in the big moments of your part. These moments may not be physical but are equivalent to a difficult jump. If you hesitate, you are lost. Acrobatics prepare you for them."

He spoke of his difficulty with playwrights. "We tell him a certain scene or speech must be written in the play and he answers, 'The actor will do it.' Then the actor says, 'I can't do it. I need a speech.' Finally, there is no acting and no speech."

But he seemed to be growing tired; the noble face was drawn when I looked closely. So we thanked him and left. It had been one of the most memorable visits of my life. We were fortunate to have had this time with him—three years later, he died.

As if that hadn't been enough for one day, immediately afterward we had an appointment with Meyerhold, whose work was the antithesis of Stanislavsky's. He had begun as an actor with the Moscow Art and gradually formed his own ideas about what theatre should be. He did not believe it should be merely a reflection of life but an exaggeration, totally theatrical. Greatly influenced by commedia dell'arte, he believed that the theatre should guide spectators to use their imaginations. He opposed lifelike naturalism in acting and made great innovations in the use of scenic space. Yet he and Stanislavsky admired, respected and learned from each other. Meyerhold's apartment, which he shared with his actress wife Ziniada Reich, was spacious and comfortable, filled with books. He had an almost Mephistophelian look—a striking face, furrowed with heavy lines, and a very large nose. I could believe that he loved or hated to extremes, but his attitude toward us was direct and charming.

We were particularly interested in talking about his famous "biomechanic" method, which all of his actors and students were required to undertake. This is a series of physical exercises in the form of a playlet, usually with two characters in conflict. Each scene is based on an activity—the Chase, the Killing, the Slap—

and requires great agility, poise and constant adjustment to the partner. Meyerhold's actors did not search within themselves for the emotional reflexes the Stanislavsky system demanded.

"I must have actors with fluid, free bodies who can stand on their heads, walk on their hands, be acrobats but with a dramatic purpose," he said.

I asked how long it would take an actor to learn biomechanics.

"One winter. It is not very complicated. Each exercise is a melodrama which gives the actor a sense of performing on a stage."

Although we eventually saw a total of eight of Meyerhold's productions, when we met him we had seen two, *The Inspector General* and *Camille*. (*The Inspector General* has been described graphically, moment by moment, in *Theatre Quarterly*, Vol. II, No. 7, July–September 1972. In the same issue are excellent architectural drawings of the theatre plans Meyerhold showed us.) We knew both plays well enough to gauge how much he had altered the scripts. An admirer of his had told us that Meyerhold decided what he wanted to say through a play, then found ways of saying it—cutting out, transposing, breaking up into smaller scenes, putting in new characters, cutting out old ones, rewriting, re-interpreting conventional ideas of characters, changing the scenic backgrounds, amplifying single lines into whole scenes. In doing this he fully expressed his concept in an enlightening way; in his best productions he made these changes seem to be an integral part of the play.

Of course dead authors, like the ones whose plays we had seen, couldn't protest, but how did the live ones react? we wondered.

"I believe," he answered, "that plays should be written differently for the new theatre. But the authors don't want to learn. They all have megalomania."

"Then why don't you teach them?"

"I haven't the time," he said. "When I direct I can do nothing else, even write a letter. I think of nothing else. I see nothing else. Yes, the problem of the dramatist is now our most important problem. That and the problem of a new theatre architecture. The two are related."

"But you didn't change *Camille* much," we pointed out.

"I did, but it's less noticeable. I took monologues from the novel and put them into the play."

"Why did you choose this old-fashioned play?"

"Because I wanted to show the bad attitude of the bourgeoisie to women. Marguerite is treated like a slave or a servant: men bargain over her, throw money in her face—all because they love her. We in the Soviet Union have had a wrong conception of love and of women. Our attitude is too biologic. There is a deeper, loftier view of love. We must have a more delicate understanding. It used to be thought quite proletarian to be rude, but we are teaching that good manners are indispensable to a sane humanity. Recently a young man watching the play rushed to the buffet and bought a bunch of apples to offer to his girl, eagerly and tenderly like a gift of flowers. Perhaps a day or two before he beat her, but the performance had an effect on him." We all laughed.

"Do you work on your productions much before you go into rehearsal?"

"I thought about *The Inspector General* for ten years," he said. "I always knew I would do it, but I was not ready and kept on thinking about it."

Had he chosen the exquisite props and costumes for *Camille?* I asked.

"Yes, I send assistants to various shops to choose twenty possible objects. Then I go and pick one or two of them or something entirely different that I happen to see."

Proudly Meyerhold showed us the designs and plans for the new theatre that the government was building for him. Alas, he never got it. In 1937 he was accused of non-Socialist presentations. *Camille* was severely criticized by the Party, although it was packed solidly every night with an audience tired of the typical Soviet preachments. He was not permitted to work. The only people who called, offering help, were Boris Pasternak and Stanislavsky. "I have enough," he told Pasternak. "I have a car. I can sell it."

Stanislavsky, then a dying man, said, "Come and see me. I am rehearsing an opera, but I am sick and tired. Please take it over," which Meyerhold did. Stanislavsky's eminence made him untouchable, and as long as he lived, he was able to protect Meyerhold. But when Stanislavsky died, Meyerhold was sent to Lubyanka Prison. It is thought that later he was sent to Siberia or was shot in prison. His wife's eyes were put out, and she was murdered. There are several stories about that. One is that it was a political murder. Another maintains that an actor who knew her was sitting at a cafe in Yalta when another actor he knew slightly entered and sat at his table. As they talked the guest drew out a gold cigarette case, offering a smoke. The first actor recognized the case as belonging to Ziniada Reich, excused himself and called the police. The man could not explain having the case and finally confessed to the murder.

The year 1975 was the hundredth anniversary of Meyerhold's birth. His name has been rehabilitated, his working scripts and other material released. He is being celebrated in poems and honored in exhibitions. It is a great pity that he was unable to fulfill his dreams.

When we returned to the hotel, I noticed a card in my box. It was an engraved calling card—Constantin Stanislavsky. I showed it to Harold saying, "Of course. He is an aristocrat." It surprised me that such graciousness was still practiced in the Soviet Union.

Of the productions that Harold and I saw in the Soviet Union, the ones that impressed themselves permanently on my memory were plays that we already knew in English, although several of them would have been difficult to recognize in their stage presentations. We saw twenty-nine shows, most of which were at least three hours long, and I don't recall an empty seat at any performance. We never paid for tickets. If they hadn't been arranged by the theatre organizations, we simply went to the box office, said "Amerikanski regisseurs" and a pair was passed to us.

The high points of some of these productions were so stimulating that I can still remember them better than most of the theatre I have seen more recently. I shall never forget the fabulous *Romeo and Juliet* we saw at a preview at the Theatre of Revolution, which was very large. From the back of the stage, suspended high in the air, a deep red velvet curtain flowed down to the orchestra pit. As the lights dimmed a large orchestra began to play heady, romantic music that sounded like the "Romeo and Juliet Overture" by Tchaikovsky. Then a flood light from the balcony began to pulse on the curtain with a rhythm like a heart beat. The combination of the music and the beating light on the blood red drop spoke of passion and violence.

When the curtain was raised in front, its pale blue silk lining, the color of a Giotto sky, hung in loose folds above the deep stage. I discovered later that the stage was sixty-five feet deep and that every bit of it was used. On the stage were two large three-story houses with small balconies. One housed the Capulets, the other the Montagues. Each house was on a large turntable. They were separated by a series of steps, like the climbing street alleys one sees in Italy. At the top was an ornamental gate; at least thirty feet in the air, behind the gate, you could see towers of the city.

The stage was enveloped in an early morning gloom when two servants and a maid with a lantern came from the stage-left house and crossed to the other house. One of the men was playing a flute. The other man tied one end of a long string to a shoe lying on the stage and then hid, the other end of the string in his hand. When the servants from the other house entered, one of them put on the shoe and was tripped. This started a quarrel, each side slugging the other with large leather bags on sticks. The quarrel intensified and their masters began coming out of doors, windows, balconies with drawn swords. Within five minutes at least fifty men were fighting desperately up and down the stairs as others entered from above, tumbling, sparring, yelling in anger, observed by women peering and screaming from the windows. At the height of the fight, a blond young man in bright blue with a red cape rushed down, sword drawn, and died on the steps in a sensational roll down to the stage floor. Prince Escalus entered with an impressive retinue and stopped the brawl as the dead boy was carried off. I turned to Harold whispering, "My God! how are they going to top this?" My nerves were tingling with excitement. If the actors had not had extraordinary body training, there would certainly have been some real deaths on the stage.

In the banquet scene the houses were turned into soft green walls with tall medieval pictures on each panel; in front of them were long tables set with masses of food. The masquers entered downstage wearing grotesque masks and carrying flaming torches. Romeo wore a large, realistic bear costume. He first became aware of Juliet when she threw a doll on a long stick in his direction. He caught it and turned, lifting his bear snout to see her. As he began his soliloquy, "Oh, she doth teach the torches to turn bright," a huge bat, black wings spread, entered down the center passageway. It was Tybalt who recognized Romeo and started for him; he was held back by Capulet.

For the balcony scene the whole right side of the stage was a street of arcades going up to the gate. Above them was a large balcony covered with white flowering trees. Between two of the vaulted openings of the arcade was a fountain, the figure of a naked boy spouting water from his penis. The nurse bathed her face in this fountain after being baited by the young men. This nurse was as lively and spunky as the boys who teased her. When she told Juliet about Romeo, she rocked her in her arms like a child, then pushed her off, spanking her behind. On the other turntable was a very high wall with flowering trees in front and a ladder hanging from the top; Romeo descended this ladder to cross the square and climb Juliet's balcony.

The fight between Mercutio and Tybalt took place on the alley steps, the houses standing closer together than before. When Mercutio was stabbed, he dropped from one of the high balconies in a breathtaking fall. As Tybalt was led off, the men of each family came to their doors and balconies and glared at each other. The only sound was the slither of their drawn swords as the scene blacked out.

Juliet was no namby-pamby ingenue. When she was angry, she struck her nurse, then took out a dagger, slashed the wood of her bed, fell on the floor and beat her fists on it. And Friar Lawrence was not an elderly pillar of Equity but a lively human being. In their scene in the Friar's cell, Romeo rolled back and forth across the floor in anguish while the Friar attempted to stop him.

My father, Robert Kingsley Crawford, and my mother, Luella Elizabeth Parker, at the time of their marriage

Alden, Newell and I in Atlantic City

A daring actress, about age 2

My grandmother, Lavinia Lynn Parker, about 1879

Kalidasa's SHAKUNTALA in the President's garden at Smith College

THIRD SUBSCRIPTION BILL

The WHARF PLAYERS, Inc.

OF PROVINCETOWN

Present Four One-Act Plays, Aug. 15, 16 and 18

AT 8.30

BAND BOX STUDIO, *on the Shore, 595 Commercial St.*

A Provincetown theatre program, 1924

Conway Sawyer and
Cheryl Crawford

(Top right)
Some of the Provincetown
group. Standing, Cheryl
Crawford with hammer,
Frank Shay, Joe-the-
carpenter; seated, Conway
Sawyer and Betty
Collins Shay

Theresa Helburn
of the Theatre Guild

The Group Theatre directors at Brookfield Center, 1931: Lee Strasberg, Harold Clurman and Cheryl Crawford *(Blackman Photo Service)*

The three directors at Dover Furnace, 1932 *(Ralph Steiner)*

THE HOUSE OF CONNELLY: Left to right, Rose McClendon, Georgette Harvey, Margaret Barker and Franchot Tone *(Vandamm Collection, New York Public Library)*

TILL THE DAY I DIE: Among those listening to Lee Strasberg (at right) is Elia Kazan (center, with hat, glasses, hands folded) (*Vandamm Collection, New York Public Library*)

JOHNNY JOHNSON: John Garfield (right) as the German and Russell Collins (left) as Johnny fraternize on the battlefield (*Alfredo Valente, New York Public Library*)

Judith Anderson as Mary in FAMILY PORTRAIT (*Vandamm Collection, New York Public Library*)

This photograph of me, circa 1940, appeared on posters and billboards advertising the Maplewood Theatre

PORGY AND BESS: Todd Duncan, on his knees, center (*Vandamm Collection, New York Public Library*)

The crypt where Juliet lay covered with a gossamer white veil was surrounded by black velvet, and the effigies of her family were stretched on stone caskets above her. The one just behind her, covered with a black veil, was Tybalt's. The only light was from flaming torches. After Romeo killed himself before her casket, there was a pause, then Juliet's white veil began to lift gently and we knew she was alive.

The production had vigor, boldness and breadth, a Renaissance opulence and liveliness—in the acting, the scenery, the costumes and the music. Harold and I left, excited and very envious. We had seen the world Shakespeare intended, although it was not so much a play of love as a brilliant panorama of a period. Harold asked me what I thought it would cost in New York. "At least a million," I answered. That was in 1935. Today it would take at least two million, plus a hundred and twenty-five thousand a week, to break even.

We learned that a production of *Men in White* had been done by the Theatre of Sanitation, which did plays about hygiene. The translator of the play told us they had adapted it to protest our medieval laws against abortion. He also said that audiences were sick of revolutionary plays in which the typical Soviet hero they had seen so many times was portrayed as self-sacrificing, disciplined, thinking only of his task of building Socialism. "The audience wants comedy, romance, satire—love is popular again," he explained.

The wife of a dramatist agreed, telling us, "They have had too much of political plays. They want lovely plays, nice costumes, music, no politics. A happy ending is obligatory." Harold and I grinned at each other. They might have been talking about Broadway.

The Lower Depths was the first play we saw at the Moscow Art, sitting in Stanislavsky's seats, which had a brass plaque with his name. Their famous actor Moskvin played Louka, the simple-minded servant, a character I had seen played in New York as a fumbling, dreamy fool, spouting philosophical platitudes. When Moskvin spouted the platitudes, he would scratch his behind or keep busy sweeping, eating, serving, sewing, making a sandal. One couldn't think of him as an actor except with difficulty. He was Louka "to the life," not a mystical idealist but a simple, homely peasant with practical wisdom, never sentimental.

Katchalov, another of their top actors, played the Baron. His face was a noble ruin. He was all aristocrat, manicuring his nails to a high polish with an old rag, putting on his cotton gloves with holes where his fingers came through as though they were the finest yellow chamois. The way he smelled his food, the dainty way he ate and drank showed a refined sensibility, but his slightly shaking head bespoke senility. Moskvin was so real he did not seem to be acting at all, but one was aware of Katchalov's intellect, carefully planning all the small details of his character as an aristocrat in spite of his seedy clothes. Yet we were dissatisfied. Most of the other actors were uninteresting and the performance as a whole did not ignite, did not seem to be kindled with any fusing idea or purpose. It made us realize that more is needed than technique, good actors and a good play. As Harold said, "There must be a common vision, consciously directed. In the Moscow Art the little things are good. In the Meyerhold theatre it is the big things that are good."

The Cherry Orchard was the most satisfying production we saw at the Moscow Art. Two of the original company, Moskvin and Olga Knipper Chekhova, Chekhov's wife, performed. She was playing Madame Ranevskaya, a part she had originated in 1913. Twenty-two years later she and Moskvin were still playing freshly, the realism perfect, warm and human. "This is the cream of bourgeois art," Harold said. I had seen Alla Nazimova play Ranevskaya at Eva Le Gallienne's Civic Repertory Theatre. She was wayward, sexually attractive, careless of her precarious situation, glamorous; whereas Knipper Chekhova was old, too ample and unable to bring these qualities to the part. But when she sat at the table opposite Lopachin and learned that everything had been lost due to her improvidence, she was extremely touching. The truth hit her slowly; her hands fluttered on the table, her face grew immobile as she faced reality for the first time. At this moment she surpassed Nazimova's performance and moved me more deeply.

When we saw *Camille* or *The Lady of the Camellias,* as Meyerhold called it, I didn't particularly like it because of the poor acting. The production was nevertheless more vivid than many other versions of this play have been. On Meyerhold's small stage it was not possible to fly any scenery, so Meyerhold used three curtains—one blue, one white, one green—hanging at angles to each other from perceptible wires about ten feet high. There was one large French window with a curving top that was used in various positions for different scenes. In spite of these simple, primitive curtains, the opulence of the furniture, props and costumes enabled you almost to smell the period, its extravagance and sexual seductiveness: the enormous white grand piano with elegant golden candelabra and lighted tapers, the oriental hangings, the intricately carved mirror, the white fur bear rug still with its head, the expensively brocaded period sofa, the languid chairs upholstered in sea green, the small round table covered with a cloth of gold and silver and holding a carved glass vase of white camellias, the intricately chased gold clock.

Marguerite never coughed. Her seizures took her at the piano. She would start to play Chopin, then suddenly hit a sour note— stop—start again—another mistake. You knew at once that she was ill, so the usual handkerchief to her face was eliminated.

When Armand expressed his love, he threw a veil over Marguerite's face and kissed her through it. When he left, she hugged and kissed her maid violently.

When Armand got angry, Marguerite shrugged, raised him to his feet, put her arm through his and walked his temper off.

The farewell scene took place in a garden backed by the white curtain, which was separated by the large window. Behind the window on a raised, invisible platform stood a table with delicate curved legs, inlaid with mother-of-pearl. On the table was a large cloisonné vase filled with vari-colored roses; beside it was a large yellow straw hat with a white plume hanging down over the side. This was backed by the blue curtain. There was a low carved white fence in front of the scene downstage. A green bench on one side had a trellis of vines above it. On the other side, leaving room for an entrance into the house, was the green curtain with a bell pull attached. There was also a large country table on which sat a parrot in a fancy cage and a large bowl of varied fruits. With these rather simple, elegantly chosen means, Meyerhold had created something that resembled a French impressionist painting. The farewell scene opened with the servant bringing out a long black coat, which had fifteen or twenty buttons from the neck to the floor, for Marguerite to wear. Armand thought she was just going for a drive, and he put the coat on her and began closing the buttons. Working his way from her neck to the floor, he eventually had to kneel. So, instead of the usual vis-à-vis scene, in this production he could not look at her or see what her face showed. After she left, Armand began to walk, getting more and more uneasy as he began to realize something was wrong. He went to the bell and pulled—waited—no answer—pulled again. You heard the bell tingle, first near, then farther and farther away as the scene darkened out.

The death scene was especially impressive. There was no bed. Marguerite sat in a large chair facing the window at the back which separated the green curtain. The window was hung with thin white chiffon curtains which trembled slightly as Marguerite's hands fell to the sides of the chair and you realized she was dead. This is all as fresh to me as though I saw it last week.

The best of the new plays was *The Optimistic Tragedy* at the Kamerny Theatre directed by Tairov. It had one especially touching scene on board a ship where the sailors were having a final waltz with their girls as heavy cannon on their carriages were being rolled up a ramp to board the boat. The contrast between the wistful waltz and the heavy clanking of the death-dealing cannon expressed the pathos of war.

Harold was a splendid companion with his acute, critical observations. For hours after the performances we discussed what we had seen. By June we had been away for almost two months, and I began to feel nostalgic about the Group. We both realized how painfully we missed it—not the individuals in particular, but the sense of being a part of something larger than ourselves held together by a common purpose. Our theatre was more than an occupation; it was our life.

On the five-day boat trip from Leningrad to London and on the S.S. *Champlain* to New York we reviewed our experiences. We decided that the Moscow Art, where the only criterion seemed to be a photographic reality, a "true-to-life" experience, would be incapable of creating a variety of theatrical forms. Its naturalism tended to kill theatricality, its greatest achievement being Stanislavsky's brilliant development of a precise training method for the actor. But we concluded that stylization like Meyerhold's is only valuable when it permits one to say something that could not be said better in any other way; that there was a great difference between showmen and artists, and often the work of the latter (Meyerhold, for example) was not as agreeable, but was unforgettable.

The goal of the Group, we decided, should be to move an audience in the ethical, aesthetic sense, not to provide political theatre. We had to strive for greater discipline, personally and theatrically. We would tell our company of the attitude of the Russian actors to each other, their courtesy and forbearance, which was part of their collective strength. Our actors often behaved as though they were on the firing line—which in a way they were—giving no quarter to outsiders or even to each other. We had been bored, we confessed, with most of the classic revivals we had seen in New York, but in Moscow we had learned that many old plays could be made fresh and interesting. It was nonsense to say that classics were dated. They needed an original concept expertly carried out.

As we neared New York harbor on a June morning and saw the old lady with the torch welcoming us, our spirits soared. We had so much to tell, so much to teach. We saw members of the company waving greetings, and we were happy to be home to tackle our problems again.

Back Home

To our pleasure we found Clifford was at work on a new play, *Paradise Lost*, refusing tempting offers to go to Hollywood. Meanwhile we decided to do a play called *Weep for the Virgins* by a new author, Nelisse Child. It was about a poor working-class family in San Diego, who dreamed hopelessly of a better life. It had humor, pathos and an observant, tangy speech, but it rambled too much. John Garfield played a leading role, and I directed it. The only laugh I got from it was Bobby Lewis's naughty opening night wire, which said, *"Weep for the Virgins* Company: My dears, no one can hold a candle to you." It had nine performances. The wolf was at the door again, and this time the door was open.

But all of us believed that Odets's new play, *Paradise Lost*, might rescue us. MGM, eager to have an author like Odets in their stable, had offered him three thousand dollars a week to come to their factory. He refused, but persuaded them to put up seventeen thousand dollars for the play. When it opened in December 1935, the reviews were not favorable, even from the left-wing critics. We played seventy-three performances. Clifford left in disgust before the end to do a film for Paramount. But he had begun another play, *The Silent Partner*, which we looked forward to. Unfortunately, he was never able to get the material into suitable shape. But his interest in the Group remained, and he frequently helped financially.

Through Harold, I had met Kurt Weill and his wife, Lotte
Lenya. Fleeing Germany in 1933, they had gone first to Paris;
after some gypsying, they finally wound up in 1935 in New York,
where Max Reinhardt was producing *The Eternal Road* with a
score by Weill. I was impressed by his music, particularly *Threepenny Opera*, which I had bought in a set of German 78's. Weill
was eager to do something with an American background, and
given my perennial fondness for good popular music, I was eager
to work with him.

But before I could concentrate on discussing possibilities with
him, we had to prepare another play, *The Case of Clyde Griffiths*,
based on Theodore Dreiser's *An American Tragedy*, which Mil-
ton Shubert offered to finance. My time was spent fighting ad
nauseam with Shubert about money, attending rehearsals, buying
costumes and trying to help Lee, who was not an eager director
of this material. "Harold and Lee would never have stuck together
without me," I wrote in a consoling note to myself. "I have to
constantly introduce them to each other." For ten days or so I
worked a minimum of twelve hours a day. Daring superstition, we
opened on Friday, April 13, and in keeping with that ominous
date, we lasted a full nineteen performances. Because of this play
we missed doing Irwin Shaw's *Bury the Dead;* Shaw wanted an
immediate production. That's the play we should have done.
Presented by the New Theatre League, it was a deserved success.

Some of the company now took other jobs; some toured
Awake and Sing. But the members were increasingly dissatisfied
with our continued failures and our inability to guarantee steady
employment.

In the fall of 1935, the directors received a document headed
"Development of a Studio" and signed by twelve members of the
company, including Odets, Lewis and Kazan. Here are excerpts
from it that indicate the actors' concerns.

Dear Directors:
    Herewith we submit to you the following result of some of us
meeting together, in the assurance that it will be read and accepted,
thought about and answered, in the same simplicity of desire and
thought in which it was formulated.

As one way to make the Group inspiration a living thing again, and for other practical reasons, we want to develop studio work on a well-grounded and regular basis.

We would like to rehearse plays either old or new which are primarily actors' plays and which are cast for the sake of the development of the actors who are not likely to have the chance to work on long parts in the Broadway productions for some time, the direction of these plays to be in the hands of Lee as far as may be possible.

We would like to know what methods are being formulated other than the usual line between agent and producer to contact plays for us both here and abroad. If nothing new is being done about it, we would like to discuss and work out possible ways of going about it.

We would like to have from the directors a more definite analysis of that rather general phrase "value to the Group." We need to know some of these things:

> What do the rewards of salary and work mean to a Group actor as differentiated from what they usually mean in the commercial theatre? If there is a difference, do not the opportunities of each individual to develop and expand both in life and art have a direct bearing upon the growth and integrity of the Group as a whole? Are we definitely working toward a basis which will allow Group value to be assessed and rewarded in terms of reality rather than on the partially opportunistic ones now thought to be necessary?

The company's vocal demands for reappraisal and representation were harsh. All of the requests had merit, but there didn't seem to be a lot we could do about them, because we lacked both money and energy to implement them. However, Harold said he would write out a plan which he would announce to the company. On May 1 Lee wrote him, and I quote a portion of his letter.

Spoke to Cheryl the other day. She feels, too, that the first thing to clear is the organizational set-up of the Group. Much as I agree that the three directors are the most able to lead a theatre—it still seems to me to be necessary to do something *if the Group is to develop.* When two people marry—one may feel himself competent to run everything—but if the marriage is to be successful some mutual "giving in" is necessary. It cannot remain a "honeymoon" nor remain just as it was before. It is a new step which necessitates a certain amount of rearrangement—and no amount of "pure" logic can change that necessity. When a child grows up it *must* do certain things, possibly with dangerous results. There is no other path in life.

Collective activity despite its mistakes should not be either belittled or condescended to. If a thing is to be achieved, it can be accomplished only by collective activity utilizing to the full the individual endowments of the people it is composed of. I do not think that the Group Theatre can be built by the three directors alone—or any other three directors —except by constant replacements. But it can be built by the Group as a whole realizing and solving its own problems, even if thereby certain mistakes are made, mistakes which are inevitable in any case.

You and Cheryl must be faced by the fact that personally, I do not care to be a director. [Lee is referring to the onerous responsibility of administration, not directing plays.] I do not want to have anything to do with any of the detailed work. It is true that this may be simply the result of the existing situation, and the unpleasantness involved in serving as a director—but whatever the causes, I am absolutely unwilling to risk my personal sanity in such activity. I think that the three of us have come as near to complete nervous breakdown as I have ever seen people verge on—not because of overwork, or hard work, but because of mental worry and strain. Personally I do not wish to continue it. This is not the simple emotional reaction—I feel fine now, but I wish to continue to do so. Which means that if you decide simply to reclarify the group organization and retain the form of directorial responsibility I will have to receive a leave of absence from performance of those functions for at least a year or two.

At the time Harold was in Chicago with the *Awake and Sing* group, having followed Stella Adler there. These two extraordinary human beings had an ambivalent relationship of pursuit and flight which sometimes incapacitated Harold. I thought then that an interesting book could be written about them—not identifying either of them but expressing symbolically their hazardous interdependence. It might be called *Wolf on the Carcass*.

In response to Lee's letter and the eroding situation, Harold submitted a plan that he would become the managing director supported by a committee of actors. This was discussed endlessly and finally accepted. Since *Awake and Sing* had not made any money on tour, we had, as usual, no funds; we decided to play again for our suppers. A large camp called Pine Brook outside of Trumbull, Connecticut accepted us. Although there were several prospects of plays, there was nothing in hand, so Kurt and I began talking again.

Kurt wanted a very American subject. The most American

playwright I could think of was Paul Green, who also wrote poetry and might be able to do the lyrics. I phoned and asked if Kurt and I could come to talk with him at his home in Chapel Hill. He seemed delighted. So off we went, Kurt and I. The material that seemed most promising was on the subject of World War I, in which Paul had served, believing with Woodrow Wilson, whom he admired, that it would be the war to end all wars and make the world safe for democracy. In our search we discussed *The Good Soldier Schweik,* Buechner's *Wozzek* and *The Captain of Koepenik* for general inspiration. We spent days at the local library reading newspaper articles about the period and even *Dere Mable,* a popular novel of letters from a private soldier. At night we talked, and soon a rough scenario began to evolve. Paul credited me with being the sparkplug that fired the project. Certainly this was the kind of work I really enjoyed, inspiring new works and being a part of their development.

Since Kurt, Paul and I needed to be in close contact, we took a house about a mile from Pine Brook. This made the summer much pleasanter for me; I had had my fill of living packed like a sardine with the vacationing, fun-loving guests. Kurt worked at his piano below my bedroom, so the songs were drilled into my head day and night. We called the script *Johnny Johnson* after our hero, an ordinary simple soldier who hated war and tried to stop it. The story was told in terms of vaudeville, fantasy and poetry.

The script progressed slowly. We didn't get anything in shape to rehearse until about two weeks before we had to leave Pine Brook. Of course there was no money and I could already see that this would be our most expensive production. My budget was about sixty thousand dollars, a lot for those days. Today I would need to budget it at seven hundred and fifty thousand. Fortunately, Kurt did his own orchestrations, which saved money.

Back in New York, Kurt, Lenya, Dorothy Patten and I decided to share an apartment to economize. We found a perfect one on the East River at Fifty-first Street; Lillian and Dorothy Gish had lived there, so it had two entirely separate wings with a common kitchen and dining alcove. My bedroom overlooked the river. How peaceful it was to see the smokestacks from my bed

—and occasionally the mast of a ship. I got Rosa Johnson, an extra in the original *Porgy*, to cook and take care of us for twenty or twenty-five dollars a week. I loved that woman. She was shrewd and she was dedicated. She worked for me for fifteen years when I could pay her and when I couldn't. Later I gave her a piece of the profits in several of my shows, which helped when she became too ill to work. When I visited her in the hospital, she made one request of me—that she be buried in a particular cemetery in New Jersey. I asked her why.

"Because the birds sing there," she said.

"How do you know?"

"I can hear them on the radio when the cemetery advertises."

She *was* buried there, and if the birds aren't singing for her, they ought to be ashamed of themselves.

It was a relief to get back to that spacious apartment after the daily agonies we suffered with *Johnny Johnson*. I developed Kurt's acquaintance with American jazz since I had, and still do, a sizeable collection of records. I also taught him to like applejack, the cheapest drink we could buy during Prohibition (four dollars a gallon).

Lee rehearsed as we searched for backing. Mrs. Motty Eitingon (Bess), a wealthy woman enamoured of the theatre, had made friends with many of the company. She also admired Kurt and agreed to put up forty thousand dollars. Someone, I think it was Lewis Milestone, suggested to Harold that we should approach John Hay Whitney, who said he would send a representative to see a run-through when we were ready. He sent Robert Benchley, who saw it at a tiny theatre, now gone, and was most enthusiastic. It really looked charming in this little house, even with no scenery. The mostly untrained voices were adequate, even attractive, in the small auditorium.

A meeting was arranged for me with Mr. Whitney and his lawyer. I was escorted to a large impressive room to speak my piece. There were four men seated at a table which seemed to extend indefinitely, and I was intimidated. I told them we had forty thousand and needed twenty more. Then Mr. Whitney's lawyer spoke up.

"Since this is the final money you need, we should have an

extra inducement to become investors. What are you prepared to offer?"

This contingency had never occurred to me, but I quickly realized I was helpless. Instead of answering him, I turned directly to Mr. Whitney.

"This is nothing I can haggle over," I answered. "We need the money desperately, so whatever you think is fair we will accept."

I saw a blush come up from Mr. Whitney's neck and over his face.

He thumped a hand on the table. "No!" he said. "I don't want anything extra. We will give you the money."

My frankness had worked. I was relieved, of course, but especially delighted because my baby, *Johnny Johnson,* was going to have a chance.

We needed every penny of that money. The show was very complex. It had nineteen sets, some of them enormous since they were designed to fit into a very large musical house, the Forty-fourth Street Theatre, where today the news vans of the *New York Times* are parked. The dress rehearsals were a shambles and much more expensive than I had counted on. So we needed still more money. Harold "begged, borrowed, and stole" additional amounts.

The unfortunately huge theatre was partly responsible for the debacle that ensued. But no other theatre was available, and we couldn't afford to wait for one to open. The sets, which were quite elaborate, overpowered the actors. We communicated during the final harrowing previews mostly by screams, our faces withered with strain. We were really afraid that the production would never get together, sure that it would appear heavy, inept and unprofessional.

Surprisingly, opening night went smoothly. The three huge cannons pushed out to the audience over the top of the trenches on time, singing sweetly to the sleeping soldiers. The large Statue of Liberty appeared promptly to sing a lovely song to Johnny as he stood on board a troop ship leaving for France. The audience's response to the show was excellent, and the three directors, barely able to stand, were, as Lee would say, "flabbergasted."

But the critics were either unimpressed, or, if sympathetic, did not write money notices. We closed after sixty-eight performances. It was a heavy blow to me. I had believed that *Johnny* was a truly fresh form of musical. I didn't think I could endure much more.

Since then the play has been revived in New York and around the country a number of times. In 1974 it had a run in Germany, and in 1975 it ran successfully at the National Theatre in Helsinki. So *Johnny Johnson* was not totally misbegotten.

The Group cupboard was now bare, and we were all exhausted. In a desperate attempt to keep us going, Harold began to rehearse Odets's *The Silent Partner*, which Lee and I felt was far from ready, especially since Odets was busy in Hollywood. After a few weeks, Harold agreed with us and abandoned the project.

Some of the actors, particularly the more radical ones, were unwilling to wave the white flag. (I didn't know until many years later when the McCarthy hearings began that there actually was a cell in the Group, members who were determined to advance a complete reorganization and politization.) They presented to each director a document containing strong criticism of our activities, our inability to secure them a steady, living wage and continuing artistic activity. In this chronicle they also ran a painful juggernaut over the three directors, criticizing their characters and activities. Of me they said in part, "She's had six years of dirty jobs. She feels that she is a 'martyr' to the Group, that without her the Group would fold in a minute and, worst of all, that no one appreciates her—that what other people receive credit for doing is really her work. We should get a business manager whom we really trust to take over these tasks. Cheryl's job lies in the creation of scripts like *Johnny Johnson* and tasks of general finance and promotion."

The criticism seemed harsh but true. Still stinging from these judgments as well as our increasing criticism of each other, the three of us met and decided to resign in a body. When we presented this resolve to the company, they were startled. They hadn't expected so drastic a reaction. They had an alternative suggestion: to form a committee composed of the three directors and three members of the company to reorganize the theatre. But the few meetings of the six were futile. With no plays and no subsidy there seemed to be nothing to do but stop, at least for a time—to get back our health and sanity and find easier ways to survive. Harold went to Hollywood, where Stella was already engaged in films. He felt he needed time and some easing of the strain in order to assess the form in which we should try to continue. He was convinced that we would continue. I was doubtful. But when word came, I think through John Wildberg, that Walter Wanger was interested in making some sort of general deal for Group actors' employment in films, Wildberg and I flew to the Coast to try to work out a deal, and many of the company followed. Six had already gone and fifteen followed.

I spent some time with Doris Warner and her husband, Mervyn LeRoy, whom I had met when *Men in White* opened. LeRoy was then the wonder-boy director at Warners. We got on well, and he offered me a job as his assistant starting at seven hundred and fifty dollars a week, escalating over a period of a year and a half to fifteen hundred. After the Group's poverty and my constant worry about money, these astronomical figures boggled my mind. How tempting that salary was, not to mention the ubiquitous swimming pools. I studied many of the successful people who were in films, and I weighed the Hollywood atmosphere. It struck me as Never Never Land. Even if I could survive there, and I wasn't sure I could, it wasn't the way I wanted to spend my life; I wanted to prove myself in the theatre, as a producer. In the end I refused, though my prospects, the Group's prospects, were dim.

We were able to make a deal with Wanger for a number of the actors. They were to receive a hundred and fifty dollars a week against their salaries when they secured a film role. Most of them agreed to send back ten percent of their earnings to support a New York office. Wanger agreed to pay me a hundred a week for a limited length of time, and I returned to New York to set up a small, inexpensive office as a center for the company from which to search for scripts.

But any money from the Coast was sporadic and inadequate.

No one could be blamed for this. Most of the actors just managed to get by; some of them never got a film job. My urgent wires and letters to Roman Bohnen, who was a committee member on the Coast, produced little result.

To boot, we had no plays. No plays—and no agreement among the three directors. The friction that occurs when failure is imminent was intense. The seven-year marriage of Harold Clurman, Lee Strasberg and Cheryl Crawford was dissolving.

By March I could continue no longer. I had sat too long in an empty office grueling myself into a coma. I felt like a chicken scratching for food in a bone-dry barnyard. But what were the alternatives? I had rejected Hollywood for the live theatre. Could I go it alone? Could I find a partner?

While I was debating what to do, I received a letter from Kurt saying he was eager to do something with me. He wrote:

> I miss you very much. I have the feeling you speak my language— and that is something very seldom. And you know better than anybody here what I can do and what I want to do. Don't worry. Hollywood won't get me. A whore never loves the man who pays her. She wants to get rid of him as soon as she has rendered her services. That is my relation to Hollywood (I am the whore).
> Well, enough philosophy for this time!
> Please write me often—and let's do a fine show!

(It's curious about Hollywood: nearly every writer blasted it but most of them liked the cash.)

Not long before I got Kurt's letter I had received one from Clifford, accompanying a check for five hundred dollars to be divided among the actors. Clifford observed how easy life was for writers in Hollywood; they were given sizeable salaries and had plenty of time to do their own work. "I am getting to be pretty sure that complaints against Hollywood mean complaints really against one's own talent," he said, and closed with his plans to start a new play in two weeks. That play became *Golden Boy*.

It helped to know that Kurt thought enough of me to want to do a show with me. Would others? I didn't know. But I made up my mind. On March 17, I wrote my letter of resignation:

Dear Council,

After the most serious consideration I feel that I must leave the Group. I had thought I would write you a long explanation of my reasons, but I think that at this time they would not serve their purpose of making myself clear to you; and besides the difficulty of writing exactly what I mean on paper is very great. The shock and surprise of my determination is perhaps greater to me than it will be to you, but I have tried to deal with my problems logically and sanely and unsentimentally.

I plan to stay in the theatre and consequently will have to make an announcement of my leaving within a short time. If you wish me to write you my reasons I will try to make the attempt, or at any convenient time I will be glad to talk them over with any or all of you. I hope very much that you will not feel I am failing in responsibility to the Group in making this step, for if my interpretation of the reports I have received from the Coast is correct, I have not done so.

I would like to say that I still believe with all my heart in a Group Theatre and that the objective or outside situations which have caused us so much strain and difficulty *can* be slowly solved, but the inner situation seems to me incapable of solution at least at this time.

Believe me that I more deeply regret this than anything I have ever had to do, but it truly seems to be necessary and inevitable.

In retrospect, I feel that one of the chief failures was our inability to find or develop enough good plays to reflect what we wanted to say about life in America. And it was somewhat insane to assume such plays could be found in sufficient number to sustain a permanent company. Our blunders in rejecting *Winterset* and *Bury the Dead* were serious. They were superior in craft and content to other plays we did produce, and they would have eased our financial difficulties. After observing the Russian theatre, I realized that we could have done some classic plays, finding a point of view to make them vital and relevant to our own times.

And I wonder what would have happened if we had been given sufficient financial backing to enable us to plan our activities ahead, to commission scripts, to release our energies for greater theatrical activities, to be free from personal worry about money. There was no National Council of the Arts or State Council then. Harold and I once approached Otto Kahn, who had been a heavy benefactor of the Theatre Guild and the Civic Repertory. As he sat smoothing his distinguished White Guard's moustache, he said sadly that he couldn't help. Conditions were terrible. He even managed to look poor. I went alone to see Robert Lehman, probably in one of the rooms now deified as the Lehman Wing of the Metropolitan Museum. He also regretted. I realized that poor was relative. By their standards they felt poor; by mine they were each Maecenas.

We were criticized because some of our actors were not very talented. Talents are not created equal. The lesser ones were devoted and trained. Companies need actors willing to play the anonymous private soldiers, the maids, the unidentified bar flies, the crowd.

I think that what held us together for so long was the trust in each other that we had shared. In spite of disaffections and dissensions, we accepted each other's foibles, eccentricities, weaknesses. We were frequently annoyed by them, but always that trust existed. And there was something wonderful about its coalescing power.

Perhaps more important than any of its productions was the fact that the Group Theatre became the seed which supplied the inspiration for many theatre projects that followed. Various groups sprang up all over the country, often headed or advised by members of the Group. I didn't know then that there would ever be an Actors Studio, but I do know it would never have been born had not the Group preceded it.

Shortly after my resignation Lee followed suit. He and I then met to plan to work together if I could find a play worth doing. I had a lot to find: playwrights, an inexpensive office, someone to work with me who could afford to pay expenses—and the emotional wherewithal to go it alone. For I was on my own now both professionally and spiritually. I had lost my religion in college. Then for seven years my religion had been my faith in the ideals and values of the Group. Now that had dissolved, and I was thrown back on myself, a solitary individual. It was scary. I needed some support, some guidance.

Poetry, which I had loved since my childhood, came to my

rescue. It may seem corny, but it happens to be true that I was sustained by a passage from Walt Whitman. I learned it by heart:

I know I am solid and sound,
To me the converging objects of the universe perpetually flow,
All are written to me, and I must get what the writing means.

And I know I am deathless,
I know this orbit of mine cannot be swept by a carpenter's
     compass,
I know I shall not pass like a child's carlacue cut with a burnt
     stick at night.

I know I am august,
I do not trouble my spirit to vindicate itself or be understood,
I see that the elementary laws never apologize,
I reckon I behave no prouder than the level I plant my house
     by after all.

I exist as I am, that is enough,
If no other in the world be aware I sit content,
And if each and all be aware I sit content.

One world is aware, and by far the largest to me, and that is
     myself,
And whether I come to my own today or in ten thousand or
     ten million years,
I can cheerfully take it now, or with equal cheerfulness I can
     wait.

My foothold is tenoned and mortised in granite,
I laugh at what you call dissolution,
And I know the amplitude of time.

On My Own

Soon I felt exhilarated, even cocky, to be on my own. I was going to do great things, bring to audiences distinguished plays, quality entertainment. I was thirty-five. In a pleasant, airy two-room office in the St. James Theatre I began to search for plays with an assistant, Elizabeth Hull, an old friend who had once worked for the Theatre Guild. Since her income was substantial, she covered the secretary's salary and usually paid the rent of fifty dollars a month. Maurice Evans, Eddie Dowling and John Golden, who boasted that he produced "clean plays," occupied the rest of the floor. On several occasions Eddie Dowling paid my rent when the situation was desperate.

Starting in the fall of 1937, I began to prove what I could do. I succeeded in presenting five failures one right after another. The first had four handsome sets. On the night of the final run-through in New York, they were in a baggage car all ready to go to Philadelphia the next morning. When the run-through was over, all concerned, except the actors and director, retired to a bar across the street, where I had to tell the single bewildered backer that the show was hopeless and he had better cut his losses. The sets were removed to Cain's warehouse, and I spent the night lacerating myself for being a fool.

The second, starring Ina Claire, opened in Boston. Ina had

seen Otto Preminger's work abroad, and she insisted that he direct. He and I didn't communicate very successfully; so much for that relationship. Ina was one of the most beautiful women I have ever seen and a skilled comedienne, but she was allergic to learning lines. At night after the performance I would lie in bed at the Ritz inventing stern monologues with which to scold her the next morning. Steeled by many cups of coffee, I would go to her room determined to let her have it. She was always in bed in a lovely peignoir of pink and lace, her blond hair curling around her peaches-and-cream face, her saucy blue Irish eyes twinkling and a beguiling smile playing around perfect white teeth. I would melt. The most devastating remark I could produce was "Oh, Ina, come on now. You must learn your lines." The critics were not impressed, and I let the play die in Boston.

The third play, *All the Living*, directed by Lee Strasberg, I was rather proud of. I think it was the first time a play was located in an insane asylum, and for the first time on stage a young catatonic was cured by the injection of a newly discovered medicine. But fifty-three performances finished it.

A newspaper article at the time featured a picture of me, round-faced and grinning, with the caption, " 'A play producer takes more chances than anyone on earth and winds up with more wooden nickels. We stick to it only because it's in our blood, I guess,' explains producer in skirts." The producer in skirts went on to say, "What did I have to get me here? A ton of nerve and the same philosophy a gambler has."

Those qualities got me to my fourth play, which really had some distinction and ran for one hundred and eleven performances. Unfortunately, that didn't make it a commercial success. It was *Family Portrait*, a play about Mary, the mother of Jesus, and her children. When I first read it, it was very long and full of enough food, edible animals and descriptions of food to feed a whole village. I cut the food first. Near the end there was a brief scene between Mary and one of her sons whose wife had just given birth to a boy. The young man asked his mother what name she would choose. "Call him Jesus," she said. "I would like him not to be forgotten." When I read that line, I cut everything that followed. It was impossible to top, and some of the audience remembered it even years later.

Customarily, even before a director was chosen, I would hold conferences with writers on changes, and I often wrote my opinions for them. My next major task was the play's financing.

I want to explain how a play is set up financially, because few people seem to understand it. I have discovered that even actors and writers rarely know how it is done.

When a play is bought and scheduled for production, the producer, often with his business manager, must prepare two budgets, one for production and one for operating. The production budget covers the cost of mounting the show; the operating budget is the cost of running it weekly. Usually, we add to the production budget the possibility of a ten to twenty percent overcall to cover emergencies. Some of this has to be guesswork, as the cost of scenery, costumes, etc., cannot be determined yet. These budget estimates become part of a lengthy prospectus meant to inform and protect backers. It includes a digest of the play's story, the rules and regulations of operation, a detailed explanation of the risk to investors, a reminder that a majority of plays produced result in loss, the previous profit and loss record of the producer, an estimate of how long it would take for the play to return its investment at capacity attendance, and so on and so on until the prospectus practically becomes a book. The prospectus must be approved by the Securities and Exchange Commission before the producer can solicit backers.

Approved prospectus in hand, a producer goes looking for financing. In the old days, when productions cost five to twenty thousand dollars, many producers like Belasco, Sam Woods, Gilbert Miller and John Golden put up their own money. Today this is scarcely possible. Let's say the production cost for a play is two hundred thousand dollars now. Even a single "unit" (one percent) of a two-hundred-thousand-dollar production would require an investment of four thousand dollars. If you can secure the services of a star in advance, financing becomes easier, because backers believe, often wrongly, that the name represents insurance; even a big name doesn't guarantee a hit, especially with a bad play.

When the play opens, the backers receive all profits, from whatever source—film rights, stock, foreign and amateur rights—until their full investment has been returned. After that, the customary division of profits is fifty percent to the investors and fifty percent to the producer. However, the producer frequently has to give up some of his share to an associate who has been helpful in raising money or to a backer who invests an unusually large amount. As costs have risen, it has become customary for a producer to take at least one percent of the weekly gross, since he was supervising a show without income until it paid off. I was one of the last producers to take a percentage—a foolish gesture, because I could keep a play running for a year, and still end up having worked for nothing after I repaid most of the investment.

It was not easy to raise the financing for *Family Portrait.* However, some simple souls who were not aware of my poor record were moved by the play and put up half the money. The husband of Charlotte Greenwood, a well-known comedienne who was famous for kicking high an exceptionally long leg, promised the other half. Judith Anderson was set to star, Margaret Webster to direct and play one scene as Mary Magdalene, and Harry Horner to do the sets, including a replica of da Vinci's *Last Supper.* Things looked rosy.

On a Saturday two weeks before we were to go into rehearsal, Greenwood's husband phoned and asked for a meeting at my office. Elizabeth Hull went with me, and we both listened with shock as he told us that he had changed his mind. He had made bad investments, he said. Maybe. I didn't care. All I knew was that we were committed to expenditures we couldn't possibly afford. Where were we going to get the money? What were we going to do? Finally, I recalled that two young producers I knew, Day Tuttle and Richard Skinner, had read the play and liked it. I got hold of them and told them the circumstances. Saved! They agreed to get the money. My relief was inexpressible.

The authors of *Family Portrait,* Leonore Coffee and her husband William Cowen, were quite opposed to Judith Anderson in the role of Mary. They wanted Katharine Cornell or Jane Cowl. So the rehearsals were not very friendly, and I endured frequent blow-ups. Peggy Webster was a woman whose temper flared easily. At one rehearsal when the authors interrupted, Peggy blazed with fury, flung her new fur coat on the stage floor and stamped up and down on it before leaving the theatre to cool off. It was an extraordinary example of what we now call primal therapy. Why her fur coat should have substituted for the bodies of the writers, I never knew.

Leonore Coffee was a sort of raging Pollyanna, and Judith was not known for her easy disposition. In this part, however, she became a lamb, choosing a behavior that suited the mother of Christ. At the costume parade in Eaves Costume Shop, for instance, Judith put on her simple pale blue gown, walked over to Leonore with whom she had not spoken since rehearsals began, and, in an effort at conciliation, asked how Leonore liked her costume.

"I think it's bloody awful," was the acerbic reply. Judith, whose verbal punches I would trust to win in any battle, turned "the other cheek" and walked away. Yes, she was Mary!

After the opening Judith's notices were fantastic. Those words one longs for were there from all the critics—"superb," "sublime," "inspired," "unforgettable," "played with deep compassion and genuine spiritual beauty," "a valuable contribution to the social thought of today," "the most important play this reviewer has seen in more than twenty years," "to sit with an audience held to such reverent attention, thrilled to such emotional depths is a theatre adventure not often duplicated." Even George Jean Nathan, the John Simon of his day, had fine and stirring words for it, unlike his customary acrimonious reactions.

Pleased as I was by these encomiums, I was still critical of the production. It was nice—too nice. The dialogue was small town, the acting, although skillful, was small town too, with the exception of Judith's. With memories of what Meyerhold had accomplished in showing ordinary village life with such inventiveness, I felt this production was somewhat bloodless, lacking unusual details that would prick an audience into unexpected recognitions. Peggy was one of the most intelligent women I ever knew. She was a no-nonsense director, a "get on with it" director trained in the English repertory system, a facile and adroit craftsman with great technical knowledge. But she was not innovative. She loved to act, and if she had ever been given a part where the passion in her, mostly concealed, could have had an opportunity really to explode, she would have surprised us and herself. I thought her wrong for Mary Magdalene. The role would have been more interesting played by a sensual and vulnerable actress.

In any case, the Catholic Church banned the play, and there seemed to be too few Protestants who attended theatre. Judith, who had a high regard for money and customarily received a star salary plus a percentage of the gross, played for Equity's minimum, then one hundred and ten dollars. Even so, *Family Portrait* closed after about three months.

I was usually in financial straits in those days, but I found ways to keep my head above water and I never stopped struggling. Various devices kept me afloat. I was employed as executive administrator of the Bureau of New Plays founded by Theresa Helburn and funded, I think, by film companies. A group of young playwrights, chosen by us, met every week to have their plays read and discussed and to listen to experienced theatre people talk. For this I received fifty dollars a week, which doesn't sound like much now but would probably be the equivalent in purchasing power of four times as much today. Then, while Judith Anderson was rehearsing and performing in *Family Portrait*, I rented her my apartment—at a profit—and lived above in the apartment of a friend who had left it unoccupied for about a year.

So, one way or another, I got by and proceeded to produce my fifth failure, *Another Sun*, by Dorothy Thompson and the German actor-director Fritz Kortner. At this time Dorothy was forty-five and had been booted out of Germany for her passionate articles against Fascism. She was a world-famous journalist, one of the most influential of her time, consulted by heads of state and read by millions, including me.

Another Sun was about German intellectuals forced to flee their country and find refuge—which proved to be uncomfortable—in the United States. The theme was on the side of the angels, the writing rather mediocre. Celeste Holm played her first legitimate role in this play. ("Legitimate," by the way, has nothing to do with paternity. It means a straight play as distinguished from circuses, vaudeville, nightclubs and musicals.)

Kortner directed the play. He was a stocky, dark, powerful-looking man with a bluish jowl and wild temper. He seemed to delight in treating Dorothy as if she were an incompetent inferior. To my astonishment she accepted it, either because she felt he was a professional in the theatre and she wasn't, or because she was somewhat enamoured of him and wanted to please him. On one occasion he even frightened me with a conflagration of bellowing that shook the theatre. Dorothy sat quietly as he tore from the stage into the orchestra, looking like a crazed gorilla, his face purple, his eyes bulging. He strode up the aisle past me, yelling that he was through, through! To call his bluff, I simulated an anger I didn't feel. "Okay! Okay!" I shouted. "Let's quit! Let's forget it!" Since this was his first, and I think only, job in New York, that was the last thing he wanted to do; the suffusion of purple soon sluiced away. I must admit that in later years I read of many distinguished things he did in the German theatre. But at the time I was distressed at Dorothy's humiliation.

Dorothy and I often went together after evening rehearsals to a small, ugly bar next to the theatre. We didn't talk much about the play. We talked about ourselves, about being ambitious, independent women. Neither of us felt that we had suffered from being women in a man's world—partly, perhaps, because we were just too determined and engrossed to notice. I'm not sure we really cared whose world it was as long as we could pursue our careers. Our consciousness had not been raised. "Women's liberation" was a phrase of the future. Had it existed then, however, I think we would soon have become part of it.

There was an interesting dichotomy in Dorothy's personality. Her mind and her writing had what was called then "a masculine character"—hard-hitting, no-holds-barred; she was a powerful crusader against all injustice and evil. Her emotional side was surprisingly feminine. Her face was innocently lovely with warm, candid eyes and an apple-cheeked complexion. She had an ample and womanly figure.

Yet Dorothy, who was ruthless in exposing the political dis-

eases of her time, was insecure about her femininity. She confessed that she needed a man, talented, strong and tender.
"Well," I said, "who doesn't and where in hell are they?" I went
on to offer her the wisdom of another woman writer. When I was
about twenty-seven, I had nervily asked Edna Ferber, "Miss Ferber, how does it feel to be an old maid?"

"Well, Cheryl," she promptly replied, "it's rather like drowning—not bad once you stop struggling."

Dorothy laughed. But it was cold comfort. Her marriage to
Sinclair Lewis had become hopeless. When I became acquainted
with him a few years later, after he had ceased drinking himself
into a stupor, I found him restless and very lonely except in the
presence of a young lady whom he adored. She had a suite in his
estate in the high hills near Williamstown, Massachusetts. His
dinner soliloquies there were astonishing. He could invent the
accurate and comical dialogue of whole groups of men and
women of our average midwestern culture, mimicking perfectly
their ideas and accents. It was more fun to listen than to eat. Red,
as he was nicknamed, and Dorothy were both lively, stimulating
people to whom I was always content to listen; their minds and
awareness were much more finely honed than mine. But I didn't
envy either of them. I knew they longed for tranquil, steady hearts
and minds which the constant compulsion of their talents denied
them.

Another Sun, my fifth failure, opened and closed quickly.

By 1940, even if I had found a play, it seemed impossible to
excavate any more unenlightened investors. Elizabeth Hull
retired to her farm in Pomfret, Connecticut. She had had it and
needed to reimburse her nerves. Now there was no one to pay the
rent. I was completely alone.

The fear of failure is a particular bugaboo for theatre people,
because our work is uniquely ephemeral. Unlike artists in other
fields, whose books, paintings or music continue to exist despite
an immediate lack of reception, our work exists only as long as the
response is favorable. So we must guard ourselves by placing any
failure in perspective.

It didn't comfort me to know the Group Theatre was in

similar straits. True, while I mounted my first failure, they had had an enviable success: in 1937 Odets's *Golden Boy* had revived them like Lazarus. It was the most successful production the Group ever achieved. But only one director, Harold Clurman, remained to face the multitudinous problems, assisted by a council of the members. To ease the burden of trying to support a large company, they paid only the actors employed in a given play. And in other ways, little by little, they cut their cloth to fit the circumstances, slowly eroding the "company" idea. After *Golden Boy*, the Group produced seven more plays, none of them financially successful. In January 1941, the long-impending obituary was written.

On the other hand, there was a story I had heard years before at a revival meeting. The preacher told of a man who fell off a cliff on a dark night and managed to cling to a branch to stop his fall. He hung on for hours in misery until he simply had to loosen his hold. With a despairing farewell to life, he dropped. He fell just six inches onto a ledge.

One day John Wildberg, who had continued to be my lawyer, came to me with a proposition. He had discovered a large movie house in Maplewood, New Jersey; it had been operating as a summer stock theatre and had just been abandoned. Jack suggested I take it over with him as associate. We would produce stock too, a different play every week.

I liked the sensible location, opposite the railroad station and close enough to New York to enable us to rehearse companies there and to enable actors to live at home. Shows on tour after their New York engagement might be interested in playing their last week in Maplewood. And the house was large enough to allow us to have modestly priced tickets. I believed I would be able to persuade many of the stars I knew to perform in such a convenient spot.

Jack also unearthed a backer for the Maplewood Theatre, little Dr. Sunshine, a plastic surgeon devoutly addicted to the theatre. Dr. Sunshine was a pleasant, unobtrusive man; the only fly in the deal, I discovered, was that he regularly authored impossible plays which I had to read and criticize. A friend nicknamed me "Billikin" after a fat doll popular at the time: it had a round, weighted bottom filled with buckshot, so that if you kicked it or knocked it to the floor, it sprang back up at once. It wouldn't stay down. Neither would I.

I ran the Maplewood Theatre for a first season of twenty-two weeks in 1940, and a second of eighteen weeks in 1941. In 1942 the season was only seven weeks because the war had forced gas rationing; most of the audience came by car. Maplewood offered a different production every week, and my choice of plays was very catholic, which was of course necessary for this sort of operation. The stars varied from Helen Hayes to Bojangles Robinson, Ethel Barrymore to Canada Lee, Ingrid Bergman and Tallulah Bankhead to Paul Robeson. The top price for a ticket was a dollar sixty-five, for matinees eighty-five cents. I used professional designers who spent more money than was customary for stock, but the shows looked first-rate.

For publicity purposes, it seemed important to identify the theatre with one person, and that was me. At first it was a very painful job to address the audience during intermissions, but I developed into a ham, full of funny stories which I collected from every possible source. I memorized each week's talk so that I seemed to be speaking off the cuff.

To create an audience I also spoke around the countryside to Lions, Elks, Hadassahs, sewing circles, banks, Democrats, Republicans, Catholics, Protestants—you name it, I spoke to it. Since I also had to cast most of the plays, I was a busy lady. Oona O'Neill, Jacqueline Susann, Robert Ryan, William Bendix and MacDonald Carey gave their first professional performances in Maplewood.

I had no private life to speak of, just occasional evenings with colleagues. A social life, not to mention a love life, takes time, and I had none to spare. It was a high price to pay.

Man's best friend became this woman's best friend. Over the years dogs have given me wonderful companionship. Does any person shiver with delight every time you return from an absence? A dog does.

All the companies who played Maplewood were well behaved,

although Tallulah Bankhead tried some mischief. She invited me
to drive back to New York in her car one evening. She put me
in the back seat. I didn't know she had also put her lion cub there.

"Darling," she called back as we drove, "you don't mind
sitting there with the cat, do you?"

Cat! The cub had already begun to prowl behind my head
with a low, hungry growl.

"Why should I? Is he edible?"

She laughed. I didn't.

She looked back several times saying, "Everything all right,
darling?"

"Of course," I said each time with a rigor mortis grimace. In
the dark she took it for a smile. I was sweating when I finally
reached home in one piece, but I was damned if I would give her
the satisfaction of my showing it.

I never heard of anyone beating Tallulah to a punch line.
Much has been written about her, but I remember one anecdote
that has not been told. A young student at Yale was enamoured
of Tallulah, after seeing her performances many times and listening avidly to stories of her wild sexual activities. Eventually he
found a friend who knew her and insisted on being taken backstage to meet her. "By God," he told his friend, "I know how to
shock her." When they were introduced, he announced proudly,
"Guess what, Miss Bankhead, I am going to fuck you tonight."

Without a pause she volleyed back, "And so you shall, you
dear old-fashioned boy."

The third time Tallulah played for me was in *The Little
Foxes,* and we had quite a to-do negotiating her salary. A thousand dollars was the most I had paid any star. She insisted on
fifteen hundred. I begged her to take the thousand plus a percentage of the gross over the breakeven. She was adamant, so reluctantly I gave in. Before she arrived on Sunday for a quick rehearsal
in the set with lights, she had played a much smaller stock theatre.
When I greeted her she was very surly. I asked if it was the set.
No, she was upset because the week before she had played on a
percentage and taken almost nineteen hundred dollars. In spite
of our contract I assured her that if we did good business she

would suffer no loss. After the final Saturday matinee I sent two checks back to her dressing room, one for the agreed salary, the other for about four hundred dollars. Before the audience had evacuated the theatre, I heard fog-horn screams of "Crawford! Crawford!" I rushed backstage to find out what was wrong. She was waving the second check with tears in her eyes. "I don't believe it," she said. "I'm signing my name across this check and putting it with Daddy's letters in my portfolio." And she did.

When I knew the third season would have to end because of gas rationing, I wanted to do something big, to close with a bang. My favorite popular composer was George Gershwin. For me his music and Ira's lyrics are real "Amurrican," hard, tough, joyful, bold, cheerful, affirmative, never self-pitying, never sentimentalized. The beat is relentless. They have the punch of a smack on the kisser, a three-base strike. The love songs are celebrations that make pulses leap, make dancing irresistible. Ira doesn't say, "Oh, if my man would only come along and love me"; he says, "Someday he'll *come* along—the man I love." He doesn't say, "Oh, if I could have a hug"; he says, "Embrace me, my sweet embraceable you." He doesn't say, "Bess, won't you be my woman"; he says, "Bess, you *is* my woman now."

The Gershwins' last work together had been *Porgy and Bess*, which had closed after only a hundred performances when the Theatre Guild produced it in 1932. The glorious music was more familiar now, frequently heard on the radio as individual numbers. Wildberg agreed that *Porgy and Bess* would close Maplewood with fireworks, so we got hold of the original conductor, Alexander Smallens, and located most of the original cast. We closed the theatre for a week in order to rehearse.

When I had seen the 1932 production I had been critical of only one element, the recitatives, which, I felt, were out of keeping with the black milieu. As the Maplewood rehearsals began, Smallens and I sat in the theatre with a score between us and carefully cut recitatives we thought were out of place or unnecessary. That may seem sacrilegious to some, but I never got a thrill out of a recitative like "Oh God! Don't let them take Bess to the hospital!" The show became more of a piece and flowed swiftly and tunefully. It was joyfully received, and we blazed happily out of Maplewood.

Stock may not seem like the sort of highminded dream I had engaged myself to accomplish, but I was proud of the productions and of the low cost of seats. Every year since, as I have stood in the lobby of some theatre, people have approached me to say that they first enjoyed the theatre at Maplewood. If Maplewood did nothing but inspire love of drama in young people, it was worthwhile.

Lee Shubert came out to see *Porgy and Bess* and was impressed. Wildberg invited several Wall Street financiers who decided they could afford to invest twenty-four thousand five hundred dollars, the total cost of production. So I called on Lee Shubert to discuss a theatre. "You will have the Majestic," he said, and tears sprang to my eyes. (I cry easily, usually over injustice or anything I find beautiful and moving.) "Oh, Mr. Lee," I wept, "that big old barn has been a jinx house for years. Please don't put us there." But the silver letter opener kept scratching his head in that familiar gesture, and I knew I was licked. Of course today, because of its size and location, the Majestic is probably one of the most desirable theatres in New York. We went into the Majestic at a two dollar and fifty cent top. The "jinx house" didn't hurt us: the notices were sensational. We broke even at sixteen thousand dollars, and we ran and ran. We toured the country, and then returned to New York for two repeat engagements.

I was sitting pretty and that felt comfortable. I produced two more plays in 1942: Marc Connelly's *The Flowers of Virtue* and *A Kiss for Cinderella,* starring Luise Rainer, which I had done in Maplewood. Luckily *Porgy and Bess* was going strong, because neither of them went far.

My success with *Porgy* and my failure with straight plays made me think that my fortunes lay in the musical theatre. So I began a search for something unusual.

One Touch of Venus

The phones never stopped as the search began. I wanted something original, meaningful and entertaining—a tough combination. I called play agents in New York and Hollywood, and writers all around the country. Soon my desk was piled with scripts, novels, stories. But none of them appealed to me.

Then I thought of Kurt Weill, who had just had a walloping hit with *Lady in the Dark*. So in June of 1942 Kurt and I began to talk about doing our second show together. Aline Bernstein had given Kurt a copy of a novella by F. Anstey entitled *The Tinted Venus*, saying she thought it had possibilities. Kurt was convinced that this book would make a good musical; in fact, he told me, he had been playing around with music for it for some time.

The story concerned an "ordinary" man, Rodney Hatch, a barber, who accidentally brings a statue of Venus to life. The goddess of love immediately falls in love with him. But he is happily engaged to an "ordinary" girl, and Venus is amazed at his reluctance to reciprocate her feelings. From then on, of course, the issue is, who is right for whom: can mortal and immortal find happiness together?

This appealed to me right away because it could involve the world as we see it and as the goddess sees it and allow us to compare the two views, which would of course be quite different. I thought it could have social bearing and also be amusing. "All right," I told Kurt, "let's go."

The Tinted Venus was out of print, but when I finally got a copy and read it, I was more than ever convinced that it was a project for me. I was still sharing offices with John Wildberg and invited him to become an associate producer; I was sure he could be helpful with the financing. We knew, of course, that the story would need a lot of work—in its final form it was vastly changed —but *The Tinted Venus* served as a skeleton plot.

Kurt and I considered the writers we knew who might do a good book, and finally decided on the Spewacks, Sam and Bella. Bella was interested and began to work on the book, but we were still stuck for a lyricist. Someone suggested Ogden Nash. An inspired idea, we thought: he had that light touch with just the right social punch. It didn't particularly bother us that he'd never done lyrics. But Ogden wasn't as certain as we were, and said he'd think it over. After reading the novella, he said he'd like to give it a whirl. At last we had the composer, the lyricist and the writer.

Eventually Bella came back with a partial script which she called *One Man's Venus.* Why we didn't see on first reading the weaknesses we saw later, I don't know. I suspect it was because the role of Venus, as Bella had written it, seemed a natural for Marlene Dietrich, and we got so carried away with the idea of her that it obscured any other judgment. I didn't know Marlene, but Kurt did, and we decided to go to Hollywood to see her.

When we arrived in Hollywood and telephoned Marlene, she invited us to her home. It was a very handsome house, tasteful and charming, and she had a most impressive collection of paintings. She greeted us at the door wearing silk lounging pajamas, and my first impression of her was that she looked exactly as she did in her pictures. It was nice to find that a star could live up to one's expectations, and we were enchanted with her warmth and friendliness.

Seated in her salon, Kurt and I told her why we'd come and began to describe the musical. She was attentive and interested. Yet the meeting yielded no hint one way or another of her inclination about the show. She had, we were soon to find out, a most elusive quality.

We had many meetings with Marlene during our stay on the Coast, and we most often met at her house. At that time she was quite taken with playing the musical saw. I was accustomed to many varieties of eccentric behavior from stars, but I must confess that when Marlene placed that huge saw securely between her elegant legs and began to play, I was more than a little startled. It was an ordinary saw about five feet high and was played with a violin bow. We would talk about the show for a while, then Marlene would take up the musical saw and begin to play: that, we soon found out, was the cue that talk was finished for the evening.

Marlene particularly liked to sing Kurt's "Surabaya-Jonny" with the saw, which I will admit she did deliciously. Of course, Kurt was enchanted to have her sing his songs, but it wasn't getting us anywhere that I could see. She couldn't make up her mind whether or not she wanted to do the show. We just kept on meeting and talking. It was beginning to strain my practical midwestern mind. I couldn't stay in Hollywood forever listening to the musical saw, so I decided to go back to New York. We didn't have a completely finished script, that was true, but in my opinion we had enough for anyone to be able to decide: Marlene couldn't, or wouldn't.

I decided to take advantage of being on the Coast to explore other candidates with Hollywood agents in case Marlene refused. I telephoned several for suggestions, and when Kurt and I returned to the Beverly Wilshire one afternoon, there was a message in my box from one of the agents which had been carefully written out by the telephone operator. It read: "Ilona Massey is available for a roll." I handed it to Kurt. "This seems more like your department," I said. We did not, however, receive any suggestions that seemed right from Hollywood agents.

We decided to make one last try with Marlene before leaving, and we invited her to have dinner with us at the Cock and Bull, a steak place that was very popular in Hollywood at that time, and I believe still is. Marlene arrived with Jean Gabin, with whom she was involved romantically. There was very little talk about our project, but Marlene and Gabin were delightful to watch, two such beautiful people in love with each other. It was difficult not to construct fantasies about them, and I did. My fantasies, however, were to be short-lived. At the end of the dinner, the waiter came to take our orders for coffee. Kurt and I both said that we would love coffee, but Jean and Marlene looked horrified.

"We wouldn't think of it!" they exclaimed in unison. I was intrigued, and being curious about everything, I asked why they were so emphatic about not wanting coffee.

"But, it will keep us awake!" they explained. My fantasies were utterly shattered. How could two such beautiful people in love be concerned about being kept awake? I looked at Kurt, and he looked as stunned as I was. I knew that he had been having his own fantasies about our guests.

We told them that night that we were going back to New York, but again Marlene side-stepped an answer by saying that she'd be in New York soon and we'd talk more about it then. A few weeks later Marlene did arrive in New York and called us. On the way to her suite in the St. Regis I told Kurt that I hoped she'd left that damned musical saw in California, because I didn't plan to spend any more evenings listening to it. He agreed. Fortunately we were spared.

We resumed our talks, but got no closer to a commitment. The activities, however, were more interesting. Each day Marlene would go to the Metropolitan Museum and look at the different pictures and statues of Venus. She went so far as to purchase reproductions of the Venuses and yards of light gray chiffon material. She would return from the museum, go up to her hotel room, strip and drape herself with gray chiffon in the style of the latest Venus she had discovered. We were summoned to view her, while she would model her latest discovery. She would strike poses of the Venus and ask us for our opinions. She looked divine in all her chiffon creations and poses, but what it had to do with our show was not sufficiently clear for us to express an educated opinion. After discovering some twelve or fifteen different Venuses, she developed a fondness for a Venus known as the

Callipygian Venus—meaning the Venus with the beautiful but-
tocks. The Callipygian Venus, then, it seemed, was Marlene's
concept of our Venus-to-be.

After we'd been through several of these charming but non-
productive fashion shows, Kurt and I decided that it was high
time we heard how Marlene's voice would sound in a theatre, so
one afternoon in the excitement of swishing gray chiffon, we
suggested that we all go down to the Forty-sixth Street Theatre
and listen to her sing. She agreed, but it was instantly obvious that
she was scared. We called from her suite to make arrangements,
and Gabin, who was in New York with her and could see that she
was scared, said he would come along. When we got to the
theatre, Kurt and I removed ourselves to the third or fourth row.
Gabin, bless his considerate heart, brought Marlene on in a kind
of "Off to Buffalo" routine, with his arm around her, to the
accompaniment of a single piano in the pit. With the help of his
light antics, she loosened up and began to sing "Jonny." Kurt and
I had trouble hearing her in the third row. We knew then that
if Marlene was going to do our show we would have to use a mike
of some kind—perhaps put microphones in the foots.

Despite Marlene's voice problems, we still wanted her, but
still she would not commit herself. Time was growing short. We
wanted to make the fall season. For days I had been carrying
around an Equity contract, containing all the terms we had
managed to discuss in our many talk sessions, but the moment
hadn't arrived when it seemed auspicious to present her with it.
One afternoon I decided it was time to force the issue and arrived
at her suite determined to do so—only to find acres of luggage
neatly assembled for departure. I went into something of a state
of shock. She really meant to leave without giving us a commitment—again.

"You're leaving?" I asked with unmasked surprise.

"Yes, my darling, and I have the most terrible headache," she
replied. Her headache, I thought, couldn't possibly match the one
that I was about to have. I felt the unsigned contract in my
raincoat pocket and suddenly got a wicked idea. As it happened,
I had a pick-me-up in my other pocket, some kind of stimulant

which I used to keep me awake when I had to stay up most of the night setting up a show. (It may seem that *One Touch of Venus* was all I had to think about at that time, but I actually had other shows in the works; *Porgy and Bess* was running, and *The Perfect Marriage,* a play, was in preparation.) I don't recall exactly what we used in those days to stay awake, but whatever it was, it was harmless enough, so I produced it.

"Well," I said, "if you have a headache, I have something which I think is awfully good for that." She was delighted and reached for it without question. I got some water, and she swallowed it down. Within about a half hour Marlene was feeling no pain. Obviously she wasn't accustomed to taking stimulants, having declined even coffee that evening in Hollywood, but I hadn't thought of that when I'd offered it. However, I wasn't above taking advantage of my windfall. I felt that contract in my pocket, and I thought to myself, "Well, Cheryl, it's now or never." So I pulled it out and shoved it in front of her. Marlene signed without a moment's hesitation. I think she had been planning to do so all along but for her own reasons was playing hard to get. I finally had what I wanted, after so many meetings and so much talk. I wouldn't have given her anything harmful, but I was really desperate. We wanted her, thought her perfect for the part and had to have a commitment to move ahead.

Marlene departed for the Coast, and I went home with a signed contract. Now that I finally had my star, I sat down with Bella's script. On reading it thoughtfully, I decided that I didn't like it. The idea that had enticed me was the irreconcilable differences between the world of mundane, conventional human beings and the free untrammeled world of the gods. But this theme had not been developed. I passed the script on to Kurt, who had the same reaction. After careful deliberation we decided that what was wrong with the script couldn't be fixed; it was obvious Bella wasn't on the same wavelength we were; our concepts were miles apart. The only thing to do was to scrap the book. What a mess! Now we had the star we wanted and no script.

And the star wanted a script. Having made her commitment Marlene was anxious to start studying the part. With trepidation

I telephoned her in Hollywood to tell her that I wasn't satisfied with the script and that Kurt and I were seriously thinking of calling in another writer. To my surprise, the news didn't seem to disturb her. She said that she did like the script, but she would defer to our judgment. I later realized that having worked in pictures all her life, she was used to having several writers on a script and people called in to doctor from time to time; she simply didn't realize that things were done quite differently in the theatre.

On the strength of our belief about the script and Marlene's agreement to leave it up to us, we began to think about who might do a better book. We decided to call Ogden and get him in on our think session too. Ogden suggested Sid Perelman, an idea that appealed to us. Ogden and Sid had known each other for some time and were friends. But we agreed that the only fair thing to do was to tell Bella our decision before we involved anyone else.

Kurt and Ogden thought that I would be better at the job of telling Bella than either of them. And of course, since I was the producer, it was my job. Yet we had never stood on ceremony before. I soon found out why they had elected me for the job.

When my secretary announced Bella, both my stalwart friends fled to another office. I greeted her alone. She sat down on the couch, and I remained leaning against my desk. I told her that we weren't happy with the script and after much thought we had decided that we would like to terminate the association. To my astonishment, she fell over in a dead faint. Thank God, she was sitting on the couch. I had not expected her to be delighted with the news, but I hadn't expected anything like that. I was a little rattled by her fainting, but I went into the outer office and got some water. I came back and lifted her head and started to administer it to her. At that point she came around—rather quickly, now that I think back on it—and asked, "What did you say?" I told her what I'd said, word for word, and she fainted again! This time, however, she didn't seem about to revive with water, so I sent my secretary out to the corner pharmacy to purchase some smelling salts. A few whiffs of spirits of ammonia brought her around, but in the meantime I had the unpleasant task of watching over a woman in what I guess was a dead faint. When she came around the second time, however, she remembered what I'd said and she was mad! She told me that I would hear from her lawyer and launched a few other unpleasantries. She's never spoken to me from that day to this, although we've seen each other over the years here and there.

Once again our team was incomplete: we had a composer, a lyricist, a star and no writer. But Sid agreed to do the book with Ogden Nash; the idea of working with Ogden and Kurt intrigued him. He hadn't done a script for a musical before, but he had done two plays with his wife.

As Sid put it, they "flailed out a version at the Harvard Club, interspersed with long lunches and martinis." But when we saw that version, we liked it. The conflict of two disparate worlds was now clear. We were in business again, at last, and I happily dispatched the script to Marlene. I gave her a little time to read and consider and then telephoned her. To my astonishment, she said that she didn't like the book at all. In fact, she thought it vulgar! I was getting used to shocks, but that was a blow. I spent some time talking to her about the virtues of the show, and she eventually agreed to reread it and reconsider. I told her that I would call again on March 17 for her final answer. From the way she sounded, I feared we'd lost her.

On Saturday, March 16, 1943, Kurt, Sid, Ogden and I had a meeting, and I told them that Marlene had some reservations. Nonetheless, they were optimistic. At four P.M. on the seventeenth we met in my apartment to call Marlene for her final answer. This time I suggested that Kurt be our spokesman, and I stationed myself beside him. Sid got on the phone extension. According to him, it went something like this:

"Hello, Marlene," said Kurt.

"Hello, Kurt." There was a long pause.

"Well," asked Kurt, "have you read the script the boys have done?"

"Yes, I have," she replied in a slow, deliberate voice, and stopped.

"Well, what do you think?"

"Kurt, I cannot play this play; it is too sexy and profane."
Shocked silence from Kurt.

"It really is impossible for me to play it," she continued. "You know, Kurt, I have a daughter who is nineteen years old, and for me to get up on the stage and exhibit my legs is now impossible."

"Marlene, what are you saying?" exclaimed Kurt. "Why, this play is delightful; it's intriguing; it's witty, sophisticated." He went on at some length about its virtues.

"No, it is too sexy and profane," she kept repeating in a kind of stubborn Germanic way.

Kurt began to sputter.

"Du dummes Stück!" he roared. That told me Kurt was really mad: he and Lotte Lenya had become so depressed with events in Germany after they came to the United States that they had made a vow never to speak German again. He recovered, however, and continued in English. "How dare you! Have you lost your sense of values?" He then went on to berate her, telling her that she didn't know a really important project when she saw one, and things like that.

But Marlene remained perfectly calm and just kept repeating in a slow, determined way: "No, it is too sexy and profane. I will not now exhibit myself in that way."

So that settled it with Marlene. We were back in the same old predicament. Now we had a script, but no star. Back to square one. To console ourselves and decide what to do, we all went out to dinner, but nobody had any appetite; obviously there was only one logical thing to do—get busy and start calling people about another star.

On April 3, Ogden, Kurt and Sid read the script to Gertrude Lawrence. I liked her and she would have been good in the role of Venus, but she decided that she didn't want to do it.

On April 9, we read the script to Lenora Corbett, who had been in *Blithe Spirit.* Why she didn't want to do Venus, I never found out, but the fact was that she didn't. We were stuck on dead center, because try as we did, Lawrence and Corbett were the only two stars we could think of who seemed right. I knew pretty well what talent was around. I made some more calls, and we saw several other actresses but thought they were not possible.

A few days later Audrey Wood called me and said that Mary Martin would be available. She was just closing in Boston in a show produced by Vinton Freedly, and they had decided not to bring the show into New York. I had only seen Mary Martin once in the theatre when she had stopped the show with her song "My Heart Belongs to Daddy"; I had never seen any of her films. Certainly, I told Audrey, we would love to see Mary. She came down from Boston and we met with her. I tended to favor her, but the others weren't sure. She said later that she had been quite dispirited by our rejection.

Meanwhile, we added another member to the team, Agnes de Mille. Engaging Agnes was one of my better decisions. *Away We Go* was playing in New Haven, and Kurt and I decided to see it. We were enchanted by Agnes's choreography and told her so. She was for us. We also told her that we thought *Away We Go* (mercifully changed to *Oklahoma* before it opened in New York) was a failure, but we didn't hold it against her. So much for our judgment of one of America's biggest hits!

At some point in the star search, we saw Vera Zorina, Balanchine's former wife, who was a big name at that time. Zorina went to her ex-husband and asked if she should let that de Mille woman do the ballets. Balanchine reportedly replied: "Certainly not!" So back came Zorina to me with the proposition that she would do the show provided de Mille did not do the choreography. We hadn't settled definitely on Zorina, but she was a big star and she knew we were interested. Nevertheless, I told her that I regretted her decision, because "we are having de Mille!" I was never in the habit of letting other people tell me what to do, and my regard for Agnes de Mille's talent and brilliance is well known. I will always be indebted to her for the enormous contributions she made to my shows.

One day shortly after I had engaged Agnes, we got the team together and faced up to the problem of having no star. The name that kept coming back to all of us was Mary Martin. So we asked Mary if she would come and see us again, and she graciously consented. This time we all were delighted with her and couldn't imagine why we had had reservations.

But as Mary tells it, she had her own reservations: "When I

first read the script, I thought you'd gone out of your everloving mind, because I couldn't understand how you were looking at *me* to play Venus. Venus? It was done for Marlene Dietrich and she could certainly play Venus, but not me. Richard [Mary's husband, Richard Halliday, who had met her when he was story editor at Paramount] had to have long, long talks with me, and one day he said: 'Let's go up to the Metropolitan Museum. Have you ever been there?' I said no, and we went, and honey, we went all over the place and he kept showing me these statues, and he'd say when we'd come to one and it would be not too grand—the body wasn't great, little fat fanny here and there, and shorter, and he'd say: 'Look what it says underneath: Venus.' And I said, 'Venus?' And he said there were many forms and shapes of Venus, that sculptors had their own ideas. He finally convinced me that I didn't have to be Venus de Milo or Marlene Dietrich. So that was the beginning. Then, of course, I heard the score, and when I heard 'That's Him,' I just flipped, as we all did, I loved it so."

Even after we had all settled unanimously on Mary and it was definite that she was doing the show, some of Mary's reservations persisted. I suggested that she come up to my apartment and we'd read through a couple of scenes together. When she started reading, she got hooked, but she was still concerned about her long neck. I promised her that her costumes would be marvelous, and we'd solve her concern about her long neck.

The matter of Mary's long neck was beautifully solved by Mainbocher, who simply put a black velvet ribbon around it. Mainbocher had never done costumes for the theatre, so Mary and Richard went to persuade him. Mary described the meeting to me. "He looked just like a businessman, and it was Mainbocher, the great Mainbocher! I couldn't believe it. I had expected somebody very tall and willowy, but anyway, we adored each other. We told him what we wanted and he said no, he'd never done clothes for the theatre." But Mary was so enthusiastic we couldn't take his refusal. I decided he must hear the score. What we didn't know then was that Main adored music; in fact, he'd wanted to be an opera singer. We persuaded him to listen to the score. When Mary sang "That's Him," she picked up a little chair and brought it down right in front of him. He couldn't move. She had him pinned down: turning the chair around backwards and sitting sideways, she sang to him. When she finished, he said: "If you will sing the song exactly like that in the show, I'll do the costumes." And that's the way we got him.

It is possible I paid more for Mary's costumes than anyone had ever paid for costumes in a musical. They cost between fifteen and twenty thousand dollars, which sounds like small change now for what we got. There were fourteen costume changes, and hats too. Mary's every entrance was applauded.

There was the rest of the show to cast, and I began to move ahead. We got Kenny Baker of radio and pictures to do the male lead, Rodney Hatch the barber; John Boles, also of picture fame, to do the part of the art collector who buys the statue of Venus and has her brought to New York; and Paula Laurence for the second female lead. Paula was Moss Hart's romantic interest at that time, and Kurt and Moss were very close friends. I didn't know her work very well; she had been doing a lot of nightclub work, but I'd never seen her, and she'd only done one Broadway musical. But Jack Wildberg liked her, so I decided to have a look.

Paula has a very funny story about how she got the part. "Jean Dalrymple, who was the press agent and a great friend of mine, and Jack Wildberg and Moss used to discuss the play in my presence. There was always a part they referred to as the Paula Laurence part but which no one had asked me to play. They were talking about all sorts of other people for it, and finally I said, 'Well, why don't I play it if it's the Paula Laurence part?' That seemed to stun them. And they looked at me and said, 'Oh well, why not?' and that's how it came about."

Then I asked Elia Kazan to direct. I had kept up with Gadg since our Group Theatre days, and although he had never directed a musical before, I had a hunch he'd be good at it. The idea intrigued him, and he liked the people he'd be working with, so he agreed.

I set up a luncheon date for Mary and Gadg in the Oak Room at the Plaza Hotel so that they could meet. By this time Mary was familiar with the book and was learning the songs. She came back and told me, "We talked and we talked about everything, and we never did talk about Venus. Finally he looked at me with those piercing eyes, and he said: 'How do you think about playing Venus?'

" 'I was afraid you were going to ask me that,' I said, 'and I haven't the vaguest idea.' Then he asked me how I approach a part. I told him I hadn't done much except films so I didn't really know how I approached a part. He looked puzzled. So I said, 'I think in terms of how I will walk. If I can get that walk in my mind, then I know how I'm going to play it.'

"He was marvelous. He said: 'That's very exciting to me; then I won't have to direct you really. I'm just going to tell you what I think about Venus.' His idea was that when Venus comes to life on stage she's been dead for thousands of years and her world is so different from ours. 'In our world,' he said, 'everybody is in such a mad rush, and in Agnes's ballet when Venus comes to life, people are like puppets going wild, up and down the streets, rush, rush, rush! Venus is the only sane one in the world, and she thinks everyone she sees is crazy . . . because they seem mad; they have no joy, no fun, so your tempo and your movement should be absolutely legato. Everything else is staccato.' "

This was the approach that Gadg actually gave Mary when we finally went into rehearsal in August of 1943. He really never did say much more to her, and Mary thought that freedom was wonderful.

Not everyone appreciated Gadg as much as Mary. Some of my colleagues felt that his visual sense was not well developed. Sid and Ogden had a little run-in with Gadg over a scene in a bus station. We were all watching the rehearsals in New York prior to the Boston opening, and Gadg stopped rehearsal. The actors were suspended in the middle of the scene, and there seemed to be some great difficulty. Gadg began to stride up and down, scratching his chin, deep in thought. After about fifteen minutes of this, Sid and Ogden began to get nervous and went up to him. This was not a good idea; Gadg was somewhat impatient of interruptions. But Ogden and Sid asked him what the trouble was. After ignoring them for a few minutes, he said: "Well, I'm trying to think of some business for this scene."

Pointing to the script, they said, "There is over a half page of single-spaced business description for that scene in the script."

He stared at the script and turned on them, exclaiming, "That chicken shit? I never read that. What do you think my business is in being here? I'm the director; I have to think of the business. I never read that kind of thing!" Ogden and Sid retreated abashed to the shadows.

Yet all the people in *One Touch of Venus* were wonderful to work with, all topnotch, very professional and determined to get the best show possible. Mary, for example, grew tremendously in the show, as did her voice, and she was always willing, even eager, to take helpful suggestions. For instance, Sono Osato, our leading dancer, observed the trouble Mary had with the song "I'm a Stranger Here Myself." She never seemed really comfortable in rehearsal; she would walk up and down and then pause and stand in the traditional Hollywood position of that time, the Betty Grable stance with one knee bent. Sono, being a dancer, watched this, and it bothered her. Venus was supposed to be a goddess, with power and grace, and Sono felt she should project that physically as well. She showed Mary that if you put your feet smack on the ground solidly, legs slightly opened, that gives a visual impression of strength and assurance. Mary didn't say, "Mind your own business and go back to dancing." She took it beautifully. She was smart enough to see the difference and professional enough to accept it and use it. Then when she got the wonderful Mainbocher chiffon, she began to stride up and down the stage, plant her feet and look straight out to sing "I'm a Stranger Here Myself." It gave her a whole different look—a look of complete power and command.

As I said before, Agnes de Mille made enormous contributions to the show. But she had plenty of temperament, and she threw some scenes that were incredible. They were never personal; they were always about her work. Agnes was very professional and when she felt something was right, she could be stubborn and obstinate. If we tried to cut one minute from one of her ballets all hell broke loose. Usually she was right about the ballet sequences, but they were sometimes a little too long and cutting was a painful process for both of us—a minute here, a minute there, then a compromise.

The financing of this show was easy for a change, and I even put some of my earnings from *Porgy and Bess* into *One Touch of Venus*. My original budget for the show was a hundred and forty thousand dollars, but I always liked to bring in a show for less if possible. So before Boston, I brought it in for a hundred and fifteen thousand.

From the beginning, I knew we had a hit. I thought we all felt it, but I've since found out that my opinion was not shared by all of the team, particularly not by Agnes and Sid and Ogden. Blissfully ignorant of their doubts, I put the entire company on the train for Boston, where we were to open at the Shubert Theatre.

The first dress rehearsal there was eye-opening: we had severe scenery problems. Of course, we'd all approved the scenery. Howard Bay was the scenic designer, and we had decided that it would be interesting to cover the top of the stage, or the so-called ceiling, with a gray velveteen drape. It would hang almost like sky and would encompass the proscenium arch as well. Well, when we got a look at it in Boston, it was awful! We were all in a state of shock. At some time during that interminable night Sid slid into the seat beside me and said: "Jesus, Cheryl, it looks like the inside of a coffin." (He now claims that he actually said: "Jesus, all that gray hanging velvet looks like an enlarged prostate gland!") Mainbocher was in a state as well, and his descriptions were similar to Sid's. He thought Howard Bay's drapes had ruined his costumes and drowned everybody on stage. He referred to them as those long gray loops, those testicles hanging down and ruining Venus's costumes. Paula Laurence called it the "dirigible hangar."

The opening was less than twenty-four hours away. Nothing could be done in such a short time, and there was of course the question of money. The drapes were not the only thing wrong; some of the costumes were wrong, and there were many other ragged edges. But that's what out-of-town try-outs are for, and no one expects the final version that comes to New York to be like that first opening performance. After correcting what could be corrected that night and trying to keep the tempers of exhausted artists at a minimum, I finally got back to my suite at the Ritz about four or five A.M. I knew a lot had to be done, but I was still much more optimistic than some of my colleagues.

Shortly before the opening Mary sent for me, and I went back to her dressing room to find her in an agitated state. I asked her what was up, and she said in that earnest way of hers: "Cheryl, there's one line in the show which I simply cannot say."

"Why not?" I asked, surprised that a line should be giving her trouble at that late date.

"The line is just too vulgar," she replied.

"Which line is it that's giving you so much trouble, Mary?" I asked.

"Well, you know, it's that line I say: 'Love is not the moaning of distant violins; it's the triumphant twang of a bedspring.' Now, Cheryl, I just can't say that line." That threw me a curve because I thought it was a very funny line and I knew we'd be sorry to cut it.

"Well, Mary, suppose you say it tonight because the boys are all upset as it is. If you feel the slightest reaction from the audience that makes you uncomfortable, I'll talk to them tomorrow and see that it's cut." Mary agreed to try it that night. The roar of pleasure and delight from the audience that greeted that line opening night was so great that Mary never mentioned it again.

A lot went wrong that opening night in Boston, but one thing was unforgettable. The final number in the show was choreographed around Venus, now married to the barber; she is seated center stage in the yard of the cottage he has always wanted, a cottage where he can sit and read his paper, mow the lawn and do all the things people do in suburbia. Venus is not happy. The endless domesticity bores her. Suddenly the dancers appear, dressed as satyrs, nymphs and dryads, to circle around her in a wild bacchanal before lifting her to their shoulders to bear her triumphantly away. Stars come out and stardust drifts down. Curtain.

But when the scene began, Mary wasn't there! The dancers stamped and gestured in a circle around an empty chair as the orchestra kept playing. This shambles went on and on, making no sense at all, until Mary finally appeared and sat, just in time for the finale, which had become a disaster. The curtain fell to little applause. We ran back to find out what had happened. Backstage, during the preceding black-out, a new stagehand had moved the flat containing Mary's change of costume to the wrong side. She had searched frantically for her clothes, begging someone to find them. But the stagehands were too flustered to help. Mary had to run all the way across the back, as the stage was in full light. Panting and nearly naked she finally located her costume. She was still quivering when she told us the story. So were we.

There was a depressing party at the Ritz afterward. All of us had pages of notes for improvements scratched in the dark of the auditorium. We did not look forward to reading the reviews. The next morning we found that they were mixed, but some were surprisingly kind. Helen Eager of *The Traveler* wrote that I had another hit on my hands. And Leo Gaffney of the *Boston Daily Mirror* said, "To put it mildly, the show's a wham."

In spite of the generous words, and the subsequent financial success in Boston, much was wrong. I called a meeting of all the ten creators at ten-thirty the following morning, Sunday, in my suite at the Ritz. We sat in a semicircle and began discussing the show. Howard Bay was the target for the first attack, since he was responsible for the disaster of the gray velvet. Bay didn't take the attack lying down; he reminded us all that we had passed on the design, and further reminded us that he had a train to catch back to New York for a conference with Oscar Hammerstein at one o'clock. So everyone had a go at him. Without question the gray coverall and the brooding front portal had to be changed. Mainbocher suggested a light slender portal adorned by doves, favorites of Venus. Howard said he was not familiar with doves. Main pointed out the window where hundreds of pigeons were cavorting in the park. "Something like those," he said, and eventually that was the decoration we had, with a pale blue cyclorama as background.

Agnes complained that her final ballet was being ruined by the ugly little houses which were trucked in noisily to represent the place where the barber and Venus resided. It is true that they looked rather like troglodyte outhouses.

Ogden was bitter about the statue of Venus which he claimed looked totally unlike Mary; Lon Chaney would have loved it, he said. "Ogden," I replied, "the sculptor measured Mary's entire body, including her breasts."

Howard looked at his watch. This, at least, was not his problem. "Sorry," he said. "My train. I'll be back tomorrow." And he bowed out. Then it was Kurt's turn to complain that no one laughed at one of our comedians.

"Well, you can't fire him," I said. "He has a run-of-the-play contract. Besides, all of us laughed ourselves sick at him during rehearsals."

Gadg defended the actor. "He was relaxed then, no first-night jitters, no audience."

"Something we never counted on," Sid said sourly.

At first Gadg and I refused to make all the changes our colleagues wanted. I felt the problems could be remedied with less drastic and less expensive measures, and that when the show was tightened up, it would more than obscure the shortcomings. However, something of a mutiny developed. It had to do primarily with the scenery and the costumes being changed, and it involved most of the creative staff: Sid, Kurt, Ogden and Agnes. They felt so strongly about the changes that they formed a united delegation and threatened to go back to New York at once unless something was done. It was blackmail, but I finally gave in.

It cost twenty-five thousand dollars to make the necessary changes in the show. Jack Wildberg borrowed the sum from Mr. Lee Shubert. He didn't have much trouble because the show looked so good. Mr. Lee had seen it and pronounced it all right. That pronouncement was important to us, because it meant that we were going to get the Imperial Theatre in New York, which is the one we wanted. Shubert got his money back first, of course.

The changes Howard made for the final ballet still did not win Agnes's approval, and in the end the stage carpenter and I painted some small houses on a backdrop. They were nothing fancy, but they left the stage floor free for dancing. I took scissors and, climbing a high ladder, punched holes in the backdrop which would look like stars when lit from behind. The stagehands' union did not permit this, but I don't think anyone dared to interfere with me at that point.

To add to our troubles, one Saturday night in Boston as Mary was leaving the stage, she collapsed flat on her back. She finished the show, which fortunately was almost over, and we discovered she had a fever of 104 degrees. We had to put her in a hospital for a few days. She did not have an understudy, and the rest of us all felt ready for a hospital too because we had to cancel performances.

We also had some problems with the book. As we kept watching the show, we saw that lines that were supposed to be funny just weren't.

George Kaufman, who was in Boston working on a show at the time, used to expound with eloquence, charm and sense about the difference between writing and writing for the theatre. He would wander in and watch the show from the back now and then during our run. One evening he took Paula Laurence to dinner, and when he started talking about his favorite subject, Paula, who despaired that some of her funniest lines weren't getting laughs, asked him to do her a great favor: take Ogden and Sid out for a drink and give them the benefit of his theory about the difference between the two literary enterprises. He promised that he would within the next few days. When nothing happened in the show to indicate that George had gotten his point across, Paula asked him if he had talked to Sid and Ogden. He replied that he had and they seemed to understand very well. The next day Sid and Ogden each had occasion to take Paula aside to tell her about his talk with George. Each one of them thought that George was talking about the other, so neither of them did anything.

We still had the problem of the show's ending, and we had a scene change that we couldn't seem to cover efficiently. Everything we tried was terrible. Then Gadg, who may have fallen a little in love with Sono, suggested a solo for her, and Agnes came up with just the right thing for the scene change. Sono was such a delicious dancer, I believe the audience would have been happy to see her dance all night. Agnes devised a charming waltz, and Sono danced it with Robert Pageant as a sailor. It was one of the loveliest things I've ever seen in the theatre.

As for the end of the show problem, Agnes again came to our rescue. The bacchanal of the nymphs, satyrs, nyads and dryads who carry Venus off was very effective, but it left the audience hanging. It seemed very unsatisfactory for Venus to disappear into the clouds, leaving the poor barber all alone: the ending needed ooomph, something upbeat. It was Agnes who thought of having Venus come back as an "ordinary" human girl, dressed in a cute little dress and hat—a sort of reincarnation. In the final version, a clap of thunder sounds after Venus's disappearance in the clouds, and the stage goes dark for a brief moment. When the lights come back up, Venus is standing on the pedestal once again, as the statue with which Rodney the barber first fell in love. He goes to the statue and and says: "Why did you leave? You said I'd never be alone again." Then he sings, from their love ballad, "Speak low to me, speak love to me."

At that moment the human girl enters. Her clothes are simple, and she has an attractive, awkward grace; she might be Venus's country cousin. She carries a straw suitcase. Rodney looks at the statue of Venus and then at the girl. She asks him where she can register for the art course. He asks her where she comes from, and she tells him that she comes from Ozone Heights. He asks her if she likes it there. She says she wouldn't think of living any place else. He tells her that his name is Rodney Hatch, and then she starts to tell him her name, but he goes to her quickly and says, "You don't have to tell me, I know." He takes her suitcase and offers his arm. She takes his arm, their eyes meet, and they start off, looking into each other's eyes as the curtain falls. It was a marvelous ending to the show.

We were never too happy with the scene in which Venus makes the barber's fiancée Gloria, Venus's hated rival, disappear. Sid and Ogden took it into their heads to work out some way to actually make the girl disappear before the audience's eyes in full light. They got in touch with a magician who made a very searching examination of the situation and informed Sid that he would need twenty-four hours to ponder the thing and then he'd be back with a solution. His opening question was, "Do you plan to use this actress a second time?"

"Yes. Unfortunately, the demands of the theatre are such that we can't just use her one time," replied Sid, tongue in cheek.

"Pity," said the magician, and his face fell. "Because, you know, I could evolve a wonderful effect."

He had worked out an alternative plan, however, which involved a barber's chair with an extra thick back. The very back of the chair would actually be a curtain, and when Venus thrust Gloria backward, she would fall back into the chair—the chair would then begin to revolve and she would disappear inside the curtain and whip her knees against her chest. This disappearance, he calculated, would take three revolutions of the chair and would cost me a mere five hundred dollars. Sid and Ogden were delighted with the idea, and the magician modestly observed that it was not a very serious problem, just a simple mid-stage vanish. I said no to the five hundred dollars and the idea, though Sid and Ogden were not too pleased with me. I didn't want Ruth Bond, who was playing the role of Gloria, injured; simple or not, the plan seemed to offer too many chances for mishap.

We were to open in New York at the Imperial Theatre on the night of October 7, 1943. Along with setting up the show, which is always trying, I had housing problems, as did many other people in New York. It was the height of wartime and New York was overcrowded. I had given up my apartment when we went to Boston and was waiting to move into a new apartment. So on our return from Boston, I checked into a hotel in the East Forties. Because of the demand for rooms, you could only stay in any hotel for three days. In all the excitement of the show, I'd forgotten that, and on the sixth, the day before the opening, I was evicted. Finally I begged a bed in someone's apartment.

I slept most of the day, and in the late afternoon a friend called to make certain I wouldn't sleep through the opening. I answered sleepily that I didn't intend to go to the opening, but if she'd be good enough to get some chicken and potatoes and the like, I'd cook dinner for us. I went back to sleep while my friend did the shopping. I did indeed cook dinner, and we thoroughly enjoyed it.

As the time got on toward the final curtain, I got dressed and went down to the theatre. I got there just in time to hear the final applause as the curtain came down. It sounded good. We went to a party someone was giving for Mary up on Park Avenue in an apartment about the size of Grand Central Station. There were hundreds of elegantly dressed people, and I remember that Mary introduced me to one highly enthusiastic couple.

"Oh, you must be so excited," they said. "How was the opening night?"

"I don't know," I said. "I wasn't there." I could see the disbelief in their faces. What kind of a producer was I?

"Well, what did you do?" they blustered, hoping for some good excuse for my laxness.

"I stayed home and cooked dinner for a friend and myself," I replied. That cinched it. They thought I was mad. I let them. I didn't see the point of trying to explain to strangers unfamiliar with the workings of the theatre that when you've lived with a show intensely for a long time, from the very day of inception, you can't bear to sit through it on opening night. There's nothing on earth you can do any more, and you might as well rest your nervous system for whatever the fate may be when the papers hit the street.

Generally speaking, the reviews were good. Howard Barnes of the *New York Herald Tribune* thought it was a "cunning combination" of fantasy, music and ballet. And Lewis Nichols of the *New York Times* decided that theatre-going had once again become a pleasure. But John Chapman of the *Daily News,* after some praise, observed that the show needed pace here and there and some simple humor; he also felt the dream ballet was a couple of minutes too long. Burton Rascoe of the *World-Telegram* was harsher on us, claiming that he and most of the audience were disappointed, and that the creators had somehow never agreed on what kind of a musical *One Touch of Venus* would be—"something arty, sophisticated and abstract, or something like a Minsky burlesque only more literate."

Just to show you that sometimes we producers wonder if the reviewers saw the same show on opening night, let's contrast the Rascoe review with that of Robert Garland of the *New York Journal-American.* He wrote: "Topnotchers have certainly been assembled to make *One Touch of Venus* the smash hit it is sure to be." And *Variety's* review began: *"One Touch of Venus* is Broadway's first musical smash of the season . . . sumptuous, tuneful, artistic—and it has Mary Martin."

Kurt and I didn't need the critics to tell us we had a hit. We had felt that, through thick and thin, from the beginning.

Kurt's favorite music from *One Touch of Venus* was the ballet music, because he liked to write large music for full orchestra. Unlike many theatre composers, he did all of his own orchestrations. He always did them with the radio at full blast, because it blocked out all other noises of life in the streets of the city or of nature in the country. He thought the bacchanal he wrote for *One Touch of Venus* was the finest piece of orchestral music he had ever written. Agnes thought it the best thing he'd done since *Threepenny Opera,* but she went on to point out, "He cut the bacchanal to pieces and the dance went with it. He was ruthless about such things; he wanted a success. He was predominantly a theatre man."

Kurt used to say, "To hell with posterity; I want to hear my music now, while I'm alive. I want my things performed and I want them to be a success."

As for me, I had been right to think my fortunes lay in the musical theatre. I had the hit I had wanted: the show *was* original, meaningful and entertaining.

One Touch of Venus did well in the prize department. The 1943–1944 season saw the appearance of a new set of awards known as the First Annual Donaldson Awards. These were significant awards because, for the first time in the history of the theatre, the theatre's own people chose the outstanding achievements of the Broadway season. Voting on those awards were actors and actresses, press agents, critics, stagehands, producers, treasurers, ticket sellers and managers who worked on the main stem during the season.

One Touch of Venus was voted second place in the Best Musical Play of the Season category. Elia Kazan received the award for the Best Musical Direction. Mary Martin received first place for the Best Lead Performance (female); Kenny Baker took first place for the Best Supporting Performance (male), and second place for the Best Lead Performance (male). Sono Osato took first place for the Best Dancer (female) in the Musical Division, and Agnes de Mille took first place for the Best Choreography. Despite the scenic arguments and changes, Howard Bay came off with first place for the Best Scenic Design. Paula Laurence took second place for the Best Supporting Performance (female). *One Touch of Venus* also took second place for the Best Book of the Season for a musical play and the Best Score. Ogden Nash got second place for the Best Lyrics, which certainly wasn't bad considering that it was his first venture as a lyricist and his competition was Oscar Hammerstein II, who took first place.

Apart from winning awards, *One Touch of Venus* had its share of incidents. Paula "went up" in her lines for the first and only time in her career on the stage of *One Touch of Venus*. As she put it, "We'd been playing for some time, and the first act finale was endless. It went on forever—and I leaned against the proscenium; I wasn't permitted to take part in the dancing. At the end of the scene, Mary and Kenny and John Boles were on stage, and I had sort of drifted off, leaning against the proscenium there, waiting for them to finish. My cue to start walking and speaking was when Mary would say to Kenny, 'Cheer up, darling; don't look so glum. This is our wedding day.' And I'd walk over to John Boles and say, 'Well, cupid, you certainly loused that one up!'

"Well, on this day, I was leaning, dreaming, and suddenly I heard Mary say, 'Clean up, darling, it's the wedding . . .' and the rhythm threw me off because Mary never went up on her lines, and everything went right out of my head. I started walking and I knew I had to start speaking and I said, 'Well, cupid, you certainly fucked that one up!' I had never said that word out loud in my life. It's interesting that I should have said that, because my personal method of getting a laugh was to substitute a word in my head, so the audience is laughing at fairly innocuous words, but my intent is very clear—and that was the word I had used in my head to get a laugh, but this time it suddenly came out of my mouth.

"Well, I was afraid to leave the stage; I thought I would be arrested. A couple of guys in the orchestra made some kind of strangled noise, but I don't think anybody who was in the audience and heard it believed they'd heard it. Mary and John looked stunned, but they weren't as stunned as I was! I finally staggered off, only to find everyone was roaring with laughter backstage. I got through the rest of the performance somehow, and when I came out for my solo bow, the orchestra rose to a man and played cowbells and struck cymbals and roared! It was horrendous!"

About this time, during the hot sultry summer of 1944, Mary began to complain of the heat. It was about 112 degrees on stage for something like a week running, because the theatre was cooled by a fan and ice system and we never had enough ice. With the war on, you couldn't get your hands on an air conditioner, and I was worried about Mary. Venus was a very taxing role and the heat was getting to her; Mary was on stage almost constantly under those hot lights. The assistant stage manager used to keep a bowl of ice downstage left; when Mary would come running off for only a moment, he would put ice on her wrists to cool the blood down a little. I had an air conditioner in my new apartment and I was spending that summer in New York, but I thought if I was going to keep my star and a good show, I'd better give up my air conditioner, so I had it moved to Mary's dressing room where she could cool off while she was offstage. She played through the summer like a trouper after that, and I sweltered.

Mary's mother died during the run of the show, and she couldn't leave for the funeral since we would have had to cancel performances: no one would have wanted to see the show without Mary. It was very difficult for her. And then one night she quite lost her voice during her song "That's Him." The orchestra, realizing what had happened, slowed the tempo for her—then slowed almost to a stop. Nothing was coming out of Mary. She sat there in her little chair in a state of total shock. She was alone on the stage. Finally she began to gesture to the audience and whispered, "Please sit, just stay, I'll stay and it will come back, it will come, it will come back, I hope!" They sat and sat and sat for what Mary has said seemed like ten years, but was probably only five minutes. And then her voice came back and she finished. She says it showed her that if you don't panic, you can hold an audience.

Afterwards we found out that Mary was allergic to theatre dust and that that had caused the loss of her voice. She had to wear a gorgeous negligee in that scene, and she moved quite energetically in it, causing the skirt to billow, wiping the floor and whipping up the dust. It almost strangled her, and she had to take shots for years to overcome the allergy. Fortunately, she did finally beat it.

Part way through the run it became time to plan the road tour. Mary was a little reluctant to go on the road, and I had several long talks with her about it. I felt it was terribly important in building a theatrical career, as well as an important growing experience for an actor. Alfred Lunt, Lynn Fontanne, Katharine Cornell, Guthrie McClintic, Jessica Tandy and Hume Cronyn had all proved the importance and necessity of the road. I finally convinced Mary, and once out there she soon realized its importance herself. In fact, she went on the road thereafter every time she possibly could.

But I was not able to convince Kenny Baker to tour, and we started auditions to replace him. During the rest of the Broadway run we had about three barbers. One of the last ones we cast was apparently under some enormous emotional strain and went off the deep end during a matinee. He seemed all right until it came time for his duet with Mary, when to everyone's astonishment he walked right off the stage and straight out the stage door. A stunned Mary sang both parts, and then we rang the curtain down. Frank Coletti, my stage manager, went out and announced that there had been a technical problem and there would be a slight delay. What were we going to do? We had a full house waiting for the rest of the show. As it happened, we were in luck because one of the young men in the chorus, Geoffrey Warren, said that he knew the part and could finish the show. Frank went back out and announced that the barber had been taken ill and a young member of the company would stand in for him. Geoffrey was marvelous and went on the road with us.

On the night after the matinee episode Mary was in her dressing room preparing to make up for the evening show when through her dressing room window came the barber who had walked off the stage during the matinee. He ran to the dressing room door and locked it. Fortunately, but unknown to the young man, Mary's maid was in the bathroom washing out some things; when she heard him, she stayed in the bathroom to listen. The young actor said that the physical strain had been too much for him but that he wanted to go back on stage that night. Mary told him that he was too tired and should take a rest. Then he announced that the main reason he'd left the stage was because he was so much in love with Mary and she was so much in love with her husband, Dick Halliday, that he couldn't face another performance with her. At that point Mary's maid, Lena, thought it wise to make an appearance. Together Mary and Lena managed to get the overwrought young man calmed down and out of the theatre without further incident.

Mary was back on Broadway after an absence of five years. She settled into the part and loved it. It was obvious from the start that she was the big musical star of the season. She informed one reporter shortly after we opened in New York that she was "having more fun doing Venus than the Goddess of Love ever had in her immortal life." She told another one that Venus's "touch is supposed to bring love and happiness to everyone, and that seems to be important in times like these." About that time she also announced that she hoped never to make another picture but to remain in the theatre doing musicals and plays. Of course Broadway loved all this, and she became the darling of the press.

We were still playing to capacity houses; *Variety* reported that *One Touch of Venus* played to "capacity clean-up; gets $35,600 weekly right along." That was pretty good when you consider that the top box office ticket price was then four dollars and forty cents. I say "box office price" because the black market on hit tickets flourished, and prices could range from five to fifty dollars for a single ticket. *One Touch of Venus* was among the scalpers' favorites, a dubious tribute.

After five hundred and sixty-seven performances in New York, we were ready to go on the road; we were booked out to the Coast and back and due to make a load of money. We got to Detroit, and while we were playing there, Mary met her old friend Grace Moore, the beautiful blond opera singer (who was later killed in a plane crash). Grace gave a party for Mary. They fell to indulging in reminiscences along with champagne, and Mary had a little too much. The result of all those reminiscences and the champagne was that Mary and Dick had a little more celebration after they got back to the hotel that night and Mary wound up pregnant.

We finished the Detroit run and opened in Chicago, but by that time Mary was quite ill. It was an Rh-negative pregnancy and she lost the baby. There was nobody else of equal star billing to replace her, and that was the end of *One Touch of Venus*. As much as I love Mary, I always figured that she owed me at least a hundred and fifty thousand dollars for that episode.

Still, *One Touch of Venus* hadn't done badly by any of us. Although there were technical problems and a few personality clashes, it was Sunday School compared to some of my subsequent productions. With *Venus* I developed a technique for dealing with such difficulties. When the shouting would get loud and reasoning became impossible, I'd just retire to my hotel room or apartment and read Walt Whitman, who is a favorite of mine, or some other writer until the dust had settled. Sometimes it took a few days, but when I figured the adversaries had tired themselves out, I'd go down and make a decision. Usually my decision would be accepted, because they were all too talked out and worn out to protest any more.

Musicals are apt to have more problems and more temperament among members of the cast, because there are so many elements to organize and keep running: actors, chorus, dancers, musicians, designers, etc. Whenever I checked with my stage manager, Frank Coletti, to see if he was having difficulty keeping everybody in line and keeping things running smoothly on the show, he would reply that *One Touch of Venus* was easy. He'd been stage manager for Flo Ziegfeld on his last Ziegfeld Follies and that was, according to Frank, enough to take ten years off your life. People had a way of drifting in and out of that show and not showing up for days. Frank loved to tell about the beautiful showgirl who failed to show up for several performances over the Christmas holidays. When she reappeared, he asked her what had happened. She replied, "Santa Claus wouldn't let me out of bed."

One Touch of Venus made a handsome profit, and it put my early failures far behind me, conclusively showing that my success with *Porgy and Bess* wasn't a one-time thing. On my own, I had established myself at last.

The Battle for Repertory
and Nonprofit Theatre

The proceeds from *One Touch of Venus* enabled me to indulge my long unindulged taste for the finer things in life. I tried living like Hollywood's stereotype of a Broadway producer. There was the spacious apartment high over the East River with a terrace, a working fireplace, even a butler's pantry, and plenty of room, finally, for all the books I had acquired and the many new ones I could now afford. And there were wonderful meals cooked by Rosa Johnson. But Rosa drew the line at finger bowls, giggling each time she set one before me. She soon laughed me out of this pretense of elegance. I bought clothes, particularly a chic black dress from Valentina, who had supplied the one for my Theatre Guild interview. I also purchased six hats from a fancy milliner. I think I wore the dress once, after which it must have languished in a closet. I never actually wore the hats; I would carry one in my hand as I went about my affairs. Eventually, I forgot all six in taxis.

During this period I produced a straight play, *The Perfect Marriage*, by Samson Raphaelson on which a film company made a preproduction deal, that is, guaranteed a certain amount of money in advance to purchase the play. This made experienced investors alert. The most successful of them, Howard and Marguerite Cullman, who had wisely avoided me in some other ventures, came through with a good chunk, and the rest was easy.

It had one set and few characters. Who the set designer would be was settled when Carson McCullers invited me to an extraordinary establishment in Brooklyn known by its address, 7 Middagh Street. It was a large house owned by George Davis, an editor of *Vogue,* who had offered sanctuary to an unbelievable assortment of people. Besides Carson, Richard Wright, Gypsy Rose Lee, W. H. Auden, and Paul and Jane Bowles all lived and worked there. A young artist named Oliver Smith was ensconced in George's attic. When I studied his paintings and designs there, I offered Oliver *The Perfect Marriage.* I believe this was his first job as a set designer.

Miriam Hopkins and Victor Jory played the leading roles. Since Miriam had been busy in films and had not appeared on the stage for some time, she was nervous. The Damoclean hour grew closer. When we got to the dress rehearsal, Miriam failed to appear. I phoned, and her maid answered.

"Miss Hopkins is very sorry, but she is ill and cannot come to the rehearsal."

Suspecting that the illness was psychosomatic, I said, "I'm sorry too. I'll call my doctor and have him there to see her in two hours."

I hung up and went off to see about other things. Within an hour, Miriam arrived.

"The show must go on," she said to me bravely.

"Yes," I agreed, "it must." And it did. Although *The Perfect Marriage* wasn't a slam, it made some money.

So I was living well. I had money in the bank; *Venus* and *Porgy* were flourishing. It was lovely. And it was dull.

It wasn't really what I had hoped to accomplish. I was fascinated by difficulty, teased by challenge, hungry for something estimable. I kept thinking of Shakespeare. I had never seen a production of *King Lear* or *The Tempest.*

Peggy Webster's office was down the hall from mine, and with Maurice Evans, Peggy had been directing very successful productions of the Bard. During the summer of 1944, I discovered that her great wish was to do *The Tempest.* Now there is a reason why

The Tempest is not produced frequently, and that is that the difficulties of re-creating Shakespeare's enchantment are staggering. How do you achieve a ship at sea, a wild storm, the magical island, Caliban's cave, Prospero's cell, a set that enables Ariel to make miraculous appearances? How do you find an Ariel you would believe "could ride on the curl'd clouds," and a Caliban who is at once a monster and pitiable?

Peggy's answer was a scheme devised by Eva Le Gallienne. Eva, said Peggy, had built a model of a set that would solve the difficult technical problems of the play. I went to see it. It consisted of a large turntable built up with precipices and caves where Ariel and Caliban could make magical appearances. As it slowly revolved, it would offer the audience different aspects of the magic island. I was sold. I signed on as producer.

Casting was as difficult as it had promised to be. We chose Arnold Moss to be the magician Prospero, and he was excellent. But Ariel and Caliban, as I had expected, were tougher roles to fill. For Ariel we chose Vera Zorina, whom I had earlier approached for Venus; she had an ethereal, sprite-like quality, and she was a lovely dancer who could also act and sing. And we settled on the famous black actor Canada Lee for Caliban. He had played for me in Maplewood as the powerful, menacing star of *Native Son*. These choices immediately heightened the contrast of the characters.

I was even more concerned about the two clowns. When the clowns are badly cast, their comedy scenes can be flat and boring. As a director, Peggy could give a tart little speech on the traditional unfunniness of Shakespeare's clowns. "One gets to the punch line and one has to start wading through four pages of Variorum footnotes and a couple of Granville Baker's prefaces before one begins to get a hazy idea of what the joke is about. . . . Now, how can you ever get a laugh out of a footnote?" she would say.

I had heard exciting reports of two Czech actors, George Voskovec and Jan Werich, alias "V and W," who had written and acted in political revues in Prague with great success, escaping just before the holocaust to begin all over again in Cleveland.

When we brought them to New York to read for us, they had had five hard years of discouraging effort. We immediately took them on, and they fulfilled our hopes, contributing inspired improvisation. They felt, for instance, that the clown's dialogue, particularly Stephano's remarks about the four-legged monster and its "forward and backward voice," indicated that Trinculo's and Caliban's business in the clowns' opening scene must have been pretty funny in the original production. George designed a gabardine prop that would allow Canada to hook one end of it around his neck like a huge cape, while George crouched under the other end, his head on the stage floor and his arms outstretched, with his hands flat in two large pockets sewn to the two rear corners. When it was fully extended, there was a long green body with Caliban's greenish fishlike head and a flat tail that could flap wildly. At rehearsal they auditioned this "monster" for Peggy. Jan Werich, as Stephano, poured wine into Caliban's mouth. Hearing Trinculo call him from the tail, he cried, "Doth thy other mouth call me? Mercy! Mercy! This is a devil, and no monster—" and, taking a big leap, he landed in the very center of the monster's back, which made both ends of it jump into the air. We were completely delighted with "V and W."

Incidental music was required, and a composer had to be found. Through Carson McCullers, I had met the young composer David Diamond and had heard some of his music, particularly the premiere of his Second Symphony, conducted by Koussevitzky. We chose David to write the musical score; his contribution was correctly estimated, I think, by a critic who said, "This score was one of the most strikingly individual and beautiful scores in contemporary incidental music."

Through no fault of David's, however, the musical end of the production was to provide one of our worst problems. Even before seeing the show, the musicians' union declared it a musical. David had scored it for twelve musicians, an appropriate number for an "incidental" score. The union insisted that the twelve be paid at the larger musical scale and that four additional—unnecessary—musicians be added. I fought, I appealed to the Board, I wrote persuasive letters to Mr. Petrillo, the national union head, in

Chicago. He replied that the New York local must be the judge. The local president was adamant: "Sixteen men at the union scale is the minimum and that settles it. If they don't abide by the ruling, we close the show." They might have insisted on the twenty-two minimum musicians for a regular musical, so, I suppose, I should be grateful that they devised a new category called "a play with music." Their decision doubled our expense for music.

When we opened in Philadelphia, we still had staggering technical problems. The turntable was operated by hand, and it jerked and stopped at the stagehand's whim. Worse, the Masque of Goddesses—in wildly expensive costumes—stopped the progress of the story cold. The goddesses were eliminated at once, with regret for the misspent money. In spite of the technical problems, we were encouraged by acceptable notices. We moved on hopefully to Boston.

Enroute to Boston, the scenery was lost in a blizzard. It didn't arrive until zero hour. Not surprisingly, the opening was a shambles. To our astonishment, the reviews were favorable and business excellent.

Peggy had devised a daring and brilliant switch in the text, transposing to the end of the play Prospero's glorious monologue beginning,

> Our revels now are ended.
> These our actors
> as I foretold you, were all spirits and
> are melted into air, into thin air
> and, like the baseless fabric of this vision,
> the cloud clapped towers, the gorgeous palaces . . .

As he spoke these lines, the lights slowly dimmed and the actors vanished, leaving Prospero in his royal red robe on the height outlined against a darkening sky until, as he spoke the final lines,

> We are such stuff as dreams are made on, and
> our little life
> is rounded with a sleep

he too vanished before a hushed, spellbound audience.

The Tempest opened in New York on January 25, 1945, at the large Alvin Theatre. It had a longer run than any other production of the play had ever achieved. It went on tour in the fall and returned to re-open at City Center about December 1. It was a gratifying success.

Working closely with Eva and Peggy, I discovered that they longed to start a repertory company. Eva, of course, had had the taste of a successful repertory company during the years when she had run the Civic on Fourteenth Street. And Peggy had been brought up in English repertory. I didn't have their familiarity, but I had my own fervor. The Old Vic had recently presented four plays in repertory in New York; I had seen all four and had been deeply impressed, along with everyone else. The Old Vic had been received with such rapture that everyone felt an imperative need for a similar American company. Their visit had convinced me that only a repertory organization could take the theatre and actors out of mere "show biz" and put them into the cultural haven they deserved. With plays rotating, the actors could stay fresh and develop their talents in a variety of roles. To see Olivier go from Henry IV, to Oedipus, to Doctor Astrov in Uncle Vanya, to Mr. Puff in The Critic in the space of a few weeks had been a revelation of the actor's art to me. Moreover, repertory seemed to offer the opportunity to sustain a worthy but less popular play which would have to close quickly if it played every night. Ideals! Ideals!

Eva and Peggy and I began to have long conferences to plan the founding of the American Repertory Company, as we decided to call it. There were two main points to settle: how much money we would need and where we were going to get it. I did some figuring and came up with three hundred thousand dollars to mount six productions, which I thought would not only cover the cost of mounting but leave an adequate reserve for operating. A lot of guesswork went into this sum. For example, I believed it was possible to get the cooperation of the various unions with the promise of a full season's engagement. I was wrong. Actors Equity was the only helpful union. The company agreed to play for considerably less than their customary salaries, and we were allowed six weeks' rehearsal period by their union. Eva, who during her Civic Repertory days had received aid from Local No. 1, the stagehands' union, used all her persuasive powers with their Council. It was not until we were almost ready to open that Local No. 1 laid down their onerous conditions: they had decided that twenty-eight stagehands must be hired for *Henry VIII,* our largest production, and kept on permanently and idly for the much less elaborate productions. The musicians' union insisted that whatever number of men were needed in any play which used music, they too should be kept on for the plays that required none. All this played hell with my operating estimate.

Today three hundred thousand dollars isn't peanuts, but it was even more then, and we had to raise it. Peggy said, "Let's make a list of possible donors. Since it will be nonprofit, we have to go to civic-minded people, people who care about the theatre." Each of us made lists, preparing to use all our powers of persuasion.

The only theatre we could require on a four-walls basis (i.e., the producer rents only the building and supplies everything else, including light and heat, and does not give a percentage of the gross to the owners) was the now-demolished International on Columbus Circle, where the Old Vic had played. Its stage was large enough to store our productions, which eliminated expensive trucking costs. But it was, for those days, regrettably far from Broadway, where all theatrical activity then centered.

The next question was who to proselytize for the company. We needed "names," actors whose work we admired and who would attract audiences. So we began to hold meetings, tempting recruits with roles they would never have an opportunity to play in a regular Broadway run.

"Wonderful parts!" we told them. "Leading roles in any great classic you might wish to play."

"Great! Great!" went the response. "What I've wanted all my life. A dream come true at last."

Then we got to the part about the salary and the work schedule. "Top salary five hundred dollars a week," we said, "and everyone signs for two seasons." The sparkling eyes glazed over. Visions of money they might receive elsewhere, from films, TV, a Broadway smash, won over our quixotic dream. The three middle-aged sirens wooed to no avail.

Eventually, our efforts won us an excellent company of able, experienced "pros," and we auditioned endlessly for young, unknown actors. Our choice of these was not bad: Eli Wallach, Anne Jackson, Efrem Zimbalist, Jr., William Windom and later Julie Harris, who played the White Rabbit in *Alice in Wonderland.*

Acknowledging the problems we were aware of and fortunately, or unfortunately, ignorant of the many that would explode unexpectedly as we proceeded, we began to promote the necessary three hundred thousand dollars.

It was a seemingly endless chore involving talks with moneyed individuals and daily speeches in New York and the adjacent countryside to stimulate prospective audiences. Our speeches went something like this:

The American theatre has almost abandoned the entire dramatic heritage of the past. America is the only great country in the world where no classic repertory theatre exists. The public has proved by its support of isolated productions of classic plays that it is still vitally theatre-minded and hungry for the best. Our productions will include Shakespeare, Shaw, Ibsen, a classic comedy and a new play. We believe it is important to tour the entire country with the same plays and company. We believe that a sufficient number of people share our faith in the importance of this plan to make the American Repertory Theatre a reality.

Finally, I wrote Peggy, "I find I'm tired, not physically, but my spiritual bin is empty from money-raising, money-cutting, glad-handing and the grinding repetition of our aims." Then sunshine: after a lunch with Joseph Verner Reed, Peggy returned with a check for one hundred thousand dollars, the first I had ever seen (and the last). Other public-spirited individuals came along: William Paley contributed ten thousand, Mrs. Efrem Zimbalist the same amount, Mrs. Samuel Goldwyn five thousand, Mrs.

Donald Stralen five thousand, Leonard Hanna the same, the Wertheim Fund another five, Mr. and Mrs. Harry Schloss forty-five hundred, Libby Holman thirty-five hundred, Mrs. Mike Hogg two thousand, J. S. Seidman two thousand, Bobby Clark one thousand combined with lesser amounts from a nurse, a GI, a college fraternity and others. Their generosity moves me to this day.

During this period I also managed to donate some time to the birth of the American National Theatre and Academy, known as ANTA. After Herculean efforts Robert Breen had finally persuaded Congress that the cultural life of the country merited an organization of theatre services, information and activities. Originally chartered by Congress in 1935, ANTA was inactive for its first ten years, first because of Hallie Flanagan's Federal Theatre Project and then because of World War II. But in 1945–1946, it came to life, a nonprofit group, independently financed, and dedicated ". . . to extend the living theatre beyond its present limitations by bringing the best in the theatre to every state in the Union."

One of our immediate aims was to develop new talents, playwrights and actors under the guidance of experienced professionals. Accordingly, the first move of the Board of Directors, on which I served as a vice-president, was to inaugurate an experimental theatre, giving new plays a brief, limited engagement at the small Princess Theatre. We hoped that some of the plays would be worth continuing and that new actors would be encouraged by the opportunity to display their talent.

Meanwhile, the American Rep was preparing its season and rehearsing. On November 6, 1946, we opened *Henry VIII* at the International Theatre with Victor Jory, Eva Le Gallienne and Walter Hampden playing the leads; *What Every Woman Knows* was our second play. On November 12, *John Gabriel Borkman* debuted; and on December 19, *Androcles and the Lion.*

But for all our pains and for all the marvelous acting, the notices were discouraging. Critics who had been wild about the Old Vic in 1944 and had cried out for a similar American troupe seemed, two years later when they got one, to have no understanding or appreciation of the repertory idea. Only *Androcles* impressed them.

I had frequent nightmares about money. In my sleep I clutched for greenbacks which turned before my eyes into endless bills for stagehands, musicians, costumes and scenery, through which I tried to push, flailing my arms for escape. There would never be enough money, there would never be enough money. And in the end there wasn't.

Unlike the critics, the audiences who came were appreciative —but they came in insufficient numbers. Eva felt that more would have come if the seats were cheaper. She wanted a people's theatre with low-priced seats. I didn't object to that at all—but just to break even we would have had to fill the house every night. And the fact was, we weren't filling the house. The deficit grew. My nightmares continued.

By January 1947 there was practically no money left. For a few days I retired to bed with a flu virus and passed the time reading Thoreau. For no reason I still remember a line from his book on Sir Walter Raleigh: "The fire which the Chaldeans worshipped for a God is crept into every man's chimney."

Then two events occurred that temporarily saved the ART. Rita Hassan offered to put up all the financing for *Alice in Wonderland,* which we thus were able to open on April 5. And a group from Actors Equity, to the astonishment and anger of some of its members, presented us with five thousand dollars. That money enabled us to produce Sidney Howard's *Yellow Jack. Alice* was a delightful production, which had a fair run but never repaid its production cost. No one seemed to want to see *Yellow Jack.* For all our efforts and ideals, we were without audiences and without money. The situation was desperate.

One evening the three of us sat gaunt, exhausted and silent. There was nothing to say. Nothing to do. We had tried and failed. It was no comfort to know that the great Old Vic in London had endured early seasons of comparative mediocrity before it became world-famous; that even in its wildly successful New York run, it had incurred losses. I didn't think there was a laugh left in us. Then Eva told a story.

At the Civic Repertory during the Depression, she one day

ordered wigs for a new production from Jean, her wig maker. Jean was bald and always wore a full head of hair. When she glanced at him, she noticed his toupee was heavily streaked with gray. "Why, Jean," she asked, "what have you done?"

"Oh, Miss G," he answered, stroking his gray sideburns, "you know—for business troubles."

At least we could laugh. I told a story, again about repertory. Leslie Banks, an eminent English actor, was approached by Jane Cowl, a famous star, with an appeal to join her in heading a repertory company. "Just think," she said, "one night I will play Hedda or Magda, and you will play a bit. But the next night *you* will play a great leading role, and I will simply carry a tray."

Banks returned to his wife in great excitement to report this marvelous idea. "Oh yes?" she said. "And you know what will be on that tray? The head of John the Baptist!"

Pain can sometimes be exorcized only by laughter.

Distraction also helps. ANTA had meanwhile been carrying forward its plans for an experimental theatre. For once, the financial responsibility was not mine, and that freedom made work seem like play. On February 9, 1947, we began to present five new plays for five performances each at the Princess Theatre. This was the first time that try-outs were done to help new authors and actors—it was an early "showcase"—and the effort won the Sidney Howard Award as the season's most important development in the theatre. As it eventually turned out, the Experimental Theatre paved the way for Off-Broadway.

But the American Rep in New York was, effectively, finished. Peggy was still determined and began to plan a bus-and-truck touring company of Shakespearean plays. I was not tempted. Zealot that I was, I was also a businesswoman, and I could not shake the memory of the relentless fund-raising, the unending bills and the pages of numbers in red ink. I had made up my mind to cut loose. Soon afterwards an unforgettable note arrived from one of the two playwrights in my life whose initials are T. W.:

Take three years off from the cultural drama and the better things in the theatre—even from that literate shade that skirted *One Touch of Venus*. Your doctrinaire tendency has led you down the garden path.

Give it a vacation. Do popular theatre. Purge yourself in basic theatre, farces, melodrama, laughs and shudders. Really, you'd enjoy it. A three year purge. Then the big things. By that time all your friends will have deserted you but

Thornton

Peggy and Eva never deserted me. On June 10, 1947, I wrote them a letter which, having expressed my praise and admiration for their talents, said

The experience and observation of this year has left me no faith that such a theatre can exist under present conditions, and I can see no way in which these conditions can be substantially changed. Perhaps I can only be decisive and properly executive when I have to make up my mind alone and stand or fall by my decisions.

An aside to myself: why didn't I remember these words later, in 1962, when I got involved with the Actors Studio Theatre for six productions? The answer: one forgets pain after an operation; and I was never cured of my dream. This was always the problem: when I was alone, I dreamed of a company; when I was part of a company, I thought of the freedom of being on my own. And so, throughout my career, without quite realizing it at the time, I charted a zigzag course between the two.

An indication of my troubled psyche during this period is that I had three recurrences of a mysterious disease called iritis, an intensely painful inflammation of the eyes, which makes your eyes feel as though a mailed fist were being pounded into them; even the light of a match results in a scream of pain. Doctors told me that no one knows the origin of this affliction, but I think I do. George Groddeck describes such attacks very well in *The Way of the It.* My "it" didn't want to see or face the daily tasks, and that was the best way to keep from doing them.

Peggy and Eva kept on. After the run of *Alice in Wonderland* Eva undertook a season of Ibsen in repertory with Louis Singer as her producer. I have great respect for what she has achieved in the theatre.

Peggy went ahead with her touring company of Shakespearean plays. A crusader, Peggy, who matched Don Quixote fighting many more windmills: the cities and towns of forty-eight states. I saw her last at Christmas 1971, her blithe spirit still prevailing, though she had endured a number of serious operations. Soon after a party on the stage of the Imperial Theatre celebrating her book, *Don't Put Your Daughter on the Stage*, she died. The Little Church Around the Corner was filled with theatre people who loved her, some of whom recalled their experiences with her. George Voskovec captured her appropriately:

> The forever gallant Peggy who, up to the last, reminds me of a gallant British frigate with all flags snapping—and the pennant, signaling her deep sense of the ridiculous, flying the highest of all—forever with guts, style and supreme elegance. With heart, too.

Independent once again, I was able to devote more attention to ANTA. The Princess Theatre project had succeeded, yet there seemed to be too few new plays of any consequence. So the Board had decided that more substantial efforts should be undertaken to serve both the theatre and the public. In December of 1947, ANTA had opened a production of Brecht's *Galileo*, starring Charles Laughton, which had been playing on the West Coast. It was directed by Joseph Losey, who later became a fine film director based in England after the McCarthy stigma prevented his working in the United States. The production was an interesting one, and Laughton gave a fascinating performance, offering a Galileo torn between the revolutionary conviction that the earth moved around the sun and his recantation of that knowledge to save his skin. In his attempt to make Galileo human, he filled out the characterization with business of everyday living, one particular piece of which bothered me: he took an excessive amount of time bathing the top half of his naked, flabby body, a large pudding of a belly which I found most unattractive. To my regret, I was never able to convince him to cut one moment of his public bath. Laughton was a complex, inventive, highly cultured man with a strange party humor. Under the influence of a few drinks, he would recite endless scatalogical limericks that would have made even Norman Douglas, who published a book of such limericks, blush. I think Laughton made up most of his.

At ANTA I received a play called *Skipper Next to God*, written by Jan de Hartog, who later wrote *The Four Poster*, and I decided to do it as an experimental production. I was able to induce John Garfield, by now a successful film actor, to play the lead under Lee Strasberg's direction. It opened on January 4, 1948, and was so well received that Blevins Davis, a member of the Board, took it over for a commercial run. The ANTA idea was working.

John La Touche and Jerome Moross submitted to me three short musicals called *Ballet Ballads* to be performed together. I thought they were delightful and invited the Board to my apartment to hear them. Some members were unconvinced that we should do them, but Roger Stevens was enthusiastic and together we bulled through a production in May of 1948. Actually they were dance-operas, intended to fuse the arts of text, music and dance into a new dramatic unity, quite novel at that time. They turned out to be altogether charming and original, if not quite perfect. Their production was later taken over by T. Edward Hambleton, Alfred Stern and Nat Karson. My reward was the author's acknowledgment to me in the published version, "Without whom—"

By 1949 it had become more and more apparent that ANTA needed a home, a theatre that would not be operated as a business venture. Then a splendid event occurred with some financing to implement it. The City Investment Company, consisting mainly of Robert Dowling and Roger Stevens, members of ANTA's Board, bought the Theatre Guild Theatre and voted to turn it over to ANTA to be used entirely for nonprofit theatrical activity. A number of theatre people met in the large lounge to inaugurate it. I was asked to speak, among others, and I quote from my speech because that is the best way to depict the discrepancy between the dream and the eventual reality. I still feel sick when such a dream dissolves into moonshine.

There is a new question flying these days across Broadway and up from Walgren's to "21"—*What* in the name of four letters of the alphabet is ANTA?

The answer is simple. ANTA is whatever you make it. You. Everyone in every department of the theatre. For the American National Theatre and Academy is actually just a piece of paper, an official instrument, a charter from Congress for a nonprofit theatrical organization. It represents a dream, a banner, a focal point through which all theatre people can rally to help themselves, each other and the whole country to make more theatre. It would hardly be necessary to explain ANTA to an Englishman, as you would only have to mention the Arts Council of Great Britain, an organization initiated by the generous grant of an American millionaire and since 1942 backed by the British Government. Projects for special plays (even American ones such as *A Streetcar Named Desire* and *Death of a Salesman*), repertory theatres (traveling and local), Sadler's Wells Ballet, Covent Garden Opera are made possible by funds or support from this Council.

As a result, last year England had two hundred and seventy-five professional theatre productions by about thirty-eight nonprofit companies associated with the Arts Council. The successful companies, and there are many of them, must turn the profits back into new productions.

But ANTA, so far, has had to operate mostly on faith and the devotion of many volunteers. And now, miraculously, it has a theatre, the old and lovely Guild Theatre, twitched from the protean hands of television. Unpaid for, it's true, but when has that stopped us? The people of the theatre have always been in the forefront of money raising for war, for peace, for innumerable charities. Now we can begin at home, and it does not seem inconceivable that we can raise funds for ourselves. The cost of the wings of one bomber would be sufficient.

If possession is nine-tenths of the law, we now have a home, a center, the only theatre which is in the hands of theatre people and not a real-estate operation. And our object is to make it hum and bulge with theatre activity. In the morning, plays for children. In the afternoon, concerts, forums, lectures. Some of the plays will be presented at six, some at nine. We can't waste a minute of our borrowed time. Besides our own productions, we want to bring to New York some of our most famous regional theatre. It may be possible to induce some of the stars of other countries to dazzle us with their great roles for a limited engagement. Why shouldn't we have the good fortune to see Dame Edith Evans in *The Way of the World,* Sir Laurence Olivier in *Richard III,* Jouvet in *Tartuffe,* Paula Wessaly in *St. Joan?*

For this season, we are also planning ten productions to a membership audience. At least half of them will be old plays. The season will open on November 19 with Judith Anderson in *Tower Beyond Tragedy* by Robinson Jeffers, a free adaption of *The Agamemnon* and *The Libation Bearers* of Aeschylus. The second production will be a new play,

The Cellar and the Well, by a talented young American author, Phillip Pruneau. Third (we hope), Katharine Cornell will appear in a Shaw play. Then another new play—and after that, John Garfield will appear in Paul Green's new version of *Peer Gynt.* Helen Hayes will become a producer (oh, my dear) for Sir James Barrie's *Mary Rose.* We have almost concluded arrangements to bring Louis Jouvet and his company for a four-week repertory of Molière and Romains. With such activity, a theatre building is no longer an empty and fabulously expensive shell which comes to life for twenty-four hours a week. It lives twenty-four hours a day.

You want to ask questions? I know. How is this financially possible? Because everyone is working for the union minimum. The cooperation of all the unions has been extraordinary and belies the dark and bloody feuds which supposedly exist. There are some people who will work for nothing—the producers, as usual, and the many volunteers who will address envelopes, answer phones, fetch and carry and do all the onerous and anonymous work that people do for love. The costs should be carried by membership, and at the rate the public is responding, five to nine thousand dollars a day, we ought to be self-supporting except for the actual cost of the building.

The second question I can hear is, Is this going to be a temple of Culture? Oh, I hope never. That unfortunate word only brings associations with "Take the nasty medicine now. It's good for you." Culture sounds like a dead thing. The theatre's joy and pleasure is immediate, vital, alive.

So—now—we about to kill ourselves with work—and have a good time doing it—salute you. To accomplish our dreams we need the help, ideas, talents and criticism (later) of everyone in the theatre, including audience.

To paraphrase a great man, this building of ours on Fifty-second Street is a place of the theatre, by the theatre and for the theatre. It is our duty and our pride to see that it does not perish.

But from the outset things did not fall into place as we hoped. For the first presentation at ANTA's new home it was important to have a distinguished production, and as my speech had promised, Judith Anderson starred in *Tower Beyond Tragedy,* by Robinson Jeffers. We opened on November 26, 1950 to great acclaim, especially for Judith. Brooks Atkinson was overwhelmed and raved about Judith's performance. The other critics were also impressed by her achievement but not enthusiastic about the play. Its appeal was limited. We had anticipated that to some degree; after all, our avowed purpose was to do plays of distinction which would be unlikely to find a commercial production. Nonetheless, Judith had hoped to take it on tour after its ANTA run, and did not—the play's reception didn't encourage a tour.

Peer Gynt didn't fare much better. It was a very difficult play I had never seen on the stage. John Garfield was responsive to my idea of doing it, especially when Lee Strasberg agreed to direct. The version I had read was quite dated, so I persuaded Paul Green to write a new one. We opened in January 1951. Garfield was good but not astonishing, and *Peer Gynt* doesn't work unless the audience is enthralled by the performance. The production worked only in parts—and not very many parts. Perhaps it is not a produceable play; I have never heard of it being unusually successful.

Things were not working out for ANTA. Contrary to the optimism of my speech, there was never enough money. Expenses consistently outran income, even though actors like Garfield and Laughton played for ten dollars and eight dollars a week, respectively. Each production was a separate effort; there was no way to establish an ANTA company. The subscription program we had established never brought in sufficient funds, and though Equity and the Dramatists Guild gave us contributions, in the end we ran out of money.

I supervised one additional play for ANTA, a new one called *A Temporary Island*, by Halsted Welles. Although Vera Zorina played a leading part, it lasted only briefly. Two other plays were presented, their productions overseen by members of the Board.

The fabulous balloon of a nonprofit theatre had been injected with gas to little purpose. Enough was enough. I resigned; so did Robert Breen. Robert Whitehead took over the operation. He produced five plays for ANTA, some of them quite successful. But in the end, he gave up too for the same reasons: no opportunity to establish a company. Not enough money.

So there I was in 1951, back on my own, tired and disappointed. Two organizations for which I had had the highest hopes had failed. Ever since the Group days I had truly wanted to be involved in theatre that had a core and continuity, theatre that enriched the theatre itself. When the ART and ANTA died aborning, I became again that naked individual I had tried to avoid.

Musical Adventures

There's magic in a good musical. For me, the anticipation starts when the lights of the musicians' stands flick on in the pit, the violins tune softly and the trombones let out a few yelps. It grows as the conductor arrives and taps his baton for the overture to start. When there is no overture I feel cheated. I want music to make off with me, sweep me up into a special world.

So, to feed my fancy, long after *Porgy and Bess* and *One Touch of Venus*, I became involved in eight musicals.

August 1946 was a hot month. The law firm of Fitelson and Mayers was advising and aiding the American Repertory Theatre, and H. William Fitelson, called Bill, told me about a musical he thought I should hear. He also introduced me to an attractive young lady, Bea Lawrence, who wanted to participate in the theatre as an associate and investor. We went one warm afternoon in late August to an apartment in the upper fifties at the corner of Broadway. The small living room was nearly filled with a large grand piano. There we met two young men, both slender and rather short. One was a curly-haired blond with a profile like that on a Greek coin and wicked blue eyes enlarged by glasses. He introduced himself as Alan Jay Lerner. The other had a full head of brown hair which fell over his steel gray eyes when he was excited; he was often excited. He was Frederick Loewe, a Viennese, more usually known as Fritz. I noticed that he had powerful arms and hands, and later I learned he had once been a cowboy. Alan was a chain smoker with a cute habit of twisting a cigarette around his fingers, which gave me a chance to notice that his nails were bitten to the quick. I thought this might be nervousness about the audition. But no, it was a habit that continued all the years I knew him. On the piano was a balloon glass partially filled with an amber liquid I took to be brandy. This Fritz paused to sip from occasionally, returning to the keys with demonic energy.

Telling us that the name of the musical was *Brigadoon*, the two began the audition. The piano seemed to be merely an extension of Fritz's fingers; he controlled it with passion and authority. Alan read a little, told the story and sang his lyrics in a sweet, true voice. At the end both Bea and I were moved. I asked for the script and read it that weekend on a beach at Fire Island.

The story was a touching fantasy about a New York playboy who, disgusted with the emptiness of his city life, goes to the Highlands of Scotland to find himself in an enchanted town called Brigadoon, where people only come alive once every hundred years. There life has meaning. He is forced to choose between the two lives the two places offer, and in the end, he chooses Brigadoon.

Perhaps it was the Scottish blood in me that responded so strongly. I realized that *Brigadoon* was probably not for the tired businessman who supposedly supports musicals, but I couldn't let that deter me. (Over the years many businessmen, still tired, have told me *Brigadoon* was their favorite show.) I decided to do it. Bea decided to join me.

Billy Rose was flirting with *Brigadoon*, but not with a pen and a contract. While he hemmed and hawed, I signed. Figuring that two hundred thousand dollars would be sufficient to produce it, we began to have auditions for investors. In between my other obligations—opening the ART plays out of town and supervising ANTA's Experimental Theatre—Alan, Fritz and I, sometimes with Bea, who held several auditions in her apartment, trotted out bearing the score and the book to play for anywhere from six to twenty people who had money. We performed thirty-two auditions. It seemed as if we would never assemble the entire backing. Some of the backers urged me to change the title. "No one will pronounce it properly," they said. I answered, "If it's a hit, they'll learn." Then Bill Fitelson introduced me to J. S. Seidman, head of a world-famous accounting firm. Seidman liked the show enough to gather acquaintances in his apartment frequently to hear the work. The more he heard it, the more he loved it. He finally decided to invest ninety-six thousand dollars with some friends. The rest was like pulling teeth; it came in bits and pieces. The authors became so adept at performing that some listeners wondered if the full production could possibly be as good. There were moments when it seemed to me that if I really wanted to get *Brigadoon* before the public, I should do it as a two-man show!

Nonetheless, with the euphoria customary to those in the theatre at the start of a promising venture, we chose our director, Robert Lewis, whom I had known from Group Theatre days; Agnes de Mille, the choreographer who had done such a fine job on *One Touch of Venus;* the set designer, Oliver Smith; and David Ffolkes, whom Agnes suggested for the costumes. We also held casting auditions and chose actors with no star names, since most of the characters were too young to be played by stars. We set out-of-town theatres and arranged for Billy Rose's Ziegfeld Theatre in New York, although we were still twenty thousand dollars shy of our total investment. At the last moment we were rescued by Harriett Ames, who took the entire twenty.

It was a dedicated and charming company with even greater rapport than the *Porgy* company, greater than any I have ever known. We were a happy family. Our last run-through at the Ziegfeld before opening in New Haven went very well. Billy Rose saw it and gave his accolade.

We weren't sanguine, however, about the leading comedy performer, Pamela Britten. She had an attractive stage presence, but where was the comedy? We were concerned enough to audition possible replacements, though we didn't give up on Britten. Before we opened in New Haven I asked Bobby Lewis if I could work with her. For two days she and I rehearsed in the ladies' room whenever she was free. For every moment of her big number I gave her exact and detailed business.

Her song was called "The Love of My Life," and it described her attempts to attract four different men, all of whom abandoned her. All alone on the stage, Pamela didn't know what to do with her hands. I gave her a piece of heather to play with for greeting and flirting, and showed her how to imitate the different men as she sang about them. These bits of business relaxed her, and the song came to life. When the last man had had his pleasure and disappeared, she tossed the heather over her shoulder in disgust.

On opening night her performance was so well received that we decided she should have a number in Act Two. It turned out to be "My Mother's Wedding Day," verse upon verse of which was greeted with laughter and abetted by a chorus dancing and singing a drunken bacchanal. The notices were sensational, and we moved on to Boston dreaming of sugar plums. Our first performance there was a benefit for the Smith College Club.

When the curtain rose on the second scene at the square with the entire chorus on stage, we were stunned to see only an enormous white cloth backdrop. Where was the backdrop showing the village with hills behind? What was wrong with the lights? Only a dead white glare fell on the stage. All of us were making anxious sounds but David Ffolkes, staring with us, gasped, "My God! Ann has on the wrong color stockings!" Now *that* is a one-track mind.

We opened to critics the following night; all of the reviews were excellent except one. Business was poor the first week, and somewhat better the second. We headed for Philadelphia with some trepidation. But there the notices were wonderful and business excellent. Returning to New York for a few days, I discovered that that miracle of all media, word of mouth, was working for us. Mail orders and window sales at the Ziegfeld were astonishing. On a Monday, thirteen thousand dollars window sales and twelve hundred and fifty dollars mail orders. The next day, sixty-five hundred dollars over the window and twenty-five hundred dollars mail orders. And the top orchestra ticket was four dollars and fifty cents!

When opening night came, even I couldn't stay away. It is my unfortunate habit to predict the success of a production by buying something expensive, at least by my standards, just before an opening. It seems to buoy my confidence, though I often regret it after the notices. On this occasion my largesse to myself was a party dress I was happily able to afford. I wore it to the opening with great optimism. I sat in the house manager's office reading the *New Yorker* cover to cover while listening for applause. Each time I began to tense up, the house manager took me next door for a drink. By the time the show was over I was feeling no pain. My father and mother had arrived that morning to see their first opening night of one of my productions and went with me to a very large party—the sixty members of the company as well as other guests—at Bea's apartment. The tables were handsomely decorated with gay tartans. Champagne flowed endlessly. I asked Father what he had done that day. He had gone to see a matinee performance of *Oklahoma.* "I tell you, Cheryl," he pontificated, "*Brigadoon* is better."

The next morning every review was a rave. We took an ad that said simply one hundred percent raves from the critics.

Even if a honeymoon is all it's cracked up to be, it can scarcely be more exciting than being wedded to a smash hit. Every day around noon various friends and I would stand across from the box office to watch the lines of ticket buyers stretching around the corner. Fritz was the only one who didn't enjoy the glowing reviews that rained down on us. He became depressed. I suspect he may have felt that *Brigadoon* was his zenith, that he could never match it again. When the Critics Award was given to us at the end of April, Fritz bought a farm near Poundridge, New York, and settled there. He and Alan had a mysterious falling out, and he wasn't active in the theatre again for four years.

The company of young people had an admirable and sturdy discipline that I valued. So after a few months, without being asked, I raised the chorus salaries and instituted Blue Cross for each member of the company. This gesture was sufficiently unusual to make news, and it was not appreciated by other producers. Yet I felt it was richly deserved. Theatre folk lead too insecure a life as it is. Why shouldn't they have the benefits workers in other fields take for granted?

Lee Strasberg had just returned from a long stint of work in

Hollywood coaching film actors. There was nothing for him immediately available in New York so I invited him to work on acting problems on a weekly basis with the entire company on the Ziegfeld stage. I can't forget how they said, with astonishment, "Free acting lessons?" I saw it as an opportunity to encourage and extend them. I attended the first meeting. Listening to Lee speak again after such a long interlude, hearing the brilliance and perception of his comments affected me so deeply that I went home and lay in a hot bath for a long time to calm down.

Although Fritz had decided to rest on his laurels for a while, Alan was eager to begin another show. He had an idea of telling the history of a marriage from colonial times to the present, using one couple who are trying to save their relationship in the face of economic progress that threatens to kill it, and interspersing the scenes with pertinent vaudeville interludes illustrating the development of a materialistic society. I asked Fritz if he had any objection to my working with Alan and another composer. He said he couldn't care less. So I introduced Alan to Kurt Weill, who responded to the idea with enthusiasm. Kurt and Alan went to work at once and by September 1947 had completed eleven songs and some scenes. They decided to call the musical *Love Life*. Elia Kazan signed on as director.

While Kurt and Alan were at work, I was still involved with ANTA and ART, but best of all, I was busy arranging the London production of *Brigadoon* for the following year with Prince Littler, a distinguished theatre owner there.

Mary Martin was playing a very successful tour of *Annie Get Your Gun* and generously loaned me her home outside Norwalk, Connecticut so that I could have weekends of rest. Mary seemed ideal for the wife in *Love Life*, so I made arrangements for Alan, Kurt and me to play it for her one November Sunday in 1947, in Chicago. Unfortunately, the one song that really sent her was called "Susan's Dream," a lovely number for a black woman to be done in one of the interludes. The words were very touching, but it was impossible to conceive of them being sung by a white woman. Mary decided against the show. Ironically, "Susan's Dream" was never used. For the two leads we settled on Nanette

Fabray and Ray Middleton; Ray had made a great success opposite Ethel Merman in *Annie*.

The Christmas Eve party for *Brigadoon* was held in the large basement lounge of the theatre. I shall never forget it. Having discovered my love of poetry in general and Walt Whitman in particular, the company gave me the most cherished present I ever received: a rare "Butterfly" edition of *Leaves of Grass* signed by Walt Whitman in 1861, printed by Thayer and Eldridge, and dated "Year 85 of The States"; it was interspersed with actual newspaper reviews of the period, good and bad, which I have preserved. It still takes no more than two drinks and a guest who likes poetry for me to exhibit it proudly.

A dream had begun to nudge me. I wanted a weekend retreat of my own. On a blazing hot Sunday in August 1948 I finally found the home for me. I had seen an elaborate brochure of a small estate only four miles from Mary and Dick's place. It looked perfect and much too expensive, but my brother Newell, his wife, and my friend Ruth Norman decided to have a look anyway. Fatal. It was my dream come true. Two old houses from Eastham on Cape Cod had been moved and reconstructed on thirteen acres of pasture and woodland; the rooms had been expanded and modern facilities installed. The paneling in each room dated from 1690 to 1705, with handsome old wallpapers; there were seven working fireplaces. The exterior had a charming old-fashioned garden in back, looking up to stands of birch and tall firs, and a stone wall covered with red roses. The picket fence in front was covered with pale pink roses. None of us dared to look at each other for fear we would expose our delight. We returned to visit Mary and Dick, who plied us with martinis, which only increased our delirium. They wanted to see the place too, so back we went. I told Mary, who is given to exuberance, to make no sound so that I could negotiate a price. One look through the Dutch door of the large living room and Mary screamed with pleasure. I've told her ever since that that outburst cost me ten thousand dollars. (That plus the money for the tour of *Venus* makes a tidy sum!) Luckily I was able to make a deal for the house and five acres of land, which brought the price down to something I dared to undertake.

The next day *Love Life* went into rehearsal.

Rising very early each morning, I would go to furniture shops and at the end of the day to auctioneers' establishments, picking early American tables, chairs and knicknacks for my new home, which had been named Eastham. Once a week my purchases were piled in the back of an ancient Ford station wagon and chugged up to the country. By spring I had discovered additional charms —lilacs of blue, purple and white, pink and white dogwoods and MacIntosh apple trees. A swimming pool was obligatory, removed from the house so that no bathing suit would be necessary, only cardinals, noisy bluejays and an occasional chipmunk observing. I think this retreat saved my sanity and health. I relaxed under transparent summer skies and stalked through the white snows of winter. Ruth Norman planted vegetables, and I picked them. She was a partner with James Beard in his famous cooking classes, and since he became a frequent visitor, I ate very well. One remarkable thing about Jim, not well known, is that from childhood he wished to be an opera singer and is hence a storehouse of opera knowledge. I would play recordings of operas, and he would guess who was singing. I seldom fooled him, even with Hugo Schmidt, Supervia, Muzio, Tetrazzini and Ponselle.

Like many others who suddenly acquire more money than they need, I lived it up. I bought a Lincoln Continental and employed a succession of mostly unsatisfactory butlers who also cooked and cleaned.

There were many weekend guests: Thornton Wilder, Tennessee Williams, Janet Flanner, Tallulah Bankhead, Harvey Schmidt and Tom Jones. Kurt Weill, Fritz Loewe, Marc Blitzstein, whom I had known from Group days, and Bart Howard played their hearts out on the grand piano. Bart frequently played a song he had written called "In Other Words." We all loved it, but it seemed to get nowhere. Then the title was changed to "Fly Me to the Moon." It flew!

Marilyn Monroe came to swim. One special afternoon one of Jim Beard's friends, a monumental man with a Santa Claus belly, asked her to dance on the small back porch. She graciously accepted, allowing herself to be pushed around on his stomach. I expect he dined out on that experience for a long time. There were bucolic Christmas days in the snow with crackling fires and laughing visitors, Mary Martin and Richard Halliday with their child Heller, Burl and Helen Ives and other friends.

Love Life opened in the fall of 1948 and had a respectable run of two hundred and fifty-two performances. Why only respectable? Its theme was fresh, the form unusual, the cast exceptional, the settings by Boris Aaronson delightful. But it had no heart, no passion. The audience couldn't get emotionally involved in the marital problems of the couple. And though it was satirical, it lacked penetrating wit for the most part. Because Kurt's score served the style of the writing, it didn't have the warmth of his best ballads. But in 1948 Alan had been married only twice. Now, after six marriages, he would probably have more emotional material at his command.

In February I flew to London for casting and rehearsals of *Brigadoon.* Alan, Fritz and Bobby Lewis were already there. I had a small modern room at the Savoy, but when I saw Fritz's suite high above the Thames, I vowed that someday I would occupy such a suite, if only for a few days. Much later, I did.

When *Brigadoon* played in Manchester to spellbound audiences, I decided I was free to go to Rome before the London opening. It was my first visit, and I was lucky to have a Roman friend there, Natalia Danesi Murray, who had left New York temporarily to do radio broadcasts for the Voice of America. In ten days I had a fascinating, exhausting view of a Rome most tourists don't see, and met many charming theatre and literary people.

I returned to London a few days before we were to open *Brigadoon* at what was then called His Majesty's Theatre. Bobby and I went there to watch the set and light rehearsal. To our dismay, the lights were haywire; the forest glade, instead of having green shadows, glowed a deep red, looking like Dante's Inferno. Fortunately, my training as a stage manager stood me in good stead: I was still able to remember most of the lighting we had used previously. Between the two of us we slowly set about locating the proper lamps. But late that night we were still in a mess, and when Prince Littler dropped by, happily smoking an aromatic cigar, I had to tell him that I didn't see how we could possibly open. He left. We worked steadily on, and by dawn we got the lights corrected. I will always remember walking back with Bobby to the Savoy in the morning mist, completely exhausted, hoping the electricians would be alert enough that evening to remember. They did.

That night, sitting in a box at the opening with Prince's wife Nora, I saw tears streaming down her face at the close of Act One.

"What is wrong, Nora?" I asked.

"Oh, it's Prince," she answered. "He has been so upset about the lights, you know!"

The critics were full of praise, so I knew we were secure for a long time. I set out to enjoy myself, and had a wonderful time.

Before I had left for London, Marc Blitzstein had played a musical version of Lillian Hellman's play *The Little Foxes* for me. He called it *Regina*. I was sufficiently impressed by its power and originality to option it. When I returned, we set to work. Bobby Lewis signed to direct and the search began for a Regina. We finally settled on an excellent one, Jane Pickens. Money raising was not easy, particularly since this material was not in the traditional style of Broadway musical theatre. Fortunately, at an audition, I met a young man named Clinton Wilder, who was not daunted by *Regina*'s nonconformity. I gave him the financial facts. A few days later, there was a pleasant surprise on my desk, a check from Clinton for eight thousand dollars. We had many auditions in his home during the hot summer months when the noise of borrowed fans forced Marc to belt out the songs in order to be heard. Clinton became my associate producer.

When *Regina* tried out in New Haven, I had a discouraging conversation with faithful Bill Fitelson, who wanted me to have a sure-fire success. He felt that my taste was too special, that *Regina* was simply not commercial. Thinking it over, I felt that his position required a rebuttal and that the issue was important enough to be put in writing.

"Dear Bill," I began,

Just want to go on record about *Regina.* How anyone ever knows what will be commercial is beyond me. I recall all the wiseacres in New Haven at *Streetcar:* "Wonderful but too special." "Not enough people will want to see this morbid thing and these sad, ugly people." Even Gadg and Irene were dubious with all their appreciation of the work.

If I want to stay in the theatre, I have to firmly believe that a sense of truth, coupled with theatrical talent, has an audience, a big one! If you tingle with a sudden awareness of things you only dimly felt before, of evil, of compassion, so that you know more about life after such an experience, that is all I ask.

I'm going to see to it that the audience sitting before *Regina* has an emotional experience they won't forget. That is theatre. That's why I'm in it. Gags and sugarstick romance have a place in a public's entertainment, but I'd like to give them something richer, truer, deeper.

As a play, this must have had a considerable catharsis for an audience or it wouldn't have run so long. I think the music adds bigger values— more emotion, more passion, more tenderness.

We opened in New York October 4, 1949 to considerable praise. Atkinson said that *Regina* was "a remarkable achievement," and Chapman thought Jane Pickens made "a gorgeous and imperious Regina." Robert Garland of the *Journal-American* chimed in that *Regina* was "the only good American grand opera" he knew. And Hawkins of the *World-Telegram* called it "the most exciting musical theatre since Rosenkavalier." Leonard Lyons summed it up with "smash hit!"

But he was wrong. Despite the praise and all our efforts, *Regina* closed after a two-month run. (Later it enjoyed a revival at City Center, and an album was recorded.) About the same time I had to close an even shorter run of a melodrama, *The Closing Door,* so I was thanking God for *Brigadoon,* which was still running in New York as well as in London. A delayed letter from the music critic of the *New York Times,* John Martin, meant a lot to me.

Though I am not much on fan letters, I cannot help writing you this one about *Regina.* I am ashamed to say that I did not get to it until the last matinee and that my enthusiasm is accordingly not even of word-of-mouth value.

I have seen a great many theatres in a great many languages over the past forty years or so, but I have rarely been so completely shattered by a performance. What Blitzstein has done is to give us a theatre of our own with heroic dimensions for perhaps the first time. I have never heard music made so integral an element in the total art of the theatre, so boldly used to heighten and create theatrical values. His figures emerge in larger-than-life proportions in a situation that, for all its specific localization, takes on universal compulsions. It is difficult not to make some comparisons with those suspect creatures, the old Greeks.

Bobby's direction is rich and superbly sensitive, the casting is inspired and the setting a real triumph. Everything in the composition manages to fuse realism with the basic grandeurs of tragic abstraction.

It is small comfort, I know, to "pass a miracle" and have it unrecognized as such, but there must be some satisfaction, nevertheless, in having produced a work which really sets the theatre way in advance of itself. Certainly you have put us all deeply in your debt.

In April of 1950, I bought a musical called *Flahooley* by Yip Harburg, Fred Saide and Sammy Fain. It told a sort of "Sorcerer's Apprentice" story: a young genius who works for a great toy factory creates a doll named Flahooley who laughs. Laughter, of course, is just what the world needs. He also fixes a magic lamp, releasing a genie. Eager to work after a lay-off of a few thousand years, the genie makes Flahooleys by the million, putting the factory out of business. The Flahooleys created for the simple purpose of making people laugh have to be destroyed.

I opened the show in April 1951 on the road. But not all the work I had hoped for was done on tour, and we opened in New York to three good and two poor notices. John Chapman said that the idea was captivating and interesting when it was being "Flahooley" but annoying when it tried for Social Significance. This was also the trouble, I think, with *Finians Rainbow* by the same writers: the enchanting story and memorable music by Burton Lane were mixed with a considerable dash of political bitters. Perhaps that is why it is not revived as often as musicals that are much less original. Barbara Cook, in her first big Broadway role, was charming in *Flahooley;* Yma Sumac displayed her miraculous voice, which ran a gamut exceeding that of a piano keyboard. And it had Bil Baird's incredible puppets, including a doll that neither piddled nor cried, just laughed. *This* doll neither cried nor laughed, just was deeply disappointed that the writers had been unable to mix properly their delightful fancy with their serious intent. *Flahooley* had a brief run.

Meanwhile, Alan and Fritz had made up, and in 1951 they began to meet at Eastham to plan a show they called *Paint Your Wagon*. I was delighted. The winning *Brigadoon* team would be together again—bound for success, I was sure. *Paint Your Wagon* was about the gold rush to California, where the mining camps were full of lusty men and empty of women until a coach brought in a group of finely dressed ladies who were no better than they should be. There was kind of a—sort of—love story between the daughter of the chief prospector and a Mexican youth.

But as Fritz and Alan progressed with the writing, mysterious things began to happen. I discovered that production meetings were being held without me. Bobby Lewis was called for them, but I wasn't. What was going on? I protested. In fact, I raised hell. Then suddenly they abandoned Bobby, whose suggestions on book changes they disagreed with, and told me to find another director. I suggested Daniel Mann, who had directed *The Rose Tattoo*, and they accepted him. If all this sounds curious, it was. It was never explained. Perhaps Alan wished to show his power by dangling people. I've never gotten to the bottom of it.

As the story began to take shape, I decided Walter Huston would be ideal for the lead. He had been so appealing in *Knickerbocker Holiday*, singing the beautiful "September Song." I told him the story before we had enough to show him, and he expressed interest. Sadly, before we were ready, he was dead.

Wonder of wonders, all the money seemed to be raised at our first audition. What a relief!

I should have known better. When I tried to reach a *Brigadoon* investor who had promised forty thousand dollars, she was always unavailable, either on her boat or ill or totally disappeared. I sweated it out until Bea Lawrence staunchly decided to join me again as investor and associate producer. Billy Rose put in ten thousand, too.

Meanwhile, more shenanigans. The writers were on the West

Coast and chose two performers whose work I had never seen, James Barton and Olga San Juan. I wasn't happy about this. A producer should be involved in casting. But Agnes de Mille compensated, outdoing herself with two spectacular scenes, the arrival of the prostitutes introduced by a chorus of miners singing "There's a Coach Comin' In," and a knock-out can-can in the Palace bar.

We approached Philadelphia with great expectations. Our euphoria quickly subsided. The critics clobbered us. Billy Rose came and said not to worry, not to worry, it was all fixable. The next I heard of him was a large ad he took in *Variety* offering to sell his interest. I was livid but helpless; there was no way to overcome the damage of that publicity. So we kept working to cut and rewrite.

On we progressed to Boston, somewhat improved. There we had a serious problem with James Barton, who played the chief prospector. As a vaudeville headliner, Barton's most famous act had been a drunk routine. Alan decided to use it for a scene in Act One when Barton brings home a new bride he has just bought. This scene was supposed to run no more than nine minutes, but by the time we played Boston Barton was stretching it to twenty, and making it a disaster. Finally one evening Fritz blew his top. Agnes and Bea were sitting in a bar in an alley behind the Shubert Theatre in Boston when Fritz entered with two large water glasses. "Fill both of these to the top," he instructed the bartender.

"What are you doing with all that liquor?" the ladies inquired.

"I'm going to talk to Barton right after the curtain," he replied with an ominous glare. Curious, they followed him. After he entered Barton's dressing room they stood outside and heard him say, "Drink this down, Barton, you're going to need it!" Silence from the dressing room: they both seemed to be bottoming up. Then Fritz said loudly and firmly, "I mean what I'm telling you; if your drunk routine ever goes beyond nine minutes again, I am going to get a gun and I'm going to kill you. I'm a fine shot and you'd better believe what I say. That's all. Good night."

We opened in New York to some split decisions, mostly

favorable. Atkinson called it "a bountiful and exultant musical jamboree." Bob Considine called it "an adult *Oklahoma.*" But Walter Kerr was much less enthusiastic, and I had to agree with some of his criticism. He thought that the chopped-up romance never got a firm enough grip on anybody's heartstrings and that the part Barton played was uncertain in tone, varying from the tenderness of his song "I Still See Elisa," as he wistfully recalls his first love, all the way to broad comedy.

And the operating expenses were excessive. I was unable to do anything about the costs, and I wanted to get the hell out. I wrote to Alan saying that I felt inept as a manager. Investors were beginning to call with complaints. Why were we making only a little over $6000 profit each week? Many were investors in *The King and I;* they said it consistently made $10,200 to $10,500 a week, even with the large company, Gertie's percentage and Yul's $1500 per. Even if we did $51,000, like *The King and I,* we couldn't make that much. To make even $7000 a week, we would have to cut two characters and five musicians and minimize our advertising budget.

My main concern, an understandable one for a producer, was for the investors. But the authors did not wish to make concessions. Nonetheless I saw *Paint Your Wagon* through. It ran for nearly three hundred performances. After all these years it has just managed to pay off—mainly because the music is popular. Virgil Thompson wrote later that he thought the score was better than *My Fair Lady* by the same writers. I still hear some of the numbers on the radio in taxicabs and grocery stores.

Alan and I were devoted friends. We dined together frequently, talking our hearts out. When *Paint Your Wagon* opened, I received a charming note from him, telling me what a friend and help I had been, and asking, before closing with love, "What do I do next?" I suggested he and Fritz do *Pygmalion* next as a musical for Mary Martin. I had been thinking of it for some time, and through Gabriel Pascal, who held the rights to Shaw's plays, I communicated with the London managers of Shaw's estate about the terms, which seemed to be reasonable. But neither Mary nor Alan was enthusiastic. Mary didn't think she could play the part, and the writers didn't think they could convert the play into a musical. So I dropped the idea.

What Alan did next, a few years later, was *My Fair Lady.* It was produced by Herman Levin. Our professional marriage was finis.

Recently while I was visiting Mary Martin in Palm Springs, Fritz Loewe, who has a magnificent estate there and whom I had not seen for years, came to lunch with Bill Fitelson and his wife. He played the score of *Brigadoon* for us with lovely embellishments. It sounded as melodic as ever. But Fritz's touch was more subtle than I remembered it. He explained that he had developed serious arthritis in his hands but was determined not to give in to it. Every day for hours he pressed his fingers one by one to the keys, suffering great pain until he finally conquered the affliction. That is indomitable spirit.

In 1955 I produced a musical offering—it might be called an opera—by Marc Blitzstein entitled *Reuben Reuben.* It told the story of a soldier returned from combat, who wandered through New York, lonely and unable to communicate, searching for contact—in a bar, at a San Gennaro festival, at a circus and finally at dawn on Brooklyn Bridge. During his progress he found a girl to care for who cared for him. It had charming ballads and pulsing jazz. Eddie Albert, who had once been an acrobat, played the young soldier; he prepared himself over a long period, studying with jugglers and black jitterbug teachers and practicing a fall from a twenty-five-foot tower into a net for the circus scene. He also wanted to learn to swallow flaming chestnuts, but at that I drew the line. The girl was played by Evelyn Lear, in her first big role. Thomas Stewart, who became her husband "in real life," had a small part. Both of them now play leading opera roles all over the world. Bobby Lewis directed. He was urged to direct *My Fair Lady* but said that he had already pledged himself to *Reuben Reuben.* He is an honorable gentleman.

We opened in Boston, announcing the show as a musical. That was a mistake. It led the audience to expect something other than what we offered, which was more like an opera. Toward the end of Act One the aisles began to fill with people pouring out.

Muttering bitter words under my breath, I stood at the head of one aisle, feet apart, arms akimbo, so that the lemmings would be forced to squeeze past me into the dark night. I was mad: mistaken announcement or no, so much blood and talent had gone into the show. Today, with the new sounds of music and new styles of writing, I doubt if it would seem at all obscure.

When I read the morning reviews I realized that we were lost. I went to Marc's room to tell him, knowing it wasn't going to be easy—he had spent about three years preparing. To my astonishment, he was at the piano rewriting, working in a sort of euphoric excitement. I couldn't believe he had read the notices. When I told him we would have to close, he looked stunned. No, no, he could fix it, he argued. I said we would be lucky to have ten people in the audience after last night's response and the reviews. We could not afford to continue. He kept protesting until I finally said "Oh, shit!" and slammed out. The last night was miserable. Most of us spent it drinking and singing sad songs in a gloomy bar to hide our sorrow.

Later I had a note from Elliot Norton, then the admired critic for the *Boston Post:*

> I should have called or written long since to tell you how bad I felt about the demise of *Reuben.* The failure of any show is unpleasant, but this one had so much talent and ingenuity and adventurous spirit behind it that it is particularly distressing. I hope your faith will be justified eventually—that Blitzstein will be able to clarify and improve it.

I was able to return thirty thousand dollars of the investment but temporarily lost a friend, Marc, with whom I was eventually reconciled.

The experience of *Reuben Reuben* made me belligerent. I would, for the Gods' sake (as James Thurber often reiterated) show that I could do another successful musical. Had Fitelson been right? Could it be true, as another friend remarked, that quality repels?

The style of musicals has steadily improved. You no longer hear songs called "Two Little Bluebirds" or "I'd Love to Waltz

Through Life with You," as you did in the old days. Although the major point of a musical is still sheer enjoyment, the story, or "book," has become more literate over the years. Some shows depend on noise, speed, vitality. *Mame, Gypsy, Hello Dolly, Call Me Madam* all depend on a starring outsize character—all women! The men have got *Fiorello, The Music Man* and *Fiddler on the Roof.* Others are based on a believable romance between two diametrically opposed characters, like the ones in *South Pacific, The King and I, Annie Get Your Gun, Camelot, Kiss Me Kate.* The more substantial ones also have a secondary story, usually involving young lovers, which enables the composer and lyricist to write a greater variety of songs. Fresh, surprising backgrounds make it possible for designers to go to town with sets and costumes.

A musical is put together like a puzzle. As my experiences illustrate, during rehearsals or out-of-town try-outs before New York, you find you need an "up ballad" here, a comedy song there, a new dance number, an effective first-act curtain. A song that doesn't work in one spot may work in another.

But the story is vital; it is the necklace on which all the beads are strung. A good story for a musical is one of the most difficult things to achieve. Each one I have mentioned had its origin in previously known material. An original is rare, a pearl of great price, since you don't have to pay royalties on the basic material or, as in some cases, a percentage of the profits as well. But of course, pre-tested material—a successful book or short story or film—is much safer. Alan Lerner is one of our top musical writers, yet he has never had a successful original.

One of the two originals I did do, *Chu Chem,* closed in Philadelphia. The other, *Celebration,* by Tom Jones and Harvey Schmidt, had a respectable run. It didn't pay off completely but is still receiving money from many more successful productions abroad.

At last in 1962 I found some material to which Mary Martin responded: the story of Laurette Taylor's early life written by her daughter, Margaret Courtenay. Mary chose Arthur Schwartz and Howard Dietz to do the music and lyrics after she fell madly in

Kurt Weill (*Blackstone Studios*)

A rehearsal of ONE TOUCH OF VENUS: Left to right, Mary Martin, John Boles, Paula Laurence and Kenny Baker with Kurt Weill at the piano (PM)

(Opposite) THE TEMPEST: Left to right, George Voskovec, Jan Werich, Canada Lee, with Vera Zorina above (Eileen Darby, Graphic House)

ONE TOUCH OF VENUS: (Bottom left) John Boles, the Venus statue and Kenny Baker. (Bottom right) Kenny Baker and Mary Martin (George Karger/Pix, Museum of the City of New York)

PAINT YOUR WAGON: The arrival of the fancy ladies (*George Karger/Pix, Museum of the City of New York*)

The wedding dance from BRIGADOON, with James Mitchell, center (*Vandamm Collection, New York Public Library*)

Marc Blitzstein and conductor Maurice Abravanel studying the REGINA score (*Alexander Bender, New York Public Library*)

Tennessee Williams and Cheryl Crawford, New York, 1976 (*Bill Yoscary*)

Tennessee Williams

Geraldine Page and Paul Newman in SWEET BIRD OF YOUTH (*George Karger/Pix, New York Public Library*)

Maureen Stapleton and Eli Wallach in THE ROSE TATTOO (*George Karger/Pix, New York Public Library*)

O MEN! O WOMEN! with Franchot Tone, Betsy von Furstenberg and Gig Young (*Alfredo Valente, Museum of the City of New York*)

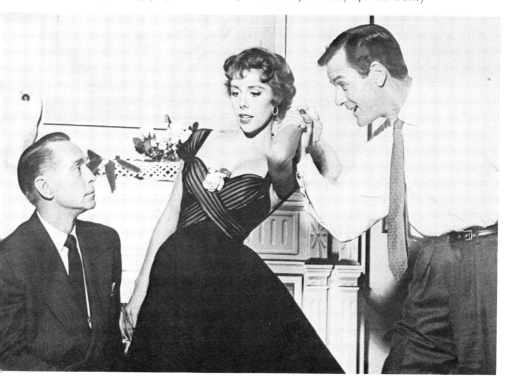

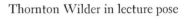

Thornton Wilder in lecture pose

Marilyn Monroe, Cheryl Crawford
and friend at Eastham

The first day of rehearsals for STRANGE INTERLUDE: Left to right,
Cheryl Crawford, Pat Hingle, Ben Gazzara, Jane Fonda, Franchot Tone,
and Geraldine Page (*Joseph Abeles*)

love with a song of theirs, "Before I Kiss the World Goodbye."
She accepted a writer whom I suggested, Arnold Schulman. I was
determined that *Jennie*, as it was called, would be the successful
musical I wanted.

Jennie turned into the toughest production I ever tackled.
Richard Halliday was co-producer. The physical production alone
was complex and difficult. *Jennie* opened with Mary at the top
of a huge waterfall—a real one, too—desperately fighting off an
enormous bear. In the nick of time her actor husband's bullet
killed the animal, and she managed not to drown. This was for
starters.

The show opened in Boston in July 1963 to mixed notices,
and all hell began to break loose between the creators and the
management over the writing and the production. I was flying
back to New York every other day to supervise other shows in the
works, so I escaped some of the unpleasant altercations. But not
all. We recast the male lead and replaced the choreographer, but
there were no other visible improvements as we limped on to
Detroit. Fortunately, business there was good, since the public
was devoted to Mary. But there was a terribly disagreeable meeting. Soon I was the only contact among the various parties, spending nights until three A.M. going up and down in elevators to the
various rooms trying to effect a compromise about what should
be done. Mary was dissatisfied with some of the lyrics. There was
also a question about which final scene to use. Finally I suggested
we bring Elliot Norton from Boston to make a judgment on which
scene to use. He had liked the show, and all parties trusted his
integrity. When he came he voted in favor of the ending Mary
preferred. I was still in the unpleasant position of being the only
one to whom the others would talk. It was a dreary, exhausting
time for me. Things deteriorated until everyone was in an unbear-
able state of tension.

After our first preview in New York, to protect myself, I was
forced to inform my attorney, Floria Lasky, of the situation:
Arthur Schwartz told me that if Mary cut any of the songs
without first informing him or Dietz or their attorneys he would
take it up at once with the Dramatists Guild and we might

lose the rights. He pointed out that he was a member of the Guild's Council and was prepared to make maximum legal trouble. I said that Mary was famous for being the most responsible star in the profession and her desire even against doctor's advice was always to play the show. He was adamant about what he said were "his rights." I felt he was ready to "cut off his nose to spite his face." I found him unmoveable by reason or anger.

Since Mary's popularity had given us over a million-dollar advance, we were able to run for a while in spite of very mixed notices. But it had all been too much. Everyone was relieved when *Jennie* closed.

My "fancy" was satiated. To date at least I have not produced another musical. But who can tell? Down deep I am still addicted.

Four by Tenn

A card to me from Tennessee Williams: "Who, if I cried, would hear me among the angelic order? Answer: Cheryl." Sadly, this was untrue. From 1960 on I saw Tennessee very rarely, no more than half a dozen times. I was shocked and ashamed when I read in his *Memoirs* of the depression and sufferings he endured during the subsequent ten years.

It has been my proudest experience to have produced four plays by our greatest playwright: *The Rose Tattoo, Camino Real, Sweet Bird of Youth* and *Period of Adjustment.* Three made money, though two, *The Rose Tattoo* and *Period of Adjustment,* were only moderate successes. *Camino Real* was a financial failure. Recently, however, Clive Barnes, who did not review it originally, called it one of Tennessee's finest plays.

I first became aware of Tennessee's work in 1940 when he won the one-hundred-dollar prize in a Group Theatre play contest with a series of four one-act plays entitled *American Blues.* I had left the Group by then, but Audrey Wood, who had become his agent, sent them to me. I was impressed by their imagination and the quality of the writing and asked Audrey to introduce us. The young man I met was slender, of medium height, with sandy, slightly curly hair, a sandy moustache, and rather pale blue eyes which scarcely seemed to notice me but, as I found out later,

never missed a trick. He was not easy to talk to. He was shy; so
was I. But I got to know him better at the Bureau of New
Playwrights, which he had joined and where I helped out with
Theresa Helburn when I was first on my own. As we worked
together over the years we developed a comfortable rapport. I
particularly enjoyed our correspondence.

I have noticed that I can say scarcely anything about Tennessee without saying the opposite. He is courageous and fearful,
suspicious and trusting, generous and acquisitive, sanguine and
despairing, impulsive and cautious. Perhaps that explains his extraordinary comprehension of the great variety of characters he
has created. Tennessee has an endearing cackle which turns into
a gulping roar when he is amused, sometimes at things I am
unable to perceive. I think these excessive explosions are a cover
for his shyness. The gossip about his private life which he candidly
and generously reveals tends to obscure the depth of his dedication to writing. His sense of humor sometimes baffles more
straightlaced people. On one occasion he invited a group of
friends to attend a preliminary showing of the film *The Glass
Menagerie* for newspaper and magazine critics. At the door stood
a lady with a pad and pencil to check the names. "Where are you
from?" she asked Tennessee.

"I'm from Mississippi," he replied.

"Well, I can't let you in."

"All right," said Tenn and started for the elevator.

His friend, Frank Merlo, yelled after him, "Tennessee, where
are you going?"

The surprised lady called out, "You're Tennessee Williams?
Why didn't you say so?"

"You asked me where I was from," Tenn answered. "I *am*
from Mississippi."

When *A Streetcar Named Desire* opened in New Haven in
1947, I went to see it. It was overwhelming. Tennessee was not
around, but Gadg Kazan, who had directed it, and Irene Selznick,
who had produced it, were in the lobby with the worried faces we
all have when a play opens on the road. I congratulated them with
sincere praise. But underneath I was seething that I had not had

the opportunity to read the script and make an offer to produce it.

Trying hard not to explode, I phoned Audrey Wood and asked her to have lunch with me. Audrey is a patient, as well as an extremely able, woman, and she heard me out.

"I know everyone must be trying to climb on Tenn's bandwagon now," I told her. "But I think it's wrong that a new producer was handed our best playwright on a golden platter. I hear *Streetcar* was offered to no one else. I wouldn't be angry if it had gone to others who have earned the right. Some of us have stuck with the theatre all of our working lives, taken great chances, done the first plays of many authors, taken the failures, kept going. I want to do his next play, whatever it is. Now, how about it?"

"No auspices have been set," Audrey replied calmly. "I think it's a good idea for you two to work together."

So in 1950 I was given *The Rose Tattoo* to produce. Later I discovered that Irene Selznick had rejected it, calling it an opera, not a play. I didn't agree. I realized it would be difficult to create on the stage, but that didn't deter me.

The story concerned a passionate Sicilian seamstress, Serafina, who hysterically mourns her husband, killed by accident three years earlier. Into her life comes a Sicilian truck driver, a self-confessed fool but appealing in his desperate pursuit of Serafina, who finally accepts him when she discovers that her beloved husband had been unfaithful.

Casting the two main parts was difficult. Tennessee wanted Anna Magnani for Serafina, but she was unavailable. Besides, she spoke very little English at that time and declared she would not play anything for more than four months. If I had not observed Maureen Stapleton and Eli Wallach working at the Actors Studio since 1948, I doubt I would have suggested them. It was fortunate casting. I know of no actors available then who could have given finer performances. I was deeply concerned that we have a perfect production that would satisfy Tennessee, especially because Gadg, his most trusted director, was not available. Daniel Mann, whose work I had observed at the Actors Studio, directed, Boris

Aaronson designed a lovely set, and the other parts were carefully cast. Don Murray and Sal Mineo played their first Broadway roles.

There was a flurry of alarm before the opening in Chicago. The costume designer was coming out on a train with the wardrobe. But at the final run-through she was nowhere to be found. To our horror, we discovered that she had arrived and then had taken the next train back to New York. Whether she suffered from amnesia or absentmindedness, we never learned. We never found the clothes either, and Paul Bigelow, a great friend of Tenn's and mine and a wizard in emergencies, "shopped" the complete wardrobe in one day.

Most of the Chicago reviewers were baffled by the play, but Claudia Cassidy, the doyenne of the Chicago critics, gave us an encouraging review. We ran for four weeks in the icy Windy City to a try-out loss of fifteen thousand dollars. The entire cost of the play was close to eighty thousand dollars.

The Rose Tattoo opened in New York on February 3, 1951 to very favorable reviews on the whole. But Atkinson, among others, objected to what he called "a lewd episode," which he thought showed Williams to be "curiously insensitive at times to the ordinary amenities of public communication." The scene involved the inadvertent dropping of a condom by Mangiacavallo, the truck driver, which showed Serafina, to whom he was declaring love, that he had already planned the outcome. This incident and a few other small details offended the supersensibilities of some of the audience as well. It became such an issue that I asked Tenn to express his point of view on the play.

What he wrote is, I think, one of his best pieces of writing:

The meaning of *The Rose Tattoo* is the Dionysian element in human life, its mystery, its beauty, its significance. It is that glittering quicksilver that still somehow manages to slip from under the down-pressed thumbs of the enormous man in the brass-buttoned uniform and his female partner with the pince-nez and the chalky-smelling black skirts that make you sneeze as she brushes disdainfully past you. It is the dissatisfaction with the empiric evidence that makes the poet and mystic, for it is the lyric as well as the Bacchantic impulse, and although the goat is one of its immemorial symbols, it must not be confused with mere sexuality. It is higher and more distilled than that. Its purest form is probably manifested by children and birds in their rhapsodic moments of flight and play, especially during the last few minutes of pale blue summer dusk before they light on branches and before their mothers call from the doors, *Come home!* It is not the obedient coming home and going to bed but it is the limitless world of the dream. Pagan religions were composed of it and Catholicism is drenched with it like bread soaked in wine. Protestantism and Puritanism deny or attempt to deny it. It is the *rosa mystica*, the light on the bare golden flesh of a god whose back is turned to us or whose face is covered and who flies away from us when we call *Wait!* and rushes past us when we try to stop him. It is the fruit of the vine that takes earth, sun and air and distills them into juices that deprive men not of reason but of a different thing called prudence . . .

Finally and incidentally, it is the desire of an artist to work in new forms, however awkwardly at first, to break down barriers of what he has done before and what others have done better before and after and to crash, perhaps fatally, into some area that the bell harness and rope would like to forbid him.

It may seem curious that I have chosen a woman to be the main protagonist of a play on such a theme. But in the blind and frenzied efforts of the widow, Serafina, to comprehend the mysteries of her dead husband, we sense and learn more about him than would have been possible through direct observation of the living man, the Dionysus himself. Dionysus, being mystery, is never seen clearly. He cannot be confined to memory nor an urn, nor the conventions and proprieties of a plump little seamstress who wanted to fortify her happiness with the respect of the community. It was a mistake to fill the house with dummies. It took a long while to learn that eventually the faceless dummies must be knocked over, however elaborate their trappings. It took an almost literal unclothing, a public appearance in a wine-stained rayon slip, a fierce attack on a priest and the neighbor women, to learn that the blood of the wild young daughter was better, as a memorial, than ashes kept in a crematory urn.

In its treatment of this theme the play is no doubt more allusive than direct. Still more undoubtedly its theme overshadows the play. It is the homely light of a kitchen candle burned in praise of a god. I prefer a play to be not a noose but a net with fairly wide meshes. So many of its instants of revelation are wayward flashes, not part of the plan of an author but struck accidentally off, and perhaps these are closest to being a true celebration of the inebriate god.

Dionysus slips through all of Tennessee's plays, even *Period of Adjustment,* although lightly, and it is this element that makes his creations larger than life. Our society, nurtured on the Apollonian side, which Nietzsche describes so well in *The Birth of Tragedy*, accepts the Dionysian only in dreams and fantasies. In the last few years, the Apollonian mantle has rent and the Dionysian has burst out like a streak of lightning. But having been suppressed, it is no longer "the bare golden flesh of a god" or, as another poet said, "the fair slim boy who darts along the brake, paling the morning with his silver thigh"; it is ugly and bestial, Yeats's slouching beast. This is evident in many of today's plays and films, which often foretell our social behavior.

I couldn't let Atkinson's opinion go unchallenged, so I wrote to him, asking him to look at *The Rose Tattoo* again after Tennessee's revisions. "They go in tomorrow," I wrote, "so on some cloudy day when you can't see a murmuration of starlings or an exaltation of larks in the country [Brooks is a dedicated bird watcher], I hope *The Rose Tattoo* will serve."

The condom bit had been made less offensive, and Atkinson returned to write that the changes "in the interest of public sanitation can be applauded." He also called Tennessee an artist, a lyric dramatist who had opened new horizons for the theatre, creating "a song of the earth" out of the lives of some simple people.

Condoms weren't our only problem. Some members of the audience were repelled by the fury of Serafina's passion, finding it too neurotic. Tennessee had the best answer to the charge that his work dealt only with neurotic people: "When you penetrate into almost anybody you either find madness or dullness: the only way not to find them is to stay on the surface. Madness I should put in quotes. I mean what is *considered* madness or neuroticism! —which is simply the inner distortions that any sensitive, malleable nature undergoes through experience in modern society."

Despite supersensibilities, *The Rose Tattoo* ran for most of the year. I wrote Tennessee frequently to report. In June of 1951 I wrote:

The good news continues. Despite the heat, we did $19,806 last week at *The Rose Tattoo*, almost $200 better than the previous week.

I was at the theatre last night, and the audience was loving it.

On Sunday, I gave my yearly do. A distinguished roster of guests— Carson McCullers, Lillian Hellman, Josh Logan and wife, Eli and Anne, Fritz Loewe, Santha Rama Rau (who wrote an interesting book you should read, *East of Home*) and Faubion Bowers, who is a real authority on the Far East Theatre. He got high and danced in a somewhat Oriental fashion with crippled Carson, who will never forget it. Even the next day she was saying, "I danced, Cheryl! I danced!" It was high and gay and everyone talked to everyone. Only minor accidents, two cigarette burns on my best rug, one glass broken and one gentleman fell on his face, spilling coffee on afore-mentioned rug, which now considers itself second-hand.

In the fall *The Rose Tattoo* jigsawed the country, now making, now losing money. When January of 1952 came, I decided to try to keep it open until June. I did some rebooking to concentrate on Protestant sections, as many Catholics took exception to Serafina's hysterical scene with the priest and Mangiacavallo's impassioned courtship. I urged Tennessee to forego his royalties for four weeks so that we could build up a reserve. He had made eighty thousand dollars in royalties. The backers had received only a partial return. He agreed to this, and when the play was sold to Paramount Pictures, the backers were paid off and the author got the customary sixty percent of the sale. Fortunately, the film deal included five percent of the profits. Since I had received no money during the entire two-season run, that five percent, several years later, returned about six thousand dollars to me, which was very welcome.

We all wanted Anna Magnani for the film. Tenn hurried to Rome to persuade her and succeeded. She played Serafina magnificently.

Meanwhile some scenes of a short play Tennessee had written some time earlier, which he called *Ten Blocks on the Camino Real*, were performed at the Actors Studio. The results were so exciting that Kazan persuaded Tenn to develop the script into a full evening. I was enamoured of the scenes and wanted to be the producer. So I wrote straightaway to Audrey Wood, reminding her, as I put it, that "the least of Tenn's works, if there are such, must have an audience" and that I felt that way about no other playwright.

A few months later, Tenn wrote from Rome that he had prepared a revision of *Camino Real:*

This is the one I want you to read. Gadg seemed pleased with the script and said he wanted to go into rehearsal with it in late October and would see you as soon as he returned to the States for discussion. We would both like you to produce it, but are not sure that you will consider it a good financial risk. It will have to be budgeted very liberally to ensure a full realization of its plastic values, and of course it is a gamble. We both feel that you would understand it better than anyone else.

It certainly was a gamble: the material was very unusual and there were no stars.

You might call *Camino Real* a cosmic fantasy or allegory. Kazan called it "a prayer for Romantics—a plea for the size and importance of the individual soul." It is laid in an isolated sun-baked plaza, from which there is no escape; gypsys, pimps, Fascist police, prostitutes, panderers and starving peasants inhabit the place, and streetcleaners stalk it, piling the dead into their containers. Other inhabitants are the legendary romantics, Camille, Casanova and Byron, existing fragilely in a fleabag hotel. Into the plaza comes Kilroy, a naive former boxer, lost and destitute, with a heart, as he says, "big as a baby and pure gold." He is subjected to humiliation and violence. Near the end he cries out, "Had for a button! Stewed, screwed and tattooed on the Camino Real— Did anyone say the deal is rugged?" Finally, Quixote, a ragged, stout-hearted dreamer, urges Kilroy to come away with him.

"Dónde?" Kilroy asks.

"Quién sabe?" Quixote answers.

It is a dark picture of the world, frequently lightened by macabre comedy.

Finally we had a reading of the entire play with most of the cast who would be playing in it. This reading resulted in a co-producer, Ethel Reiner, and an associate producer, Walter Chrysler, Jr. It was not easy to raise the hundred and twenty-five thousand dollars needed, but among the three of us we secured the capital. The cast of twenty-one included thirteen members of the Actors Studio who had worked there with Kazan, and that made it easier for him to find a style for this haunting fantasy.

The set never pleased me. Kazan chose to have dark, forbidding stone walls enclose the action, and they made the play even more chilling. I would have preferred a set with the off-white adobe walls one sees in the Southwest and Mexico, where the angle of the sun creates mysterious blue-black shadows and rattan blinds or ancient canvas make pools of deep shade. When Kilroy goes, I wanted the set to become transparent so that we would see him leaving the plaza to wander in an empty desert of sand stretching endlessly toward nothing.

We opened on March 19, 1953. Atkinson thought *Camino Real* was as "eloquent and rhythmic as a piece of music" and highly praised both the production and performance. But again he was outraged, finding some of it "revolting."

Some of the audience were furious and disgusted; many old ladies tottered out to meet their own streetcleaners. Others were deeply moved to the point of tears. There are still people around who say they can never forget it, that it was one of the great theatrical experiences of their lives.

The going was rough. I think we managed about one hundred performances in New York and on the road before we had to close. Tennessee thought this was premature, because the final week was almost sold out. But the closing announcement was responsible for that; there was nothing in the till for any further security. One of the things that is difficult in the theatre is doing business with your friends, particularly when it involves judgment of your actions. I often found it difficult to criticize Tennessee's writing for the same reason.

In the fall of 1954, Audrey sent me *Cat on a Hot Tin Roof* to read. I wrote to Tenn at once.

I planned to write you Friday when I was unfairly attacked by a newfangled virus which turned my stomach over and over and my head became entirely unattached. However, it wasn't on too damn tight after

I read your play. God! What a volcanic explosion, some of your very best writing and a second act that can lift the roof off the theatre if it doesn't lift the critics' hair off, or toupees, as the case may be.

I have only one really important criticism, but I think it is important for your success. Boldly put, we have no one to root for. All the people seem monstrous except Big Daddy, who is only in Act One, and I don't think an audience can take such an unrelieved attack. In *Streetcar* they had their catharsis in good Greek fashion through Blanche.

Please don't get panicky and rush. You seem to know very well what is needed, and a play of yours is too damned important for haste and unconsidered action. We have to make the critics swallow what you want to tell them, and the question is how best to do it when they eat pablum all the time. A good critic said to me recently, "Every time you go below the belt, you're bound to lose Brooks and Watts." I told him we knew that from *Tattoo* and *Camino*. I'm sure Brooks still believes in Tinker Bell, never felt a passion that wasn't tidy and believes firmly in the redeemability of man. He does like *belly dancers* though! He said so in the *Fanny* review. I think he likes his evil grandiose as in *Medea*—and preferably by a dead author to whose demise he has so often contributed. Well, perhaps a soupçon of what he calls "moral grandeur" and a layer of comedy will keep his cud in, chewing over those favorite words he once applied to you, "profoundly human sympathy, poignant, luminous" *(Streetcar)*, before he got into the depraved bit. Too bad so many Americans have such thin gastric juices.

I wait more or less patiently. I want us to have a hit.

But Kazan and Tenn were eager to get this play on quickly in the spring. I think Kazan had other plans for the fall. I argued that this was a terrible mistake, that it wasn't the sort of play to attract a summer tourist audience. No one agreed with me. Kazan was able to get Big Daddy into the last act and also to change the ending to a somewhat more hopeful scene. Since I was unable to convince them to wait, I did not produce it. As everyone knows, the time of year didn't matter at all. It was an enormous success. So much for my sense of season, and alas for me.

Our association didn't renew again until I flew to Miami in mid-April of 1956 to see the first performance of *Sweet Bird of Youth* at the Coconut Grove. I saw it twice, and I wanted to do it. After my error on *Cat on a Hot Tin Roof,* I wanted to get a bid in fast. So I wrote Audrey Wood,

I must put in the strongest appeal I can make to be in on *Sweet Bird of Youth.*

To review the past, I did keep *Tattoo* going two seasons and served it well, I think, though not to any financial advantage to myself. I worked like hell, long and hard, to get the money for *Camino,* which I think few producers would have touched, and while I am not as proud of the production as I would like to be, I think I gave it every publicity chance, expense-wise and getting the Guild subscription.

You can understand why this made me fearful of not giving such an important play as *Cat* the best break, which seemed to me would have been a fall rather than a late spring production. Unluckily for me, I had a faint heart at the wrong time, which cost me an awful lot of sleeping pills.

Then, when you returned from the Coast and told me Tenn and Gadg felt they must go ahead for a late spring opening, you also told me that Tenn had asked you to tell me that I would have first chance at his next play. I guess you know how that made me feel.

When I heard he was planning on *Orpheus Descending,* I called you to tell you I was interested, and you explained that it was a special set-up involving Anna and Marlon and a corporate holding. So I bowed.

But I want desperately to be involved with *Sweet Bird,* and I believe I can bring something of value to a production. If the trouble is fitting me into a tax relief corporate set-up, I can be hired. Not by Hollywood or TV but by The Sweet Bird of Youth, Incorporated.

When it was settled that I would do it I began to sleep nights.

Everyone was aware that the play required some revisions, and I sent Tenn my impressions. (In the following letter, Chance Wayne, a main character, to be played by Paul Newman, was named Phil.)

So now my notes on *Sweet Bird of Youth.* I am not going to mention all the wonderful and promising qualities it has. You know them. I feel some knowledge I have of Phil toward the end should be toward the beginning instead. Phil has some instincts, desires and drives of an artist —like Robert Browning's poem that starts, "I am a painter who cannot paint." His desperate frustration which forces him to do ugly things stems from this. I was horrified when, after Act One, I met people in the lobby at the Coconut Grove who said, "Well, the writing is exciting but I have no patience with the guy. Why doesn't he go out and get a job in a bank or driving a truck?" But these Fat Boys and Girls who fill the orchestra have to have their understanding pinned down for them.

The marijuana-smoking scene in Act One made me feel a little giggly, seemed like *piling* on too much and an overfamiliar way of showing vice, particularly after the extraordinarily original and brilliant image of the oxygen mask.

Had you thought of starting Act Two in Finley's house?

In the bar scene Miss Lucy seems too dragged in unless Phil reacts to her in some way, which gives a dramatic reason for her appearance.

Scene Seven—I think Phil's monologue might be more terrifying if some of the images were less direct and explicit and more secret and strange like a savage rite. Your meaning—that failure, disgrace and even death can be redeemed by a sufficiently transfiguring courage—is very powerful, moving and true, and I could take more there to be sure the dullards get it.

Tennessee kept working on *Sweet Bird.* It took him two years to prepare a new version. He was a true pro, never temperamental about rewrites. He wanted perfection. Even when he and Frank Merlo came to visit me at Eastham he would work. Every day after breakfast, he sat at the dining room table writing on a yellow pad. I doubt if there was ever a day he didn't write. It was his life.

During those years I produced three plays, none of which were successful, although one, *Girls of Summer,* returned most of its money by a film sale. At that time Tenn's situation in the theatre and mine were somewhat similar. He had been through what he called "a crushing defeat" with *Orpheus Descending* and had had only a limited Off-Broadway run for *Garden District,* although I'm sure he made some money from the film version with Elizabeth Taylor and Katharine Hepburn. "We have to come up with an artistically and commercially successful production as a matter of survival," he said.

I certainly agreed. I was hanging on by my teeth, which were loosening under the strain. We corresponded regularly. In December of 1956 Tenn wrote:

A note in Winchell's column a few days ago said that *Girls of Summer* had risen from sixteen grand to twenty-eight grand in one week, and I do hope this is an accurate report, for it pained me to find such a depressed note in a letter from someone who, to me at least, if not to us all, is synonymous with "semper invictus" as it applies to the spirit.

I find it dismaying as you do that you have this run of bad luck. But that's how it goes, rough as a cob sometimes, and sometimes smooth as silk. I have had a remarkably good time lately, feeling well and relaxed (for me!), and with a renewal of energy which made it possible for me to complete rough sketches of two plays in a few weeks' time, but now I'm exhausted again, the spurt of energy has subsided. Tonight my stomach is swollen up like a basketball and hot as fire. I can't even take a drink. I am not at all sure it is not the presence of mother. Mom is here. She could not stay in Saint Louis. She said, "That outfit would put me back in the bug-house," so she descended to Florida. I don't know why she affects me like this, but I feel that everything she says and everything she looks is an implied criticism. Guilt, I suppose. I love her and feel sorry for her, but she drives me somewhat crazy.

Poor Miss Brinda is in heat. We took her to the vet this afternoon and the vet said he had never seen a worse specimen of any breed of a dog than she is and he would not recommend the perpetuation of her line by breeding her. Funny, but I think she's the most charming animal I've ever known. Maybe because both of us are equally wall-eyed and would be equally bad bets for perpetuation of our lines.

Will be seeing you soon.

Love, 10

Finally the new script of *Sweet Bird* arrived, and I set to work at once.

"Tenn dear," I wrote on August 5, 1958,

I'm running Broadway now—'count of you. Every day people come in, call up, friends, strangers, all begging me to take their checks for *Sweet Bird*—any amount. It's like a continuous scene from *Volpone* on the cupidity of man. Fun tho! I never had it happen before. Remember how we sweated over *Camino?*

I've made a good deal on Newman—fair, not killing. The only thing I don't like is that Warner Bros. says they will release him for only nine months from rehearsal date. Wrote Gadg about that. Maybe he can do something with Warner's because of his relationship. I also told Gadg I didn't think Geraldine was right for the Princess Kosmonopolis. She's too young! I suggested Micheline Presle *(Devil in the Flesh)*, Alida Valli, Madeline Robinson, Eileen Hurlie, Margaret Leighton, Michele Morgan. Do you know any of them?

I'm seeing Jack Small of the Shubert office tomorrow about the Barrymore. I've already been offered the Beck for March. It can gross $47,176 now, which is something to think about if Paul plays only seven months here.

We waited until early 1959 to pull everything together—Paul Newman's and Kazan's availability and the casting of the Princess. When I finally heard Geraldine Page read the part, I was delighted. Although I had always admired her work and had seen a lot of it at the Actors Studio, I hadn't realized she was capable of being any age required. Having observed Paul Newman at the Studio, I knew that he had a much greater range than he had been able to show in films up to that time. He once performed a monologue from *The Taming of the Shrew* there brilliantly. Bruce Dern played his first Broadway role in *Sweet Bird*. Things went so well that I didn't have to watch too much. Rehearsals were a pleasure with Kazan and the company in top form. At last Tenn and I had the larger-than-life hit we had wanted. I reveled in it. We *were* "running" Broadway, and it was wonderful.

Tennessee never stopped. He was working on two plays, *Night of the Iguana* and *Period of Adjustment*. When the latter was given a try-out in Miami I was unable to get there, but I got hold of a script and decided I wanted to do it. It is a funny and touching story of a delicate time in the marriages of two young couples. Casting young actors, I felt, would make the characters' problems more sympathetic, but Tennessee was pleased with the Miami cast, headed by Barbara Baxley, and I went along with him. It was an excellent company directed by George Roy Hill, now famous for directing *Butch Cassidy and the Sundance Kid* and *The Sting*.

We opened in November of 1960 to critics who were not as responsive as I had hoped. I thought and still think that it is a much better play than they reviewed. The characters are endearing and pitiful, and the comedy is delightful, using the vivid idiom of rather ordinary Americans. *Period of Adjustment* was sold to a film company, so eventually we didn't come out too badly. But the run wasn't more than fair, and Tennessee was unhappy. In February I had to write to him:

I've been quite "flabbergasted," as Strasberg would say, that you felt it necessary to call Jack Phelps twice about the show running two more weeks when I gave you my word on the phone that it would and you said that you accepted my word. What's wrong with our communication? I've been working like hell the last six weeks to find a big enough name to tour the show, calling the Coast, getting in touch with agents for important names. For a few days I thought I had Hugh O'Brien. For a few more days I thought James Garner was going to do it. I'm working now to arrange a summer package which I think can do very well.

Audrey was at the meeting when we looked over the financial situation, found that we had no advance, that only about twenty-five mail orders a day were coming in even after the very extensive two weeks of TV advertising. The closing was a *mutual* decision. I assumed she had written or phoned you about it. We can break for the next two weeks on $11,000 to $11,500 a week. We will probably lose quite a lot this week, as so far the closing announcement has not worked. But *we are playing,* and I did not do anything arbitrarily.

You seemed to indicate on the phone that you thought you had lost your investment in the play. At present there is enough money to repay all investors entirely. Leaving the investment aside, you have made $105,000 from the author's share of the first movie payment plus $60,000 due from the next payment plus about $7,000 from the gross on profitable weeks plus $30,000 on weekly royalties. This totals $202,000 minus $20,200, which represents the ten percent of your earnings to MCA.

The show itself has so far made around $6,000 in profits, but we will probably lose that this week. I haven't made anything so far. Not a complaint, just facts. This week on five performances we have taken $6,806.

The performances are excellent. The cast is working well. You and I have faced too much together over too many years not to understand each other now.

As a result of the letter, Tennessee also cut royalties. But *Period of Adjustment* closed early in March.

In 1960 the Actors Studio presented an early draft of *Night of the Iguana,* directed by Frank Corsaro, for Tenn to see. Afterwards, I wrote him:

Remember you said last Sunday that you wish people would level with you? You said it quite insistently. I'm not sure I believe you. But I'm going to pretend I do because I think in *Iguana* you can have your finest play to date and a play, stealing movie slogans, I would be proud to present. I don't think it is all there yet. Put on as is, it would appeal to people sensitive and aware enough to dig it. The majority, I think, would be intrigued and baffled.

I'm judging entirely by the performance I saw at the Studio, realizing how many points were lost, scenes unrealized, some casting all wrong.

Now I'm going to sound arbitrary: I'm going to omit "I think," "I feel," "I believe" and I'm not going to lard the criticism by mentioning the thrilling and moving scenes.

In the first half (Acts One and Two) some simple plot situation is needed. Perhaps it should be in developing Shannon's desire to return to the church. During the intermission I want an audience to be saying "What's going to happen next?" *"What* is he (or she) going to do?" They weren't. They were saying, "Interesting; isn't that actor, what's his name, good?" You often speak of having no plot in *Period of Adjustment.* You're wrong: People will rush back to their seats to find out what is going to happen. They didn't at *Iguana.* They strolled. That's dangerous.

The Iguana. I was moved by the scene around the cutting loose of the Iguana before, but I was not moved Sunday night. I don't know why. Was anything changed? Also there seemed to be a closer relationship between Shannon and Hannah before. The circumstances between them were deeper.

I wish I had words of fire or iron to put my first point to you with greater impact. The audience simply does not know who or what to follow by the end of Act Two. Consequently, they were not identifying and not caring.

This is all for now. Are you still speaking?

There was a considerable hubbub about how this play would be produced. When it appeared that it might be under the auspices of Audrey Wood and her husband Bill Liebling, I wrote again:

Every night before dinner I look at the phone and think I will call you—and don't. And every day I think I will write you—and can't. So, I think of you, Tenn. My heart is still sore with the realization that you and I will probably never be associated again. It makes my life in the theatre, which is my whole life, seem empty of purpose.

It's not that I blame Audrey for wanting her taste. I guess it's just that I feel only people who have dedicated themselves for better or for worse to the crazy theatre should have the privilege of a chance to leap for the best. You are the best.

Maybe you think I'm talking about money. I'm not. *Sweet Bird* has paid me fifteen thousand dollars since it opened, whereas Audrey must have received three times as much as your agent. And you know my luck in the other two shows. So it hasn't been the long green. Perhaps I'm all muddled, but I think of it as the principle. I've taken a chance on more plays by new authors than any other producer except the now-leaking Theatre Guild. So once in a while I look forward to leaping where there is a net.

My lament is probably tedious, but I have to get it off my chest. When I can I will write you without groans or moans or tears. I don't think they become me either.

"Dearest Cheryl," Tenn answered on January 8, 1961,

I've written you three or four letters but none went off, a couple didn't seem right and the other one or two simply got lost among my debris of papers.

I never thought that you really wanted *Iguana;* I thought that, being a truly kind person, you wanted to encourage me by seeming to want it, just that, and when I got your notes, I realized I couldn't please you with it and still please myself. This play is a dramatic poem of the most intensely personal nature and Bowden [Charles Bowden, the producer], for some unknown reason, seemed to want it like that. What threw me off in your notes was your saying that after the second act the audience ought to go out, for intermission, just as intensely concerned with what would happen next as they do after the second act of *Period of Adjustment.*

Now I've never met anyone who liked poetry better than you, but this did indicate a resistance to what I was aiming at in this probably last play. I think you need this play like a hole in the head. Surely you know that, don't you?

We've done four plays together and none of them are failures in the true sense. I hope and trust and pray that one of the ones I am holding in reserve will be a right one for you, since working with you has always been a deeply human as well as professional satisfaction to me. God knows you took way-out chances with *Camino Real* and *The Rose Tattoo,* which Dame Selznick dismissed so brutally as a sketch for an opera libretto or a ballet.

I'll be back in New York, if the health gets better enough for travel, in a couple of weeks and then take off for Europe, and if you still don't see my point, we'll go into it further. Why do you offer to take another beating now? I love you for it, but don't think it makes sense for you.

I hope you are out of your dark room. I'm still in mine and not at all sure it isn't going to get darker before it gets brighter again.

My heart's true love to you, darling!

So I did not produce *Night of the Iguana;* as I had foreseen, our professional relationship had come to a close. I have the greatest admiration for Tennessee's ability to keep going beyond failures that affected him deeply. For his contradictory qualities include mixed feelings about success. After the Academy Awards in 1952, for which he had been nominated for writing *Streetcar,* he wrote to me—

Gadg and Marlon and I were obviously screwed out of the Academy Awards, and it was a hideous ordeal, sitting there with your bare face hanging out and pretending not to care. Gadg said he never saw anybody get so low in a chair, and I was afraid even to remove my flask from my pocket when Madame Clare Boothe Luce got up on the platform and announced the writers' awards. One part of me despises such prizes and the vulgar standards they represent, but another part of me wants to be "The Winner" of no matter what. When and how can we ever get over that, and have a dignified humility about us and a true sense of what matters?

I sometimes tried to comfort him by reminding him that the great Euripides wrote ninety-two plays but received only four prizes. I wish it had been more of a comfort.

I believe Tennessee has a very true sense of what matters. It is still difficult for me to comprehend the fury of those who hate his plays and find his characters monstrous and morbid when he is actually revealing—with respect and tenderness—the pretensions and willful folly in all of us. William James summed up this attitude better than I can in his book *The Varieties of Religious Experience,* and it is important enough to quote:

It seems to me that we are bound to say that morbid-mindedness ranges over the wider scale of experience. The method of averting one's attention from evil and living simply in the light of good is splendid as long as it will work. It will work with many persons; it will work far more generally than most of us are ready to suppose; and within the sphere of its successful operation there is nothing to be said against it as a religious solution. But it breaks down impotently as soon as melancholy comes; and even though one be quite free from melancholy one's self, there is no doubt that healthy-mindedness is inadequate as a philosophical doctrine, because the evil facts which it refuses positively to account for are a genuine portion of reality; and they may be after all the best key to life's significance, and possibly the only openers of our eyes to the deepest levels of truth.

I will always treasure a letter Tennessee wrote me after the opening of *Period of Adjustment.*

Dearest Cheryl: Thursday A.M.

My coffee has not come up from the elegantly dilatory room service of this establishment, and I have exhausted its stationery on piddling rewrites—but I must say a word to you of congratulation for last night and *all* the nights when I have observed your dedication (and gallantry) in the best uses of theatre, and say how very much I love you for it.

Sometimes it is a tattered ensign that we may seem to be playing —but to play it because it still has our devotion, the purest part of us, is a thing in you that I want to salute with my heart this early morning, late in my life. Forgive the rhetoric, love, when I come back I hope to visit you.

Love, ever,
Tenn

Errors and Abortions

The theatre is full of regrettable mistakes. Everyone in the theatre, films, TV—the most astute, the most experienced—makes his share; no one is exempt. And one person's error becomes another's fortune. Years ago a play called *Green Pastures* went the rounds of every producer's office only to be turned down. Then a stockbroker who had never produced a play bought it and made a pile of money. The Theatre Guild offered *Pygmalion* to Rodgers and Hammerstein when I couldn't arouse Lerner and Loewe's enthusiasm; they turned it down. They also turned down *Fiddler on the Roof.* Joseph Papp produced *Hair* at his Off-Broadway festival theatre, but did not choose to bring it to Broadway. Oscar Serlin, who had done the wildly successful *Life with Father,* took a play called *Washington Square* as far as New Haven, where he closed it; Jed Harris picked it up and brought it in as *The Heiress.* Everyone turned down *Music Man* until Kermit Bloomgarden, who had done only one musical, took it with very happy results. *Picnic* was produced by the Theatre Guild, Leland Hayward and Joshua Logan; when Hayward saw a run-through, he bowed out, saying he didn't think it had a chance. It won a Pulitzer Prize. Joshua Logan decided not to direct *Hello Dolly.* When David Merrick saw his production of *Hello Dolly* in Detroit, he was tempted to leave it there; it took some urging to get him to bring it to New York. These are just a few examples out of hundreds.

There are two basic ways of falling on your face. You can make a downright error and reject a play that then becomes a hit. That hurts. A subtler pain, perhaps more insidious over the years, comes from what I call an abortion: when you and a project "miss" after you have expended precious time and money on it. I've had my fair share of both errors and abortions.

First let me take the abortions, those sperm that find the egg but don't produce a bouncing child. Some are only wooing letters of inquiry; some get far enough for Dramatists Guild contracts and for money to be advanced for scripts that, when they're written, turn out for various reasons to be unsatisfactory. Every producer has many of these.

Some years ago Meyer Levin brought me a book from which he wanted to make a play. The book was *The Diary of Anne Frank,* and it affected me deeply. Anne Frank's father, Otto Frank, was in New York, and in spite of some formidable competition, I was able to induce him to give me the rights. We both promised Meyer Levin he could work on it and submit it for our approval. We did not care for the result, but allowed him to submit it to several producers I chose. The agreement was that if they did not accept it, the rights reverted to me. None of them optioned the work, so it became mine. I approached Carson McCullers, who was then living in France. She answered that for three days she had been reading *The Diary* and crying, that she had never felt such love and wonder and grief, that she wanted to write the play. Meanwhile, Mr. Levin was unable to accept the arrangements he had agreed to and was being very difficult. At the time I was very busy trying to keep *Camino Real* going, and I finally got weary of all the complications and abandoned the project. Kermit Bloomgarden picked up the rights, persuaded two writers, Frances and Albert Hackett, to write the play and had a deserved success.

But that was not the end of my involvement. Meyer Levin brought suit in court against Kermit, the Hacketts and me, claiming his script had been stolen. Why he included me, I couldn't imagine: I had lost my advance, endured his anger and enjoyed none of the pleasures of having a hit. My rewards were legal fees and several days in a courtroom when I could have been more pleasantly employed!

There's more. Searching for material for a musical, I discovered that Vincent Youmans had written a number of unpublished songs. I arranged for a pianist to play them for Mary Martin, Richard Halliday and myself. Some of them were charming, but we could never find a good idea for a book. The same thing happened with a lot of unpublished George Gershwin songs. Then I heard that Jerome Kern had left the largest trunk of material. Dorothy Fields, the famous lyricist, had written many songs with Kern, so I interested her in the idea of helping to find a story. We finally hit on an old successful film, *Hold Back the Dawn*, which had been adapted from a book by Ketti Frings. The rights were available. The first writer I approached was Peter Schaffer. He wrote a few scenes and then begged off, since he was working on a play. He is now the triumphant author of *Equus*. So I went to Arnold Schulman, who had written the successful play *A Hole in the Head*. He agreed to try. Act One went quite well; Dorothy completed four delightful lyrics based on some of Kern's music, and we chose six songs without lyrics. We had enough to tempt a male star and Yves Montand seemed ideal, so off Dorothy and I flew to Hollywood. Marilyn Monroe helped persuade Montand to listen to the records we had made. One warm Sunday at David Selznick's charming home high in the hills, Marilyn and Paula Strasberg, who was then Marilyn's teacher, arrived with Montand. He listened thoughtfully and was interested—but not to the point of committing himself before he had read an entire book. That we didn't have. However, we thought we would explore possibilities for a feminine star, since both leads were equally important. I made arrangements to have Judy Garland hear the songs. She was very responsive and asked to hear more. We recorded seventeen numbers, sent them to her and never heard from her again. Act Two became an insoluble problem and finally, after a frantic search for other story material, we abandoned the whole project. A hell of a lot of time and money wasted!

Any time Clifford Odets came to New York we would meet. Over a vodka he would tell me he had eleven ideas for plays and I would urge him to get to it. One letter from him asked me what kind of play he should write. "Cliff, dear," I answered, in June of 1961,

You ask "what do I think" is the best choice between comedy, drama, melodrama. I don't think it matters a damn. Whichever bubbles with the most life, whichever is the one you wake up thinking about most often at burglar time. I figure I've got twelve more years of real action. I haven't done half of what I want to do. I want to do a play of yours, at least one. Time slips by too fast, so let's get cracking and by God, say whatever you have to say that is important to you.

Sadly, I did not receive a play from him.

Never sufficiently discouraged, I kept searching. In the sixties Dorothy Fields had an idea of doing a musical on the Peace Corps, which was in full operation then. So we got in touch with Sargent Shriver. He was enthusiastic and invited us to Washington to read the files of letters from members of the Corps. We spent a few days there reading and copying a series of interesting reports of their activities, which gave us a title, *Side by Side.* Then we pulled in Burton Lane, composer of the lovely songs for *Finians Rainbow,* and the writer A. E. Hotchner, who had done a successful biography of Hemingway. After a number of meetings and a partial script, the project didn't seem to jell. More time down the drain.

At one point I recalled a minor classic, *Precious Bane,* which I had enjoyed and thought might make a fine film. When I gave it to Paul Newman to read, he agreed and joined me in securing the rights and advancing money for a playwright, a young Irishman named Tom Murphy, whom I discovered in London. Paul and I spent a considerable amount of money on this project, including a trip to New York for Tom in order to have conference meetings. When we had a complete draft, I wrote Olivier, inviting him to direct it if he liked the script. He replied that his work at the National Theatre made it impossible. "It's silly to go around flirting when you're already married, isn't it?" he said, and signed himself "Larry O."

We approached John Huston, Bryan Forbes, Jack Clayton, Ken Russell, Jack Carter and Albert Finney. They were either engaged on long-term projects or not sufficiently enthusiastic about the script. As time passed, Paul and I reviewed the script with more reflective eyes, deciding finally that it did not fulfill its promise. Another burial. I have concluded over the years that if a project doesn't "take" in time, no matter how worthy it is, it won't go. Momentum is a necessary ingredient, and sometimes momentum seems almost independent of the people, the idea and the situation. It graces some projects, ignores others and cuts out in the middle of some. But then, it's just one of the many disguises of Lady Luck.

In 1970 I heard about the hundreds of performances a play called *The Night Thoreau Spent in Jail* had received at colleges and universities around the country. Being a Thoreau fanatic, I got in touch with the authors, Jerome Lawrence and Robert Lee. They sent me a script, which I liked, but explained that Universal Pictures had purchased it to be produced by Hal Wallis. So I flew to Hollywood to see if I could arrange for a stage production. Practically under guard I went to the top of the great black phallus which houses Universal Pictures and had a pleasant but inconclusive interview with a top executive, Edd Henry. He suggested I talk with Hal Wallis, who was then making a film in Santa Fe. So off to Santa Fe I went to have pleasant and inconclusive interviews with Mr. Wallis. The project was on again, off again, over a considerable period of time. We were never able to reach an agreement. The film has never been made.

One of my projects was unique because I pursued it for twenty years: I wanted a play from Thornton Wilder. In the course of the pursuit I secured a warm, enduring friendship with many enjoyable lunches and evenings spiced with drinks. Speaking with swiftness and exuberance, Thornton would hold forth on a great range of topics. He had an exhaustive knowledge of history, literature and music. And he loved to have fun. One splendid weekend in Newport we visited all the sailors' bars and danced. Thornton dancing is something to remember. He loped, nearly off the ground, covering a large floor as swiftly as a bird in flight. Oh, how my feet ached the next morning.

For reasons that will quickly become clear, our correspondence was one of the pleasures of my life. I would write, appealing for a play, and Thornton, elusive as an eel, would, for one reason or another or none, but always irresistibly, put me off. At the outset I tried to persuade him to do a musical book for Mary Martin. He replied:

I have no organ "for entering into" a musical comedy. I'd have walked out of *My Fair Lady* if I hadn't been a guest. One part of my head could appreciate music, performance and a lot of charm; the other half was successively bewildered, confused, resentful. It kept saying, why?

(Later, of course, his play *The Merchant of Yonkers* became *Hello Dolly*, which enabled him to live as richly as he wished— and he wished to live richly. He had a huge zest for life.)

In 1947 he wrote:

Dear, I've been in hiding—theoretically, at least, but really hugging great libraries in order to pursue my Lope de Vega studies.

Of course I should have been writing plays to sweep you off your feet —but that's the way I am.

Anyway, I'm well, impenitently happy, fifty-one, and I'm much given to laughing, for reasons which I seldom divulge.

I hope to be striding up and down your office before long. Hugs.

In 1948 he was off on another of his constant travels, and I wrote to him in Ireland,

Thornton, Thornton—

I just read in *The Saturday Review* that you are in Dublin for the winter writing a novel! But it's a play, isn't it? Because as the two Black Crows insisted, Dey *is* more black hosses den white hosses: there are more good novels than good plays.

Plays have opened and closed here as fast as the jaws of a hungry shark and I am still unable to find one I want to do.

Later Thornton wrote me about a new play by Sartre which he admired. I sent him a check to give Sartre for an option. He answered,

You gambler.

You didn't even know the theme of the play.

I must say that if I were C. C. I'd have taken the same risk—not because Wilder said it was a good play, but because living dramatists are so rare and because the Theatre Business is Most Fun when you can get hold of a play by a living dramatist.

I haven't told you the plot yet. Its subject is the dignity of man and the existential doctrine of freedom. There's not a wartime cliché in it.

I have passed on your offer to Sartre.

The Maître leaves in a day or two. If he decides for you, I'll rush to New York, arrange the meeting between you and give the check back to you for you to give him.

Did you know that the gesture you made is pure existentialism: the soul of freedom is choice: the soul of choice is risk—you will hear from me soon.

For reasons I have forgotten, Sartre and I never met and the play was not done in New York.

Not long after, when Thornton returned my check, he told me about a new play he was working on entitled *Emporium.* I was haunted by his description of it and wrote,

Dear Roman Candle, dear—

On the brief occasions I see you, and they are occasions to me, I feel shot up into a brilliant vari-colored world, but it bursts and vanishes too soon. Then I spend nights thinking about the things you've said and discuss and argue with your shadow.

Emporium has me in a real spin. It feels like the kind of thing I've stayed twenty years in the theatre to do. If Jed [Harris] is to direct it, would you have any objection to my finding out if I could make a deal with him to manage it? Then you might eat your royalties and have them too! You would have the advantage of his genius and my capacities for brood hen detail.

I shall, of course, do nothing until I hear from you.

He seemed to be having trouble with it. Meanwhile I read Colette's *Cheri,* with which I attempted to arouse him.

Thorny dear—

What I'm writing you about now, aside from the pleasure of saying "hello," is that I have just read Colette's *Cheri.* It has been on my library shelf for years, and it has made my winter, I think it is so wonderful. I also read a version of the play which was turned into a boulevard farce and does no justice to the book.

Can't you, won't you, turn it into a good play for Judith Anderson who is crazy to play Lea? It can be a wonderful play and I can think of no one but you for it. I can afford a large advance pittance at once and feel sure I can arrange to free it.

Why a midwestern provincial with a strong sense of duty and a slight sense of amour should feel so close to this material, I doubt if even a psychiatrist's couch could disclose, but I do. And I hope, hope, hope that you have a similar empathy.

To this letter he answered:

I love *Cheri* but I wouldn't like to see it. (Besides, all the big scenes take place just the other side of a keyhole.)

I don't tell anybody that I've finished another play because they wouldn't believe it. And the disposition of it is still a secret. It's not the *Emporium*. It's just terrible the way I wring hearts, including my own.

All I'll say now, dear, is that Jed must get at least the refusal of it first—and if Provence continues to agree with me as it's done so far, maybe there'll be lots.

Jokingly, he signed himself Euripides. I hastened to answer:

You may call yourself anything, darling, but remember that Euripides, if he is your model, wrote *ninety-two* plays—you'd better hurry. Wouldn't it be nice to have that many to split among your swarm of admirers? It is exciting news to me that you have finished a new play, and if Jed is silly enough to say "no" after reading it, I'm silly enough to say "yes" before reading it. *Anything* you write has got to be better than this season's crop.

The play in question was his version of *The Alcestiad*. He had promised it to a theatre in Edinburgh, Scotland. It was not a success. Still I didn't give up. After a meeting I wrote him, enclosing a check,

. . . I'll say it again, that the crown of my theatre life would be to produce a play by you. You must be free to say no without any explanation. I will never press or plead as I might with a stranger. It's that Scotch and one thirty-second Indian blood in me. Besides I have recourse to a prayer which runs like this:

> Now I lay me down to sleep
> I pray the Lord my soul to keep
> You let me do a play by Thorn
> And I'll thank you for being born.

He replied,

You have the methods of a condottiere.

Once before you snowstormed me with bullion. How often must I tell you *I'm rich,* but I'm honest. How could I pocket an advance on a play which may never be completed? Will *The Hell of the Vizier of Kabaar* ever be seen or *Emporium* or *The Martians* or *The Sandusky Ohio Mystery Play?*

Anyway dear—if I live, if I produce—you will get a play—

As you lie in the pool say over and over to yourself, "Thornton loves me—"

We saw each other frequently when he returned from extended visits to various parts of Europe and America. In 1960 he invited me to his home in Hamden, Connecticut to listen to him read some one-acts he was writing, to be called *The Seven Ages of Man.* Afterwards, I wrote him,

Last Saturday was one of the great evenings. I guess you know by now that I admire you t.s.i. [this side idolatry], as rare Ben said about another playwright.

But what can we do about you before people eat you all up? Of course, it's your fault too, you're such an inviting feast that everyone wants to gobble. With all this important work in progress, I agree you *must* hole in—desert, mountain, cave, wherever all of us can't get at you.

If it would be interesting or helpful to you, would you like to see any of the one-acts at the Actors Studio this fall, no obligation on your part? I'm sure any director you wanted would find them an irresistible challenge.

But when the one-acts were finished they seemed to belong properly to Off-Broadway and were done by the Circle in the Square. In 1961 I was planning a trip to France and hoped to see him there but, as usual, he was somewhere else. So I wrote—

Subterrannean reports have it that you have written a new play. Thornton! If this is true, I must produce it. I'll do it anywhere, anyhow you say. I'll do it off Broadway, on Broadway, on my head, in the square, in the round, in the ellipse. If anyone else gets it, I will murder him or her. Promise. For thirty-six years I have worked at nothing but theatre, no TV, no movies to keep me solvent, and I can't give way to *anyone* where you are concerned.

That didn't yield a play, either!
In 1963 he was in Douglas, Arizona, and wrote,

Here are my plans.
By the end of this month I shall have been a year here. A good year. But now I'm hankering for Rain and a sight of Green. And oh, the Ocean. So in a few weeks I'm going to seek out another small town.
I'm not ready to return to civilization yet. I'm on an extended work —not drama—which gives a core of discipline to my days. It's going surprisingly fast and I may be ready for another project . . .

But his next project was a series of lectures, which I heard were jammed with eager students. In 1966 he wrote—

It's fun to write you.
There's something about you that makes me feel young and sportive and intellectually reckless. At the University of Chicago and at Harvard I had lots of girls in my classes (classes of hundreds in big amphitheatres on Homer and Dante and Don Quixote) and I'd hear myself saying the most preposterous things—from sheer brio—because girls are such ready, self-forgetting listeners. Oh, to be forty again.

In 1967 I finally gave up. He sent me a copy of his new book *The Eighth Day*, and with his last letter I realized that my fate was to enjoy his extraordinary conversations and his friendship. What we—no, what *he*—talked about is evidenced in his last letter to me.

Now:

Don't tell anybody.

Before long—in New York—in the middle of the week—a strange man will call you up—disguising his voice by speaking through a tear-drenched handkerchief—asking you to lunch at some obscure den, like Sardi's.

There are some new exciting discoveries he must share with you. Agenda:

1. Mahler's symphonies esp. the Fourth.

2. The new intellectual craze that has engrossed the young in Paris—totally dethroning Sartre and existentialisme—structuralisme.

3. The greatest scientific discovery since nuclear fission—and completely beneficial to man. An answer to Rachel Carson's *Silent Spring.* A mode of providing an insecticide that (1) kills only the noxious insect (2) does not reach us in food poisoning (3) the insect cannot adjust himself to. (The amopheles mosquito now loves D.D.T.) Beautiful on the mountains are the feet of those who bring tidings of joy. Economic consequences far, far reaching.

4. First there were the Beats, then the Hippies, then the "Flower" people—what next?

5.

6. Too fascinating to transmit through the mails.

> See you soon,
> Thy
> Thornt.

If I had to lose out, it was a charming way to do so.

I don't like to dwell on my outright errors. There were five major ones. As my favorite mayor, La Guardia, put it, they were "beauts."

First, of course, there was *Cat on a Hot Tin Roof.* And then there was *Member of the Wedding.*

Although I saw Carson McCullers frequently, she did not tell me she was writing a play until she came to Eastham one weekend. She presented me with *Member of the Wedding,* which I read at once. Then I sat her down opposite me before the living room fireplace.

"Carson, dear," I said, "no one doubts your writing ability. And your dialogue here is charming. But the play's story is so slight, so small. I doubt a Broadway audience would be interested in a young tomboy full of fantasies. And the third act is very weak. I'm sorry to say it, but I really think you'd be better off sticking to novels. You're a master at them."

Such a play—a genre play—is very deceptive. It depends a great deal on the quality of the dialogue and the talent of the performers. *Member of the Wedding* had both wonderful dialogue and marvelously talented performers. I lived to regret my stupidity.

During our work on *Regina*, Marc Blitzstein and I spoke often of *Threepenny Opera*. We admired it—except for the English translation, which, we felt, had made for the show's failure on Broadway. I persuaded Marc to write a new version of several of the songs. His lyrics were so good that I drove him out to Kurt Weill's home in New City to have Kurt listen to them. He too was impressed and gave Marc the rights to translate the entire work. Then I got cold feet. I couldn't shake the memory of *Threepenny*'s earlier failure. So Marc's version languished. Two years later Carmen Capalbo picked it up for an Off-Broadway production at the Theatre de Lys, where it ran, of course, for years. I thought it was stunning.

I made another of my howling mistakes during rehearsals of *Love Life* in 1948. One day at the end of rehearsal, Kazan gave me a manuscript, which he said I must read and decide on overnight. My mind was considerably cluttered with problems of the musical, but I didn't want to pass up an opportunity, so I dutifully spent the evening with the manuscript, which proved to be a play by Arthur Miller. I didn't care much for the title, *Death of a Salesman*, but what really bothered me was the flashbacks—I couldn't see how they would work out. And the main character struck me as pathetic rather than tragic. Who would want to see a play about an unhappy traveling salesman? Too depressing. In short, I was not swept away, so the next day I thanked Kazan and said no. It was presented to Kermit Bloomgarden, who opened it in Philadelphia to a six-hundred-dollar advance. A few days after the notices and word of mouth had their effects, police had to be called to control the throngs storming the box office there. The rest is history.

You might think these were enough blunders for one career, but no, there was another to come.

In 1956 Leonard Bernstein came to see me to tell me that he and Stephen Sondheim were going to write the score and lyrics for a show based on *Romeo and Juliet.* Arthur Laurents was writing the book, and Jerome Robbins would work with them and direct it. Was I interested? Of course! They asked for an advance that was more than I felt able to afford at the time, so I asked Roger Stevens if he would join me in a co-production. The quality of the talent made him answer yes. While they were preparing the work, I was busy with three plays. Bit by bit I heard the score, wishing they would develop one great soaring ballad for it. Then one day Lenny phoned in great excitement: they had finished a wonderful new number. Sure enough, when I heard it at his apartment, I was delighted. The song was "Maria." The show was *West Side Story.*

By April of 1957 the work was ready to audition. Bea Lawrence permitted us to use her large living room, where we gathered about twenty prospective backers. Jerry presented a synopsis of the story as Lenny played the score with several singers. The reaction was less favorable than I had hoped. Indeed, I didn't believe anyone there was going to invest. Richard Rodgers and Oscar Hammerstein were present and felt that it would have to be cast with very youthful actors—and where were we going to find youngsters who could sing that score? I was discouraged, especially knowing that the production would cost more than any show I had ever produced.

In this mood, I restudied the book. It was thin, somehow . . . and really, there wasn't any leavening, any humor. . . . (The one funny song was added later.) I agonized for a while and then made the tough decision to abandon it, informing Roger of my decision and calling the writers and Jerry Robbins into my office to tell them. It was a miserable meeting, but at least I was able to soften the blow by telling them that Roger wanted to continue. I will always remember their unbelieving, angry faces as they walked out. Only Jerry stayed to shake my hand. I told Roger I was certain they would work harder than ever to prove me wrong.

They sure did.

Once in a while before dawn, when I can "knit up the ravelled sleeve of care" no longer, I lie fantasizing about what might have happened to me if I had produced these scripts. Rich, I'd be rich, if the government let me keep anything after taxes. And proud, very proud, instead of feeling stupid. And what would I have done with the money? Trips to exotic places? No, I'm really an armchair traveler. I prefer imaginings of Samarkand, Persepolis, and the Greeks' wine-dark sea.

A repertory theatre? Today, I think, I would know how to plan and execute one. That's it: the fascination of what's difficult —first, last, always. Some people never learn.

The Actors Studio

April 17, 1947 was a landmark day for me, the day the Actors Studio was born. I had lunch with Elia Kazan at a small Greek restaurant on the south side of Fifty-ninth Street, west of Broadway. At Kazan's request, we always lunched at a Greek restaurant, and I had learned to enjoy its special dishes—except feta cheese. "No feta for me, thank you, Gadg," I would say, as he ordered. He would order it anyway, thinking, I guess, that in time I would learn to like it. I never have.

The conversation that day began with mutual congratulations on our current successes, mine *Brigadoon*, his *All My Sons* by Arthur Miller. This led, circuitously, to reminiscences of the Group Theatre, which in turn led to a discussion of the plight of young actors and actresses who had no such resource.

"It's a damn shame they have so few opportunities to learn their craft," I said. "If they're good in a role, they get cast in another just like it. They're only part of a labor pool."

"It's not just the kids," said Kazan, between bites. "The more experienced ones need a place where they can stretch. Who has time to train them? You know how it is. When I'm directing a play, I'm on a schedule." He paused. "We ought to do something about it, get a bunch together, get 'em out of that goddamned Walgreen's drugstore. I've been talking to Bobby Lewis. He's all for it."

"He did wonderful work with the young singers in *Brigadoon*," I said, nodding. "I'm not a teacher, but I'll help. And there were three talented youngsters in the American Rep I know would be interested—Julie Harris, Anne Jackson and Eli Wallach."

And so we decided to proceed. Gadg, Bobby Lewis and I became the original directors of what was called the Actors Studio. (Although everyone associates Lee Strasberg with the Studio, he didn't become a director until 1951, four years later.) Bill Fitelson was the attorney for all three of us and set up the Studio legally, establishing it as a tax-exempt organization with a Board of Directors. He served on the Board without fee, as did a well-to-do woman named Dorothy Willard, who made considerable contributions of time and money in the early years.

Our idea was to offer a sort of artistic home to the many young actors and actresses who wanted to stretch their capabilities, a sympathetic atmosphere in which they could tackle their limitations. Classes taught by Bobby and Gadg were the obvious format, and we wanted to keep them small, about twenty each. My role at the outset was a vague one of coordinating classes and giving general help where it was needed.

We spent the next few months talking to actors we knew and interviewing actors we didn't know who were sent to us by agents and by others who learned of our plan. The response was so great that we had to expand almost immediately. It was decided that Bobby would take the more experienced group, which finally numbered fifty-two, including Montgomery Clift, Marlon Brando, Mildred Dunnock, John Forsythe, Tom Ewell, Kevin McCarthy, Karl Malden, Patricia Neal, Sidney Lumet, Jerome Robbins, E. G. Marshall, Eli Wallach, Anne Jackson, Maureen Stapleton, Beatrice Straight, David Wayne and Herbert Berghoff. Kazan chose a less experienced group of about twenty-six, which included Julie Harris, Cloris Leachman and James Whitmore. (Any discussion of the Studio quickly becomes an orgy of name-dropping. From the outset it was a nest of the finest talent of its time.)

Our first meeting was held in a dingy room on the top floor of what originally was the Princess Theatre, then called the Labor Stage. Gadg told the assembled actors that they were expected to

work, that if they missed two classes in a row they would be asked
to leave. Since we had no money, the actors each agreed to
contribute two dollars a week to pay for a place to work. On
October 5, 1947, the classes began in a room in the old Union
Methodist Church on West Forty-eighth, now a parking lot for
Mama Leone's restaurant.

Bobby's and Gadg's teaching derived largely from the work
they had done in the Group Theatre. The general procedure was
that an actor prepared a scene or an exercise and performed it
before his colleagues, after which it was discussed. Bobby's teaching was always well prepared and disciplined, embodying his own
interpretation of Stanislavsky. He objected to what he called the
dogmatic approach of that system. He brought to the students his
quirky, original humor, wonderfully exemplified in the brochure
he prepared for his private teaching: it offered one hundred and
twenty-nine courses, including Theatre of Sexual Shock, Horse
Opera and Poor Theatre. His group worked mainly on scenes,
preparing roles they could not expect to play in Broadway productions. For instance, Tom Ewell, who was playing a lead in the
light comedy *John Loves Mary*, prepared the part of Lenny, the
retarded unfortunate in *Mice and Men*. After the scene was
performed Tom said happily, "My God! No one ever cried at me
before." I think I saw tears in his own eyes.

Marlon attended regularly, although he was often inattentive,
reading a newspaper; he seemed to object to Bobby's sometimes
longwinded lectures. On one occasion Bobby stopped and asked,
"Marlon, what was I saying?"

Without looking up, Marlon replied, "Why did you step in
it?" Later on, Marlon performed a scene from *Reunion in
Vienna*, playing a former White Russian officer reduced to driving a cab in the south of France. At a fancy ball where a group
of expatriates tried to relive their former splendor he appeared in
a stunning costume he had rented, complete with a pencil moustache and an ivory cigarette holder. When he removed a glisten-
ing polished boot, he revealed a dirty, holey sock. It was a charming piece of business that showed effectively how he had disguised
his poverty for the night.

Gadg brought to his classes the voltage of a high electric charge. His vitality and enthusiasm kept the actors in a state of creative ferment. His younger group largely did exercises meant to extend the actor's imagination, to sharpen his senses, to develop his concentration and to differentiate between indicating his emotions and really experiencing them.

To expand the imagination, the actors were sometimes given a single word, such as "freedom," "America" or "war," and asked to illustrate it immediately. Or two actors would be given three words, such as "wine, hair, sing" and a couple of minutes to consult; then they would perform a scene based on these three words. They studied pictures by Lautrec and George Grosz, and improvised scenes using them as models. Another task involved memorizing a poem and figuring out ten different actions to use with it. Sometimes Gadg would ask his group to perform animal exercises. On one such occasion, James Whitmore acted out what the class thought was a seal, and they congratulated him on the acuteness of his perception. Whitmore looked disturbed. What was wrong? they asked. Whitmore confessed he had been a dachshund.

When Kazan was engaged with a play or film, Martin Ritt, now a successful film director, took his group. But Kazan found time to direct a play with Studio members, a first play by Bessie Bruer called *Sundown Beach;* it was laid near a Florida psychiatric hospital for convalescing Air Force combat crews, where wives and children waited anxiously for their young men to recover. It had a brilliant cast of unknowns, including Julie Harris, Cloris Leachman and Alec Nicol. As it took shape in the Studio, it seemed worthy of a more extended life, and the young people were very eager to perform it in public. It seemed to be another kind of opportunity for them to grow, so I offered to book it for a few weeks in the summer. The Westport Theatre took it rather reluctantly, because it had no names. On the other hand, it was inexpensive. Although the stage lights went out on opening night and part of the play had to be lit by large flashlights, it was very well received and made more money for the theatre than anything else that summer. It then played Marblehead and several weeks

in Boston. On a hot September night we brought it into the
Belasco Theatre, which was not air-conditioned. That didn't help.
A few days before the opening Kazan came to re-rehearse the cast.
Instead of helping, this unfortunately made them tense and push-
ing, with disastrous results. The play closed quickly.

But this production was in a way inadvertent: Kazan and I had
no intention of turning the workshop into a producing organization. Bobby Lewis disagreed. He believed we *should* develop into
a theatre. He was also disappointed, with some justice, that the
brilliant production of *The Sea Gull*, which he had prepared over
months in his class, had not received a public production. He
decided to resign in the summer of 1948, parting company with
us amicably. Kazan and I wanted Lee Strasberg to replace him,
but although Lee took sessions occasionally, he was reluctant to
take over a permanent responsibility. So Daniel Mann and others
took over for a time.

Reminiscent of Group Theatre days, we operated pillar to
post in various locations. In 1948 Dorothy Willard found us some
space on the fourteenth floor of 1697 Broadway. In the fall of that
year financial support came easily for the only time in the Studio's
existence, when we were approached by a major TV network to
produce weekly dramatic programs. They were prepared at the
Studio and broadcast live. Jessica Tandy played Tennessee's *Portrait of a Madonna* for the first show, followed by a second one
called *Night Club* with Maureen Stapleton, Cloris Leachman and
Lee Grant. We lasted for fifty-six weeks, receiving consistently
good reviews and winning the renowned Peabody Award.

The TV exposure and the growing word of mouth about the
Studio put pressure on us to open our classes to more talents. So
we began a series of auditions. In the period between 1948 and
1951, over two thousand aspirants were auditioned, having been
screened first by members of the Studio. Those who passed had
final auditions for the directors. It was curious that many of the
auditioners used scenes where they removed most of their clothing. I suspect that they wished to show us how free and uninhib-
·ited they were. We certainly witnessed a good number of bare
breasts and jock straps. About thirty actors were accepted, only

occasionally the unconstrained ones. Among the men accepted over the years were Paul Newman, Anthony Franciosa, Ben Gazzara, Walter Matthau, Pat Hingle, Rod Steiger, Cliff Robertson, Sidney Poitier, Patrick O'Neal, Darren McGavin, Nick Persoff, Martin Balsam, James Dean, Dennis Weaver, Gene Saks, Richard Boone, Al Pacino, Bruce Dern, Steve McQueen, George Peppard, Martin Landau, Burgess Meredith, Dane Clark, Carroll O'Connor, Gabe Dell, Robert de Niro and Dustin Hoffman. And the women: Joanne Woodward, Jane Fonda, Kim Stanley, Geraldine Page, Estelle Parsons, Shelley Winters, Anne Bancroft, Madeline Sherwood, Barbara Baxley, Kim Hunter, Jo Van Fleet, Eva Marie Saint, Carol Baker, Barbara Harris, Lois Nettleton, Lee Grant, Bea Arthur, Susan Strasberg, Ellen Burstyn, and Diana Sands. This is a remarkable list of stage and film stars. Altogether they have received ninety-eight Academy Award nominations and twenty-one Oscars. Some of them worked very hard at the Studio. Others seemed satisfied with the accolade— for in time it came to be a distinction to belong to the Studio— and took little advantage of the opportunity to explore their craft.

To have instructors coming in and out as they got jobs in the theatre and films was not very satisfactory. We needed someone permanent. Finally in 1951 Kazan persuaded Lee Strasberg to become the artistic director, and eventually the two groups of classes were consolidated under Lee's guidance. The actors prepared scenes from plays or often from novels or short stories, which they presented for criticism. They got it! Sessions were held twice a week from eleven A.M. to one P.M., often spilling over into heated discussions. Scene rehearsals had to be carefully scheduled. They frequently went on until three A.M. Again, as he had in the Group Theatre, Lee became a father figure, the final arbiter.

Many of the actors flourished under Lee's guidance, but a few were hurt when their scenes were poorly received. James Dean was one of these. His audition had been an original scene written by an actress, Chris White, who auditioned with him and was also accepted. The scene was an encounter between an intelligent drifter and an aristocratic Southern girl. To prepare the scene

Dean stopped strangers in Central Park and noted their responses to lines of the character he was working on; he wanted to ascertain if he was believable. There was no question of his exceptional magnetism. It was the best scene he did there. But he did two scenes later on that were not well received, and he turned bitter and left.

James Dean was credited, if it could be called credit, with representing what was thought of as the Actors Studio style. It involved slouching, mumbling and wearing dirty, torn jeans. In truth, there was no such style. If a lot of Studio people wore T-shirts and jeans, it was usually out of economic necessity; they were, after all, struggling young actors. The notion of a Studio actor as a self-absorbed, inarticulate proletarian derived mainly, I think, from the much-publicized tough, sensitive loners that Brando and Dean played in films. Today, of course, every stratum of society is devoted to jeans, preferably frayed. But the fifties were such a conformist period that any emblem of nonconformity, whatever its *raison d'être*, took on an exaggerated importance.

The actors responded to Lee's teaching the way hungry people respond to bread. It fed them. And for many of them, proud and anointed, it seemed natural to develop a clannish, almost religious, cult, which angered directors who worked with them on Broadway. They questioned, they argued, to the annoyance of the director, who had to get a play ready for public performance in only four weeks. One famous question-and-answer occurred when a Studio actor demanded of his director, "I want to know my motivation for your asking me to move on that line." The director snapped, "Your paycheck!"

One of the most important activities was the work on new scripts. It is astonishing to realize how many plays came out of the Studio. The most successful were *Camino Real, Hatful of Rain, End as a Man, Zoo Story, Night of the Iguana, Any Wednesday, The Rose Tattoo, Take a Giant Step, The Death of Bessie Smith, Dynamite Tonight, Shadow of a Gunman, The Thirteen Clocks* and Edna St. Vincent Millay's long poem *Conversations at Midnight*, edited and to some extent reorganized by Eli Rill, who also directed it. We invited a few guests to see it.

They were surprised that Actors Studio members could stand up straight, speak good English, be heard clearly and wear tuxedos. Not subhuman at all! Thornton Wilder and Archibald MacLeish said they were absolutely dazzled by it, that it was the most inspiring theatre experience they had had in ages. But Norma Millay, the author's sister, was upset by the cuts and rearrangements, and unwilling to grant permission to carry the production further, although Wilder and MacLeish urged her to do so. (Soon afterwards I drove up to Steepletop, the country home she had inherited from her sister, in another effort to persuade her. No luck, even with two bottles of good wine.)

As time passed the Actors Studio became more and more the talk not only of Broadway and Hollywood, but of theatre people in countries all over the world. The State Department requested that we allow foreign theatre workers to attend, and observers came from England, Japan, Turkey, Israel, Uruguay, Colombia, Canada, Brazil, Sweden, Italy, Mexico, Argentina, South Africa, Spain, Burma and Poland, some staying for a season, some more briefly. Everybody wanted to get into the act—literally. There was no other place where they could observe, ask questions, meet and discuss theatre with professionals.

In 1955 I was invited to a delightful dinner party given by Paul Bigelow and found myself seated opposite Marilyn Monroe. We had a lengthy discussion about acting, and I invited her to come to the Studio. On the day of her visit, I picked her up at the Ritz Towers, getting there early since I had heard she was consistently late for appointments. She was enthralled by the work and by Lee, to whom I introduced her. She came constantly —on time—and also enrolled in Lee's private class, which provided his income. I tried to persuade her to do a scene. After much hesitation she finally chose the first scene of *Anna Christie*, working with Maureen Stapleton. Its performance was canceled many times because of Marilyn's fear. Eventually she and Maureen acted the scene for an audience of members, and her performance was luminous with exciting gradations of feeling. Unfortunately, it was the only scene she ever managed to do there. But over the years she was a staunch supporter of the Studio, and her presence helped to bring it into further prominence.

For a while we occupied several rooms on the top floor of the American National Theatre and Academy, given to us, rent free, by Roger Stevens and Robert Dowling. That top floor had of course been the scene of the Theatre Guild school, and it was a haunting experience for me to be in the spot where I had been born theatrically. But the space was not large enough to accommodate all our doings. With all the play activity and an increasing number of members, we needed a permanent home with enough space for the presentation of scenes and plays as well as for offices and rehearsal rooms. After a search, in 1955 we purchased a hundred-year-old church on West Forty-fourth Street between Nineth and Tenth Avenues. The membership raised twelve thousand dollars, Kazan and Roger Stevens contributed ten thousand, and a special preview benefit of the film *East of Eden* raised additional money. Peter Larkin, a scene designer, redesigned the main room to give it the feeling of an American meeting place of New England origin. Members worked very hard carpentering and repainting under the guidance and aid of one of the original members, Fred Stewart, who became the invaluable coordinator of activity there, initiating many interesting projects and advising the new young members. This he was doing as usual when he suddenly died of a stroke in the place he cherished. It was an irreplaceable loss.

Another invaluable person is fortunately still there—Liska March, a lady dedicated to the theatre, an excellent organizer who has spearheaded fund-raising through benefits and foundations.

Although we had started by concentrating on actors, we began to enlarge our activities to include more directors and playwrights. Among the directors have been Jerome Robbins, who occasionally taught dancing classes; Vincent Donahue, who directed *The Sound of Music* and *I Do! I Do!;* Frank Corsaro, now a noted director of operas, including the current *Treemonisha;* Alan Schneider, director of *Who's Afraid of Virginia Woolf?* and many other plays; Michael Bennett, who conceived and directed *A Chorus Line;* Arthur Penn; Joseph Anthony; Stuart Vaughan; John Frankenheimer; Gene Saks, recently director of *Same Time Next Year;* Frank Perry; Gerald Freedman; Ulu Grosbard;

Michael Kahn; Jose Quintero; Herbert Berghoff; and Word Baker, director of the perennial *The Fantasticks.* They prepared scenes or worked on new plays with any actors they chose, often with actors who were not members. Strasberg conducted and criticized the directors' sessions for a time, guiding the directors toward fresh insights into the meaning of a scene. The work was taken over eventually by Arthur Penn.

A playwrights group was also organized, both to criticize first drafts by members and to see if a play in progress would work or not. It included Edward Albee, Lorraine Hansberry, Terrence McNally, Arthur Kopit, James Baldwin, Arthur Laurents, William Inge, and Norman Mailer. This was conducted mostly by Molly Kazan, Elia's wife, who had been a playreader for the Theatre Guild and wrote plays as well.

Eventually the two groups merged, the directors working with the playwrights. Edward Albee was instrumental in setting this up and invited Tennessee Williams—who had never been an official member, although the Studio had worked on some of his plays— to participate.

Tennessee answered,

... it sounds like a rather formidable unit, but what isn't? I am not scared off. And I certainly do have things I would love to have tried out. My career has turned to a try-out it seems, anyway. I can't think of any better place to have a try-out. Most of my work now, and from now on, I suspect is in the short-long or long-short form, intensely personal and highly eclectic, and may be unfit for public exposure. But I know from past experience with plays such as the short form of *Camino Real* and *Night of the Iguana,* both of which were explored by the Studio, that the atmosphere there is sympathetically creative and experimental—and it would be of the greatest help to me to have one or two of them tried out as classroom exercises, culminating in the sort of in-group presentation that the Studio provides to nerve-shattered playwrights.

So if you will accept me as a probationary or novitiate sort of a contributor, I will *gladly* contribute.

However, nothing developed from this, since Tennessee was very rarely in New York.

We did not seek publicity, but the rising fame of many of our actors and playwrights inevitably brought newsmen, who wrote a stream of featured articles, and stars, who were curious to see what we did. Permitting famous people to come was unfortunate. Usually they based their judgments on a single session and came anticipating something astonishing. We were expected to put on a show. Yet the whole purpose of the work was to allow actors to fall on their faces, to experiment, to fail.

The presence of celebrities put pressure on the performers, which erupted in unexpected ways. For example, there was a memorable scene of Strindberg's play *The Stranger*, played by Anne Bancroft and Viveca Lindfors before an audience that included a number of famous people. Viveca's part called for her to be totally silent; we were to see her reactions to Anne's monologue only from her behavior. But Viveca was not content to remain silent and began to make little noises, which infuriated Anne. A wild fight of screaming and hair pulling began. It was both frightening and hilarious. I never knew what the shopworn expression "tempers flew" meant until I saw this. Madeline Sherwood attempted to stop it and was knocked down. Lee yelled, "Keep out of it, Madeline!" As they began to wear out, Lee rose and stopped them. Naturally, this scene caused quite a commotion in the audience.

Most of our famous guests left a session wondering, "What was all the shootin' fer?" and delighted in gossiping about the ineptitude of some trial-and-error scene they had witnessed. Olivier and Gielgud were different. They understood and appreciated what the work meant and spoke to the actors warmly and appreciatively of their own experiences.

The old church now buzzed and nearly burst with various activities from morning until after midnight. Alice Hermes, a fine speech teacher, was hired. Anna Sokolow began her first experiments with what became later her famous dance *Rooms*. Etienne Decroux, Marcel Marceau's teacher, was brought from France to teach mime. When the great Kabuki performers arrived in New York, they came to lecture on their style. Moscow Art actors also came while they were performing in the city.

I gave a course in play producing, which opened some of the actors' eyes to the many problems involved. It was a reward to watch the young actors develop. Actors who were stereotyped by a succession of similar parts tried to break out of these molds, frequently with success. This was of course one of the things we had hoped to achieve, and it was a gratifying accomplishment.

My major task was to keep us solvent. I was trying to raise money simultaneously for my own productions, and it was a nearly impossible job. Investors in Broadway plays are different from those who might be persuaded to assist a nonprofit enterprise. The former expect to make money. The latter are people interested in theatre development, who may take a tax deduction for their contribution. But neither foundations nor wealthy people seemed to find our oyster bed, the workshop, worthy of their altruism. We got this reaction in spite of the many pearls we uncovered in those oysters. Their negative responses reminded me of the story of two elderly women rocking side by side on the porch of a summer hotel. One was knitting, the other reading. The reader asked the other why she knitted all the time. The answer was, "Oh, but if you read you have nothing to show!" Money wants something to show. I think that is why so many impressive and expensive theatre buildings have been erected to contain very minor achievements. They represent what Harold Clurman has called "edifice complexes."

Our yearly benefits helped. Marlon Brando organized one of the early ones. The benefits were quite elegant, with entertainment by the likes of Laurence Olivier, Mary Martin, Sammy Davis, Jr., Judy Garland and her three children, Marilyn Monroe, Ella Fitzgerald, and Nichols and May, who all gave their time generously.

The most controversial, and so of course the most successful, was the one for *Baby Doll,* Tennessee Williams's first film script, directed by Kazan and featuring Actors Studio members in all of the major roles. This film aroused the moral indignation of Cardinal Spellman, who denounced it from the pulpit of St. Patrick's Cathedral. Mayor Wagner protested the use of his name as a sponsor. (Unfortunately, it had been copied from an earlier authorized list.) This scandal brought out a full house attended by the rabbi of Temple Israel, the dean of St. John the Divine and the executive director of the National Council of the Churches of Christ, as well as the anonymous curious. We made forty thousand dollars.

After one benefit I spoke at length with Gene Kelly about Studio problems, and a few days later he sent me a check for ten thousand dollars. In periods of financial desperation, which occurred every single season, some help always came, but never enough. At one time Marilyn Monroe sent ten thousand dollars, at another Elizabeth Taylor sent the same. Paul Newman helped greatly in various emergencies. The William Morris Agency was also generous. MCA was less so, even though they derived more talent from the Actors Studio than William Morris did.

Eventually, I was able to get between five hundred and a thousand dollars each season, at least for a few seasons, from each of various theatre-loving individuals. Kazan persuaded many people to give. In order to sustain the Studio properly, we needed at least sixty thousand dollars a year for salaries, mortgage, building maintenance and the limited production of new plays. We never got it. It was my unfortunate task to announce each season that we were practically bankrupt.

Meanwhile, starting in 1956, the Lincoln Square project, which resulted in New York City's great cultural complex, Lincoln Center, was flirting with the Actors Studio to decide if we would be suitable to occupy the theatre they were building. The idea of having a theatre of our own, a home, of being in a sense a resident company, thrilled us. We were all eager to become a part of the project: visions of productions of new American plays and American classics such as O'Neill, Williams, Miller, danced in our heads. Happily, we three directors supplied documents of our intent and and attended meetings. But Rockefeller's advisors were oriented to a classical theatre on the European model. Their visions and ours did not coincide. And they were put off by our authoritarian manner. Although I was willing to make some compromises, or at least appear to do so, Lee's stubborn declarations indicated that he would brook no interference. In 1959 the Lincoln Square people decided to turn the theatre over to Robert Whitehead and Elia Kazan. Kazan nursed hopes that somehow he could sneak the Studio in, but he was never able to. When he later approached a number of the members to join his enterprise, he was turned down. The actors' hopes had been very high, and they were furiously disappointed. They felt betrayed.

Theatre or no, by 1958 Studio members were putting considerable pressure on the directors to have public productions. The issue became a turning point in the Studio's history. All three of us were hesitant, remembering the Group Theatre's vicissitudes. Kazan and Strasberg had different points of view. If there had to be a theatre, Kazan wanted it to be a small nonprofit one, something like the English Club Theatre or America's own Off-Broadway. By contrast, Lee felt we should be involved in something on a larger scale that would represent the apex of the Studio's work. He didn't care if it was profit or nonprofit, but he wanted it to be big-time. I agreed with Kazan that it would be best to start modestly. I also felt it was important to develop and produce plays by our own authors. These different approaches were finally reconciled by compromise. The choice for a large-scale production was Archibald MacLeish's play *J.B.*, to be directed by Kazan. On a smaller scale we would take over a little theatre to present a series of plays, starting with O'Casey's *Shadow of a Gunman*, which Jack Garfein had been directing in the workshop for months.

At first Kazan was hesitant about *J.B.* By the time he decided to direct it, Alfred de Liagre, a producer and college friend of MacLeish, had optioned it. We offered to co-produce, which would have allowed us to share de Liagre's share in the production. Knowing that Kazan wanted to do it and that he would be able to hire any Studio actors they agreed on, de Liagre refused; there was no advantage for him in our co-producing, indeed a disadvantage. Kazan directed anyway.

This left us with the O'Casey play, but if we went into commercial production it might threaten our tax-exempt charter. I brought to the Studio Joel Schenker, president of The Webb and Knapp Construction Company and a theatre aficionado; he and I formed a partnership to present plays by the Actors Studio at the small Bijou Theatre. He raised one hundred and fifty thousand dollars to produce three plays, starting with the O'Casey play, giving the Studio a gift of twenty percent of the profits. I had not seen the play's successful presentation before Studio audiences, and when I saw a run-through I was shocked. It was dull, lifeless and totally unrepresentative of our work. I urged Strasberg to come to rehearsal to help overcome what looked to be a disaster. For the last four days he worked with the actors, and we decided to open. The notices were mixed but favorable to the actors. Brooks Atkinson reported that the performances were superb, expressing the "explosive originality" of the play. The directors did not agree. We felt the production did not truly represent our work. Indeed, there were only four members of the Studio in the cast. The play had a brief run.

Following this, Joel Schenker and I produced Norman Corwin's play about the Lincoln-Douglas debates, *The Rivalry*, at the Bijou, a non-Studio production with only one Studio actor, Richard Boone, who played Lincoln. No further play was found. Why, we wondered, did a production like the O'Casey play that was successful in a workshop setting not do as well when it went commercial? Was it the difference in scale? The difference in casting technique? The freedom of the workshop versus the constraints of the commercial theatre? It is sad that we did not find concrete answers to these questions in 1959.

The Studio retired into a private phase temporarily. The acting, playwriting, speech classes and physical activities continued unabated. At the acting sessions there were frequently two hundred in attendance—members, foreign guests and serious observers, who often participated. After each scene was performed, Strasberg opened the floor to questions and criticisms, ending with his own evaluation of the work shown. Strasberg has the ability to pinpoint the actor's problems unerringly, although his brilliant observations might sometimes be more effective if they were less verbose. An observer once voiced the wish that Lee would stop talking. Finally, he wished Lee would finish a sentence. Nonetheless, Kazan said, and I agree, that "our whole theatre would be less vital and less ambitious without the influence of this one man who has given so quietly and so unceasingly to so many people because it is his nature to study and to think and to teach."

Strasberg objected to having his teaching, inspired by Stanislavsky, called "The Method." It was rather *a* method which aids the actor in finding out what to do; and what he finds may differ from actor to actor. It is a technique, a set of tools, and not the be-all and end-all of acting. As Stanislavsky said, "Besides the method, actors must have all the qualities that constitute a real artist: inspiration, intelligence, taste, the ability to communicate, charm, temperament, fine speech and movement, quick excitability and an expressive appearance. One cannot go very far with just a method."

The playwright-directors unit was eager to put on inexpensive productions in the Studio with minimum sets and props, paying a small sum to the participants to cover expenses. The Ford Foundation turned us down on this, but when I brought an official of the Rockefeller Brothers Fund, a Mr. Crawford (unfortunately no relation), to see our work, we received from them a grant of $56,400 for this purpose. Over several seasons they contributed $100,000. Two of the plays worked on under this grant later became part of the Actors Studio Theatre productions.

The disappointment of being left out of Lincoln Center was still with us. Resentment made the actors' determination to start a theatre even stronger. They would "show them" their worth. They talked to Roger Stevens about their willingness to commit themselves to such an enterprise. Roger was enthusiastic, volunteering to speak to the Ford Foundation and private people to raise financing. In the spring of 1962, the formation of the Actors Studio Theatre was announced; it would be a branch of the Studio, functioning under its tax-exempt umbrella, using only Studio actors and directors. In response, Laurence Olivier wrote, "The Actors Studio has, without question, made Herculean efforts to meet the creative needs of the American actor. As a privileged witness to some of their work, I can say without reservation that I think this should be extended, if it is possible, so that after much careful and exploratory nursing it could well become the logical center for the creation of a true ensemble in the U.S."

This expressed precisely what we believed. Strasberg was the artistic director, with final say on the choice of plays; I was the executive producer, who did all the business management; and Roger Stevens was the general administrator. (At this time Elia Kazan resigned as a director of the Studio because of a conflict of interest with his Lincoln Center activities.) It was Roger, almost unaided, who persuaded the Ford Foundation to put up a matching grant of two hundred fifty thousand dollars and who secured the other half from private individuals. A Production Board was appointed, consisting of Paul Newman, Edward Albee, Anne Bancroft, Frank Corsaro, Michael Wager and Fred Stewart.

We all met with W. McNeil Lowry at the Ford Foundation when he decided to give the Studio the matching grant. Although we were expected to be grateful, when we read of the grant of one million, two hundred thousand dollars given to the Oklahoma Mummers, we were less so. (Theirs was not a matching grant, but an outright gift given to build a theatre. In 1967 the Foundation offered the same organization seven hundred and fifty thousand dollars on a matching grant. I have heard the theatre is no longer in existence.)

As an accommodation to reality, knowing that our most successful actors would be unlikely to tie themselves up for any length of time, Lee put forth the idea of what he called a "floating company." The actors would rehearse for four weeks, then play for four months, after which, if the play ran, those who wished to leave would be replaced by their peers.

In all of the plays the Studio produced, the top salary for a few of the stars was one thousand dollars. They did not get their customary percentages. This was not a great sacrifice: we had tried to secure a top salary of five hundred dollars.

Everyone began to read plays. The classes, of course, continued as before. Albee offered us his new play, Who's Afraid of Virginia Woolf? to co-produce with his partners, Clinton Wilder and Richard Barr. He wanted Geraldine Page to play the lead. She was reluctant, because she did not care for the play. Stevens didn't either, saying he would not help subsidize the speaking of dirty words on the stage. I was scared of its bitterness and brutality. So we passed it up. Of course we made a mistake. Geraldine later wrote me, "It would have put a stamp on us of bitterness, hostility and infantilism that would have taken us years to struggle out from under." Perhaps, but we could have used a big hit.

We considered O'Neill's *Strange Interlude*, which we liked, but since Carlotta O'Neill had given the rights to all of O'Neill's plays to Jose Quintero, it seemed impossible to acquire. Not to Rip Torn, a member. He succeeded in persuading Quintero and Mrs. O'Neill to allow us to produce it with Quintero directing.

Strange Interlude opened in 1963 and had an extraordinary cast of Geraldine Page, Pat Hingle, Ben Gazzara, William Prince, Betty Field, Franchot Tone, Jane Fonda and Richard Thomas. It was very well received by most of the critics and made an operating profit of nearly forty-two thousand dollars in the first nine weeks. Unfortunately, the Hudson Theatre was the only one we could get at the time, and we leased it for only three months, assuming, since it was usually not in demand, that we would be able to extend our stay if we wanted to. But the owners asked for a huge increase in rent to permit us to stay. We moved to the Martin Beck at a cost of over ten thousand dollars; to make matters worse, because of that theatre's arrangement, we had to pay four musicians who did not play. Much of our early profit was expended in this transfer. That was the unhappy result of not having a permanent home.

This experience prompted us to search for a house of our own. On Broadway in the fifties we discovered an unused ballroom, the Riviera Terrace, which could be converted into an open theatre, where we could use a thrust stage, a proscenium or one where the audience sat around a central platform. Hence it could house a great variety of productions. Besides, it could operate under a cabaret license, enabling us to serve liquor and food. We worked out endless blueprints showing how wonderfully adaptable it could be, but after intensive negotiations, the damn thing fell through: the owners, Columbia University, decided to sell the building.

This was a blow, both in itself and because the Terrace would have been perfect for our first production of the fall season. It was to be *Marathon 33* by June Havoc, a member of the Studio. She had danced for endless hours during the marathon craze in order to support herself, and her memories were vivid. Because of protracted negotiations for the Terrace, our advance sale of nearly a quarter of a million dollars in theatre parties evaporated, and it took several months to engage a suitable theatre. The theatre turned out to be the ANTA again, the former Theatre Guild Theatre where I had served my novitiate. It was a strange experience to sit in the auditorium watching rehearsals and at the same time see the past unfold in double vision: *Marco Millions, Pygmalion, The Brothers Karamazov, Porgy* and the other plays of my youth. I had sat in so many auditoriums, watching so many rehearsals, since then.

For more than a year there had been exploratory rehearsals of *Marathon 33* at the Studio. June directed these, with the aid of Tim Everett; when we decided to produce it, Lee Strasberg supervised, working with June on the script to strengthen the dramatic conflicts. But the rewriting did not improve the work; the original loose structure had a striking verity which was obscured when they tried to turn it into a well-made play. And Lee and June did not see eye to eye. Some of us felt that because the play was autobiographical, June tended to sentimentalize. Nonetheless, it was a theatrical tour de force, a production I, for one, would enjoy seeing again.

Marathon 33 opened in December of 1963. Julie Harris played the Havoc part most skillfully, singing and dancing like a true vaudevillian. Lee Allen, not a Studio member but an actor we had observed in a performance at Grossingers, gave an excellent comedic performance as the male lead. Some of the others have become well known since: Ralph Waite, now of "The Waltons"; Gabriel Dell, Joe Don Baker of "Walking Tall"; and Conrad Janis with his Tail Gate Band.

Our third production was also first presented in exploratory rehearsals at the Studio under the Rockefeller grant. *Dynamite Tonight* was a comic opera by Arnold Weinstein and Bill Bolcom, which we presented at an Off-Broadway theatre now famous as the restaurant Maxwell's Plum. But the work suffered an inexplicable sea change from the hilarious presentation which had charmed us at the Studio. It closed after one performance. Recently a Yale University production of *Dynamite Tonight* received very high praise. Does a mordant satire on war, which this is, seem more relevant to our current derangements?

A month after *Dynamite, Baby Want a Kiss* by James Costigan opened at the Little Theatre with only one set, three characters and a sheepdog. Paul Newman and Joanne Woodward, close friends of Costigan, were eager to do it. They played for the Equity minimum, $117.50, less than even the understudies. Costigan, also an actor, played the third role. Paul and Joanne gave brilliantly satirical performances, but the audience did not really enjoy seeing two famous actors playing parts that ridiculed the stupid egos of two smug film stars. Nonetheless, their illustrious names and their minimum salaries made us a considerable amount of money.

Four days after the opening of *Baby Want a Kiss*, we opened the fifth production, James Baldwin's *Blues for Mr. Charlie*, a play of vigorous social comment. This exciting and inciting play had an interesting history. Kazan had given Baldwin the idea of writing a play based on the Emmett Till case and advised him during the writing. He expected to direct it for Lincoln Center, but Baldwin refused on the grounds that there were no blacks on the Lincoln Center Board. He finally confessed another reason—that he believed he would defer too much to Kazan, whom he revered. Rip Torn pursued Baldwin, helping with the script and urging him steadily to give it to the Studio. He finally agreed, after Torn promised him that it would be done exactly as he wrote it. I objected to some of the raw language, particularly "motherfucker," but I was voted down. Burgess Meredith, who directed the play and was aware of the arguments about the language, told me recently that he had just been sent a play to direct entitled *Motherfucker.* O tempora! O mores!

The Studio's Production Board had voted that because the play was five hours long and not really in shape to produce on Broadway, it should be done first as a workshop production. After the meeting Lee left for Kennedy Airport. From there he phoned to say that he had decided we should proceed at once to put it into professional production. This decision was final, and it is an example of the kind of administration that became our downfall. We never planned to give the artistic director the power to overrule the Board; it simply happened. The decision was a mistake for several reasons. First, given time to experiment I am sure a much finer play would have evolved. In his preface to the play, Baldwin expressed his feeling that it presented "the tragedy of the whites." This was not achieved in the rush to get it on.

Moreover, the time necessary to condense the play made it difficult to set a date for opening and to build up any advance sale. To make it possible for a subway audience to come, a top price of four dollars and eighty cents a ticket was set. We didn't expect to attract the carriage trade.

To boot, rehearsals were difficult. Rip Torn, who played one of the leading parts, and Burgess Meredith did not agree on how the part should be played. I was called in several times to try to smooth things over. On one occasion on the bare stage with the whole company present, Baldwin climbed to the top of a tall stage ladder to shout a long diatribe about the ineptitude of the Studio's work. All of us, including Strasberg, looked up, silently waiting for him to tire. He finally did, but he stayed above us on his perch while Strasberg answered him.

Blues replaced *Marathon* at the ANTA theatre on April 23, 1964. The reviewers praised the performances of Rip Torn, Pat Hingle, Diana Sands and Al Freeman, Jr.; in fact, they praised the entire company and "the fierce energy and passion" of the play, but criticized its lack of structure and the simplistic characterizations of the Southern whites.

Although the play was well attended—eventually the audience came to be composed of about eighty percent blacks—there were twenty-seven actors in the cast, and with the low ticket prices, we lost money every week.

It looked as if we must close for lack of money. Baldwin began a campaign to keep the play running. One large ad was taken through the efforts of Reverend Sidney Lanier, signed by a long list of imposing names. Two daughters of Nelson Rockefeller contributed ten thousand dollars. Roy Wilkins, the Executive Director of NAACP, wrote a letter on official stationery to NAACP members, appealing for their attendance. These efforts kept the play running longer, but by the end of the summer the theatre had been booked for another production and we could not raise the eight thousand dollars required to move. We had played to a consistent loss for four months. I cabled Baldwin, who was then in Beirut, that we had to close. He cabled back vehemently and at length, protesting that whatever it cost to move "the most underproduced show in recent Broadway history" a few blocks was not too much; that the show had proved it had an audience. He absolutely rejected our reasons for closing and threatened to take us to court. He finished with, "The only cause which I will accept is your declaration of bankruptcy. Home in a few days. Best regards."

We closed. Nothing happened. The erupting volcano was a smokepot.

The sixth—and as it turned out, the last—production was Chekhov's *The Three Sisters*, which was dedicated to Marilyn Monroe, whose tragic death in 1962 had been a great shock to all of us. She died in August; at the time I was spending a brief holiday on Cape Cod. When I drove into Cotuit to get the newspaper one morning, I was stunned to see the headline announcing her death. I sat in the car alone for a long time.

To direct *The Three Sisters* had been a dream of Strasberg's for many years. He believed that the Moscow Art production, which he had seen in 1924 with the original company, did not fully reflect Chekhov's vision: the emotional life was too rich. He thought the play required more simplicity and emotion that was not obvious or sentimental.

I had read that the poet Randall Jarrell was working on a version of *The Three Sisters*. I wrote to ask for his script, and his is the one we used. The sisters were played by Kim Stanley (Masha), Geraldine Page (Olga) and Shirley Knight (Irina). Barbara Baxley played the sister-in-law Natasha, and Kevin McCarthy played Stanislavsky's role, Vershinin. The reviews were mixed. Atkinson's and Jerry Tallmer's were full of praise; others reported that there was a failure of ensemble acting. But Lee was pleased, and so was I. The production was moving and well acted, superior to the tired production the Moscow Art Theatre brought over later with aging actresses and slow, stolid movement. Everyone praised the performance of Kim Stanley as Masha, although Harold Clurman, who considered her a wonderful actress, thought that her Masha "was going crazy." She insisted that Masha *was* going crazy; when some of the company said that her performance was too strong, she agreed, saying that her Masha would really *have* gone to Moscow. It ran for about three months, closing in October 1964.

After the closing, Ely Landau, then a TV producer, made an agreement to film the play for television presentation as the first of a series of films of our productions over a three-year period. This was arranged by Carl Schaeffer, a lawyer who replaced Roger Stevens as general administrator after Roger became involved with the Kennedy Center. Profits were to be split fifty–fifty, with Landau paying all costs and each production receiving a fifty-thousand-dollar advance. This was a windfall to us, and we received it with hurrahs: it would partially subsidize future productions, especially since the Ford Foundation had decided not to continue its grant.

Alas, the TV film of *The Three Sisters* was made too quickly, and, like many classics that are filmed, it was not a success. In the wake of its failure, the hoped-for subsidy vanished. We were fresh out of funds.

This looked like the end of the Actors Studio Theatre. For better or worse, we had produced six plays, two classics and four by new American authors, for a total cost of $462,500, remarkably little money for such productions.

We may have been economical, but our miscalculations were severe and painful to avow. The planning had been helter-skelter, suffering from mixed motives. The Actors Studio Theatre had not functioned as an ensemble company; it had presented a series of productions with completely different actors; it had not obeyed its own casting policy. It had not been different from Broadway but a part of it; nor had it created a theatre with an aesthetic monogram, so to speak. No definite stamp was revealed in our choice of plays. They had been presented on a haphazard schedule like random shots from a BB gun, scattered without aim or objective.

Disillusion set in for everyone. And everyone wondered where the blame lay. How had a group of gifted, dedicated, experienced people drifted so far away from their intentions?

I believe that W. McNeil Lowry, head of the Ford Foundation, asked a telling question when he refused to continue the Foundation's support: "Who is minding the store?" Everyone, and thus no one, was minding the store. The administrative structure was never clear. True, we had three directors and a Production Board. But in practice, power and decisions did not obey the rules of the structure. Lee's image as father figure and head of the Studio emotionally overwhelmed the executive organization. We let things happen rather than organizing them. Instead of functioning as an executive, I found myself the vehicle for carrying out decisions, frequently haphazard, of the Board and the artistic director. Moreover, we were all distracted. Most of us were engaged in other theatrical activities: I with several productions of my own, Lee with his private and Studio classes, Roger with the Kennedy Center. Only Michael Wager was in the office daily. But he had little authority, only his intelligence and dedication.

Then, just as the production company was about to be shoveled under, I received a letter from Peter Daubeny, an English producer who, for some seasons, had organized a spring World Theatre Festival at the Aldwych Theatre in London. The famous companies of many nations came to play two weeks of repertory there. Daubeny invited the Actors Studio to participate. There was great excitement among all the board members—except me. I realized that fifty or sixty thousand dollars would have to be raised rapidly and also that a number of actors from the original companies of *The Three Sisters* and *Blues for Mr. Charlie,* the plays we could offer, would be unavailable. However, it was determined by vote that we should go.

Our first appeal for money was to the State Department. They rejected it. So Paul Newman and I talked with a top official of Pan American Airways. This resulted in a free round-trip flight for the company, as well as for the sets and furniture. Paul was instrumental in raising most of the additional fifty-five thousand dollars from Columbia Pictures, MGM, Paramount, Seven Arts, Twentieth Century Fox and Warner Brothers. He also made a personal contribution.

But the money came through belatedly, hampering preparations. There was not adequate rehearsal time—a serious problem, since, as I had expected, a number of leading actors had to be replaced by some who were not members of the Studio. Kim Stanley refused to go if Kevin McCarthy played Vershinin again; she wanted George C. Scott, a splendid actor but one I thought completely wrong for the dreamy, sentimental Vershinin. However, Lee accepted her demand. Geraldine Page had the best excuse for not going—she was pregnant. Nan Martin replaced her. Shirley Knight was replaced by Sandy Dennis. So only one of the original sisters went, not to Moscow but to London. With one week for rehearsals, Kim declined to fly and left alone by boat.

Since Rip Torn disagreed violently with Burgess Meredith's re-rehearsing of *Blues* and with Baldwin's changes and cuts made for the English censor, Ralph Waite took over his part. Diana Sands, who had been so brilliant in the play, was in a success and unable to leave. For me, the result of these changes blew the theory of a "floating company" to pieces. A new actor, however excellent, cannot come into an established company without tearing the existing fabric; the entire company has to re-rehearse sufficiently to accommodate the change. Otherwise, the result is expedience, not art.

The London opening of *Blues* was a disaster. Much of the effectiveness of the production depended on complex, subtle lighting, since there was practically no set. But we did not have enough time or equipment to light properly. The play was performed in ghostly, gloomy half-light. During the second act members of the British National Party began shouting, "Filth! Why don't you go back to Africa?" The London critics panned the hell out of it.

Before we recovered from the blasts, the heavy sets of *The Three Sisters* had to be set up swiftly on a raked stage not very adaptable to our scenery. On the afternoon of the opening I went to watch Kim and George rehearse, to find him playing a poignant scene in long johns that had a sagging back flap. (His uniform was being pressed.) The British stagehands peered out from the wings, their faces incredulous. It was almost an omen.

That evening a distinguished audience waited and waited for the play to start. The actors couldn't seem to get organized in an unfamiliar theatre. When they finally did start, they gave an unbelievable, self-indulgent performance. Kim was lethargic and allowed herself a performance one of the actors said "you could drive a truck through." The play took almost four hours because of the pauses during the scenes and between the acts. Some of the audience disappeared. When Sandy Dennis came out toward the end saying her line, "Oh, it's been a terrible evening," the audience laughed. At the end there were boos, petrifying the cast.

The reviews were awful. Penelope Gilliatt, long a great admirer of the Studio's work, was intensely disappointed and wrote in *The Observer*, "The admirable World Theatre's dismal task has been to mount the suicide of the Actors' Studio—the whole endeavour is absurd and agonizing, like playing the harpsichord in boxing gloves, like filling the Spanish riding school with hippopotami." A very few reviews by critics who saw the play later in its week's run were sympathetic. But the overall result was a humiliating, lacerating blow to the reputation of the Actors Studio. And it was the end of the Actors Studio Theatre.

I was too sick at heart to return to New York, and stayed over for a week to assess why and how the Studio Theatre had failed. As I saw it, Lee, as the artistic head, had seesawed between caution and the assertion of his authority without being able to delegate responsibility. Lee's great gifts are teaching and inspirational guidance, not administration and management. And where I might have complemented his talents, I had somehow fizzled. Dazzled, as always, by Lee's brilliant theories, I did not assert enough of the expertise my long practical experience had given me.

And, overall, the Actors Studio Theatre had been in too much of a hurry. Some of our play choices were arrived at too hastily. Our course should have been more thoroughly mapped out. Instead of trying to do a number of plays so rapidly, we should have taken the time to oversee each one properly. We should have had at least one theatre, our home, where we might have developed a subscription plan. And we were too star-conscious, without sufficient concern for an ensemble, such as the Group Theatre had had, which would express our method of work.

An infinitely sounder plan would have been to produce the wealth of material developed in the Studio, beginning with *Zoo Story*. Eight successful plays came out of the Studio and were presented by other managements; the Studio derived nothing from them. We should have taken advantage of our own talented playwrights.

As a workshop the Actors Studio still exists. A few of the older members are still there; new ones enter each year. Lee does not take classes as often as he used to. He has become a successful film actor and has private classes here and on the West Coast. Some older members carry on the work. Since the London debacle I have not returned more than a few times.

So another dream exploded. This was the most painful disappointment of my life: when I had failed before, I had at least failed with honor. That is one thing. It is quite another to fail ignobly. What was lost was so valuable, and the way it was lost so unworthy.

Actors—the Third Sex

It may not come as a shock that in the course of fifty years in the theatre, I have developed some views on actors as a breed. Indeed, I have come to think of them as the third sex. That designation is not meant to imply that actors are androgynous. Some are, some aren't. But so are many people in the arts. Nor am I alluding to sexuality at all, but to the breadth of understanding of the entire human spectrum that actors must be able to express. Social scientists have stated that no human being is totally male or totally female except in his physical body. How dull we would be, how unable to reach any mutual understanding between the sexes if it were otherwise.

Almost every human being has a latent desire to be an actor —to masquerade, to get out of his or her skin and be another person. Perhaps those who become actors are the ones who feel this longing so keenly that they do something about it.

Actors are like other people, *only more so.* They have to be. Their responses must be swifter, keener, fuller. All art is an effort to create human experience, but only the actor creates it directly. Other arts translate it. As John Donne said of the actress Elizabeth Drury, "One might almost say her body thought."

I have heard "regular" citizens complain that actors are like children, self-centered, emotional, impulsive, unpredictable, with quick angers and easy tears. Of course they are like children in the sense that they are full of fantasy and faith, willing to believe the unbelievable. As St. John Gogarty, prototype for the doctor in Joyce's *Ulysses,* said about the Irish, "They believe only in that which they know to be untrue." Children create a world from their imaginations: just as in my youth I transformed our truck gardener's wagon and stolid old horse into a dashing chariot, children make the space under a table into a house where they live with their doll children, or a cave where they hide from Indians, or a wigwam where they are Indians hiding from soldiers. But most adults lose that transforming imagination. So the first problem of an actor is to react to imaginary stimuli. The carafe of tea is whiskey on which the actor gets drunk; the vial of water is poison—the actress must die of it; the rubber dagger kills the king. The actor must make an entrance from a snowstorm, although he can hear the gurgles and grunts of the heat pipes spread against the back wall of the theatre. As he brushes the prop snow from his coat, he must make the audience believe in the storm. It is not simply a matter of stamping feet and rubbing hands. That is, not if he is a good actor. Only lesser ones use these clichéd imitations. The good actor has learned through his technical training to arouse the feeling of the cold throughout his body.

Since their professional lives depend on illusion, actors are probably more prone to illusion in their personal lives too. For instance, Mrs. Jacob Adler decided after a long interval to return to acting. A reporter came to her dressing room for an interview, during which he asked, "By the way, Mrs. Adler, how old are you?"

"I am sixty-one," she answered firmly.

"How odd," the reporter said. "I interviewed your son Jake last week, and he told me he was fifty."

"Oh well," Mrs. Adler replied, "he lives his life and I live mine."

By what Stanislavsky called the "magic if," an actor enters whatever part he is called upon to play. I had an unusual experience of that some years ago. Thornton Wilder and Robert Edmond Jones had told me about the transcendent performances of

Edith Evans, the English actress, as Rosalind in *As You Like It*
and Millamant in *The Way of the World.* They raved about her
beauty, her femininity, her alluring charm. Not too many years
after hearing these praises, Peggy Webster and I went to Sardi's
one evening after rehearsal for a drink. "Why, there's Edith
Evans over there alone," Peggy exclaimed.

Following her gaze, I stared. There was an aging woman with
no remnants of beauty, a rather heavy, hawklike face, one eye
placed lower than the other. "My God!" I thought. "Thornton
and Bobby must have been blind."

Would I like to meet her? asked Peggy, heading for her table.
Edith Evans graciously invited us to join her, and I sat on her
right. She told us that Lawrence Langner had done some "fixing"
on a new version he planned of *The Way of the World,* and he
had recently invited her to play it. Since Millamant's final speech
is one of the glories of the drama, I asked if she would speak it
to us. She consented, and I closed my eyes to see if I could
comprehend what my friends meant from her voice. After a few
sentences I was compelled to open my eyes: there, close beside
me, sat a most entrancing woman, sexy, flirtatious, desirable. It
was a miracle of transformation. As Millamant she knew she had
all those qualities, and her will and imagination made them real.

Geraldine Page accomplished a difficult and astonishing transformation in *Sweet Bird of Youth.* Although she must have been
in her early thirties at the time, she had to play an aging woman
burnt out with drugs and other excesses. I don't recall that she
used much makeup, perhaps a bit around the eyes and a gashed
red mouth. But her voice, her manner, her gestures all conveyed
the decadent, pitiful monster.

Part of the ideal training of an actor is to develop a flexible
voice capable of expressing many varieties of emotion. It is said
of Laurette Taylor that even when she murmured the top gallery
heard her. And here I must reprove many of our actors. I have
heard numerous complaints from people sitting in the back of the
orchestra that they cannot hear; and they are paying the same
price as those in the front rows. This is inexcusable, and it hurts
the acting profession. It would seem that in the players' desire to

be "real," they forget that they are not just playing to each other but to an audience that has come to hear them. Perhaps this fault is abetted by the fact that so many of our plays tend to duplicate our ordinary life, to present it realistically instead of portraying a world larger than life, more noble, more passionate, more terrifying.

On the other hand, audiences can be disappointing too. In a pinch that's convenient. Alison Skipworth, a prominent English actress, was doing a grueling series of plays in repertory on an English provincial tour. The cast had to rehearse three plays simultaneously, because the plays were changed every night. In confusion, one of the actors committed stage suicide at the end of Act One, forgetting that this occurred in another play. During intermission the company tried to decide what to do, since he was in the next two acts of the play they were performing. Miss Skipworth, looking contemptuously at the chagrined actor, said, "Oh well, let's continue with the play we began. I'm sure the audience will never know the difference."

A flexible body is as important to an actor as a flexible voice, because we often express ourselves more clearly through movement than through words. In posture, in gesture, the body speaks a language that reveals thoughts and intentions more truly than words. Recently I observed a friend talking on the telephone. In her hand she held a sharply pointed pencil. She was saying, "Oh, my dear, of course I didn't mean to hurt you. You must know how devoted I am to you. I really only did it to help. Aren't I your best friend? You must believe me!" As she was speaking she was driving the sharp point over and over into a paper on her desk. It didn't take much perception to know what she really felt.

An actor must practice releasing all muscular rigidity for perfect relaxation; contracted muscles prevent impulses and emotions from reaching the surface. Audiences are thrilled by performers capable of using their voices and their bodies with a freedom they themselves cannot achieve. I observed their delight in Jim Dale's acrobatic performances in *Scapino*, their chill at Olivier's scream of anguish when he pierced his eyes in *Oedipus*. Larger than life—that is what the theatre should be. No television or film can equal the electrical current that can pass between human beings on either side of the stage.

Actors must also be sensitive to their own emotions in order to re-create them for a part. It is not necessary to have killed in order to play the role of a murderer. If you have ever gone wild with a swatter trying to kill an annoying mosquito, you have the emotional material available for taking a life. It is essential that actors also be attentive to all human behavior in order to interpret what Wilhelm Reich calls "character armor," the patterns of gestures, voice, movements of which a person is unconscious. A good analyst can discern almost as much about his neurotic patient by watching these activities as he can from free association and the interpretation of dreams.

We are told that Richard the Third was a hunchback. It is not sufficient to put a heavy pad across the actor's back. The actor must determine how this disfiguration came about. Whatever he chooses as the reason—and he must find a specific reason—will color his performance in a particular and individual way.

Our theatrical history begins with actors as vagabonds, strolling players, clowns and minstrels. They were not accepted by polite society then, and even today society looks askance. Theatrical folk find it difficult to get insurance, loans, superior housing.

I feel strongly that actors in the United States have a rough time. If they are lucky enough to be in a hit, it becomes very difficult to re-create a fresh performance every night for a long period of time. The repertory system customary in most other countries, where different plays alternate nightly or weekly, gives the actor an opportunity to play a number of different parts, classical and modern, in the same season. This system affords them a much better opportunity to develop their craft. There has never been a really successful repertory theatre in New York City. With the aid of private endowments, Eva Le Gallienne's Civic Repertory lasted the longest. Lately some distinguished repertory companies have developed across the country, in Minneapolis, Chicago, Cleveland and Pasadena, for example, and I wish them long life. Our government and various foundations have just begun to give our arts some assistance. Nonetheless, in 1972 the

United States spent fifteen cents per head on aid to the arts, while Germany spent two dollars and forty cents and Canada one dollar and forty cents. Sweden spends more than the United States, and so does England.

When a piece of machinery in a factory becomes obsolete, the owner replaces it and receives tax credit. When an actor becomes obsolete through age or a change in styles of acting, there are only a few homes for actors where he can subsist with his memories. Heavy taxes do not permit him to retain enough from the years when he was successful to sustain him through the lean, unsuccessful years. This is unfair. Not even a gold watch or a small pension rewards him for a life spent entertaining and illuminating his fellowman.

I wish that actors were more respected in our country. When the Japanese Kabuki Theatre came to New York and the stars spent an evening at my apartment, I was thrilled to learn that the Japanese government had appointed them "national treasures." In England many actors are given the Order of the British Empire or made Dames or Sirs or, as in the case of Laurence Olivier, Lords. In France some are given the red ribbon, which enrolls them in the Legion of Honor.

In the United States actors are used to sell war bonds, to entertain troops in desolate outposts. The highest honor an actor receives here is to be invited, without fee of course, to the White House to entertain foreign dignitaries. And that honor is only likely to be accorded an actor if he has proselytized for the incumbent.

If I had my druthers, I would choose the lovely designation "national treasures" for the most talented of the theatre people who have devoted their lives to interpreting our habits, our terrors, our guilt. While I welcome our new concern with landmarks, with the protection of our wild land and our wet land, I wish there were more concern for the artists who enlarge us through exposing our pretensions and our inherited taboos or who inspire us with an image of what we might be, or have been.

English audiences allegedly cherish their older stars more than Americans do and will go to see them even in an indifferent play.

Recently, however, I heard a charming story which disproves America's indifference. Mary Martin's son, Larry Hagman, is widely known, especially for his lengthy TV serials. Joel Gray, a close friend of Larry's, was opening in Las Vegas, and he invited Larry to come with his wife and daughter. Mary was asked too. When they all left their hotel to go to the one where Joel was to perform, a large crowd of teenagers spotted Larry, surrounding him with squeaks and squawks, begging for his autograph, trying to hug and kiss him. Mary stood aside with a friend, unnoticed. The doorman hastened to put Larry and his family into a taxi. As it departed, Larry leaned out of the window, waved to his mother and called, "See, Mom! This is show biz."

At the opening they all sat together at a table. When Joel appeared, he announced, "I don't usually do this, but I have a great friend here tonight whom I would like to introduce, Larry Hagman." There was great applause. Then Joel continued, "And there is someone else here. You many have seen her in *Peter Pan* or *South Pacific* or—" At this, as Mary rose, the entire audience stood up clapping and shouting. When Mary sat down, she turned to Larry and said, "You see, son, *that's* show biz."

Why do actors act? Think what they go through: humiliating auditions which so often end before the actor has finished with "Enough! Thank you," or "Don't call us—we'll call you if we want you"; the uncertainty of income, since there are more failures than successes—and an arid desert between as they await another call; the boredom of that great desideratum, the long run. I think actors put up with all this because their need to get out of their skins is so great—their need to be someone else, to hear the applause, to feel the love of which they are frequently deprived in their personal lives. I have seen them obey the hallowed "the show must go on" beyond the call of duty: Lynn Fontanne striding down a long flight of stairs in *The Taming of the Shrew*, a whip in one hand, a leg in a plaster cast going clunk-clunk, clunk-clunk; an actor playing with a temperature of 104 degrees or a strep throat; an actor with an upset stomach hastening offstage to a vomitorium. They can be heroic.

And actors often have a consideration for the needs and

despairs of others in their profession that could well be emulated in other professions. Leonore Ulric was a great star for David Belasco. But after his death she was not asked to perform, and her good fortune decreased. When Katharine Cornell decided to play Cleopatra in *Antony and Cleopatra,* she asked Miss Ulric if she would care to play a minor part in the play. She would. She was delighted. When the dressing rooms were apportioned, Katharine Cornell gave her the star dressing room and took number two. That is grace.

But sometimes actors are a pain in the neck, so self-concerned, hysterical, and interested only in where their vis-à-vis is standing and how they can upstage him or her and take stage center. When they are difficult, it is because they have to use themselves, expose themselves in the most direct, immediate fashion. That is not an easy thing to do.

In a way all theatre people are lunatics—in a good sense, revolutionary. Tom o' Bedlam, the anonymous seventeenth-century poet of visions and inspired fantasies, expresses in the final verse of his song the incredible dream of belief beyond reality:

> With a heart of furious fancies
> Whereof I am commander,
> With a burning spear
> And a horse of air
> To the wilderness I wander;
> By a knight of ghosts and shadows
> I summoned am to tourney
> Ten leagues beyond
> The wide world's end
> —Methink it is no journey.

Bless them! They're all Tom o' Bedlams, without whose lunacy the theatre could not exist.

Upward, Downward, Onward

In 1952, in the wake of ART and ANTA, I helped cast a revival of *Porgy and Bess* for a continental tour, and then decided to take a trip abroad. On the April afternoon before I was to leave, a writer named Edward Chodorov called my office. I had not seen him since Theatre Guild days, when he had submitted a quite interesting script. He had since become a successful writer-producer with such films as *Pasteur* and *Zola*, plus a successful Broadway play, *Kind Lady*, to his credit. He had to talk to me, he said. I explained that I was flying to Europe the next morning, but if he wanted to, he could ride home with me in a cab. Work in Hollywood was no longer available to Eddie—he, like many others, having been caught in the McCarthy spider web—so he rode with me. Enroute he rapidly outlined a comedy about a psychiatrist with a number of neurotic patients who falls in love with a kooky girl only to find he is hoist on his own petard. It sounded interesting, but I couldn't commit myself so hastily. We left it that I would consider it seriously when I returned, and he would have something on paper by then.

My trip by car through France, Italy, Switzerland and the English Cotswolds was great: magnificent scenery, magnificent sinus. I returned to find that Eddie had a written scenario of sorts, enough to intrigue me, so I optioned the play. He was living in a fleabag hotel, desperate for money with which to live and to pay divorce obligations. To my astonishment I later found I had advanced him about twelve thousand dollars before April 1953, when I finally saw a complete script.

The play was called *Oh Men! Oh Women!* and almost everyone tried to dissuade me from producing it. No theatre party agents would book benefits. The general public was so disinterested that our total advance was only seven thousand dollars. One backer famous for his good judgment wrote to me, saying that it could never make a play unless all the long speeches were cut. Another complained that the analyst would never marry "a wacky girl like Myra." His acquaintance with analysts may have been slight.

But I was already committed, and I went ahead. Nonetheless, the New Haven opening in November, starring Franchot Tone, wasn't exactly encouraging. The last act was in serious trouble. Eddie's brother Jerome and Moss Hart were there, and we sat up all night discussing rewrites. That was an occasion when I observed an honest-to-God "pro" at work. I don't think Eddie ever got to bed between that Friday morning when we retired, leaving him to his typewriter, and the Tuesday night opening in Philadelphia. In that time he wrote and rehearsed—he was also the director—an almost completely new third act. And though there were still some rough edges, such as dull exit lines, throughout the play, the act worked. Luckily, I had the original manuscript with me. Searching through it, I found some hilarious one-liners, which we used effectively for various exits.

We opened in New York on December 17. After the second act I had a drink with Roger Stevens, who was a stalwart investor. He was beaming. "By God, Cheryl," he exclaimed, "it's going to be a hit." I beamed back—he was right.

Gig Young, in his first Broadway role, and Larry Blyden, whose recent accidental death made me very sad, were both excellent. My best contribution was Anne Jackson, whose work I had watched with interest since her audition for American Rep. I had decided she must play the disturbed wife of the film actor, who treated her like a dangling participle. The part had a two-and-a-half-page monologue delivered from the psychiatrist's couch that was funny, touching and required great expertise. (Contrary to "advice," the long speeches proved to be the chief laugh getters.) I told Eddie that Anne must play the part. Said Eddie, "Never heard of her." "You can try out a hundred actresses," I told him, "but you will wind up with her." He did. She did not disappoint me.

After all the dissuasion—preceded by twelve thousand dollars' worth of faith—the response from critics and audience alike was particularly satisfying. I loved the large headline that *Variety* ran: "Crawford has last laugh on 'wise' investors; *Men* looms as sock hit." By January 2 we were playing to capacity. I laughed all the way to the bank.

And a note from Tennessee Williams was a special pleasure:

Everybody who writes me from New York says, Isn't it wonderful, Cheryl has a "big hit," and each one says it with true satisfaction as if it were a personal success. I don't think anyone has ever had a hit that was enjoyed by so many people without a touch of the invidious in their reaction, and I can understand why. I feel the same way about it. I knew in Philadelphia that it would probably be a hit and it really did give me a wonderful feeling. Especially since the play is admirable. It is warm and witty and civilized and creditable to everybody in it, and I don't think I've ever seen better casting in the theatre. Of course you are justly famous for your casting. You have the greatest instinct for right actors in the theatre. I think this is the beginning of a new period for you.

Unfortunately, Tennessee was wrong. The years that followed, 1954 to 1974, may have been a new period, but not a wonderful one. They were not altogether lean, but they were too close to the bone financially and emotionally. On the good side, of course, *Oh Men! Oh Women!* toured successfully. And *Sweet Bird of Youth, Brecht on Brecht* and *Period of Adjustment* were all profitable—although in a customary arrangement, I shared the producer's portion with co-producers or distinguished directors and actors. But in those years I also had fifteen productions that failed, some of them returning a portion of their investment but nothing to me. I managed to stay afloat. That was all.

In 1955, for instance, I produced *The Honeys* by Roald Dahl, based on one of his macabre short stories about a wife who gets rid of her annoying husband by bashing him with a leg of lamb, then conceals the murder weapon by cooking it. The story of insidious evil didn't work in the theatre. Evil is often more harrowing when you use your imagination.

The next year I put on *Mr. Johnson,* adapted by Norman Rosten from a novel by Joyce Carey. George Jean Nathan said, "Its intentions are so considerably above those usually observable hereabouts and its acting and production are so superior that it seems a downright shame that its sum doesn't satisfy us as it should. But the evening is worth the attendance of theatregoers who are surfeited with the dull routine of Broadway plays and who crave something fresh and novel for a change." Not enough people were surfeited or craving anything different.

So I tried again, with *Girls of Summer* by N. Richard Nash. Shelley Winters starred, and George Peppard had his first significant part, from which he received a film contract. A film company bought the play, which helped to return most of the investment.

With this less than exhilarating run of luck, it was encouraging to learn in 1957 that Brandeis University wanted to give me its Creative Arts Award. I received it with pride and pleasure. I received something else at the same time: a subpoena to appear before the House Un-American Activities Committee in Washington.

Naturally, I had been shocked for some time by the scandalous McCarthy investigations, both for what they were in themselves and because they had succeeded in ruining so many talented people I knew. But I had not imagined McCarthy could be interested in me. I was wrong.

My attorney was able to get a list of the traitorous things I was supposed to have done. Here is what this dangerous citizen was accused of: being a faculty member of the National Training School of the New Theatre League; patron of the Manhattan Chapter of the Medical Bureau to aid Spanish Democracy; worse still, signer of an ad sponsored by the Committee for the First Amendment protesting the House Un-American Activities Committee (which, incidentally, was also signed by Myrna Loy, Eddie Cantor and Humphrey Bogart). Ah, the alarming papers I signed! A telegram of greetings to the testimonial dinner for the Hollywood Ten by the Freedom from Fear Committee; an open letter sponsored by the American Committee for Protecting of Foreign Born; a letter on behalf of Paul Robeson to *Nation* magazine regarding the Peekskill riots on September 17, 1949 (but it didn't appear in the issue). Then the explosive things I sponsored—a Committee for Equal Justice for Mrs. Recy Taylor; a Committee to End Jim Crow in Baseball. I even presented an award to Norman Corwin (whom I didn't know at that time) at an American Youth for Democracy dinner. Surely our country was in peril when I spoke at a conference of the National Council of American-Soviet Friendship. Yes, I did that—I lectured on Chekhov and Stanislavsky.

The charges were petty and ridiculous. Yet the idea of appearing made me very nervous. I hate angry voices. I had never been browbeaten, and I didn't know how I would react if I were. Just before Gadg had been summoned to appear before the Committee he had invited me for a drink at Dinty Moore's to tell me. There was gray starting in his hair. In mine too? I hadn't noticed. His face looked strained, and there were heavy lines around his mouth. I had them, too, the stigmata of too much tension. I realized we were getting older. After he appeared before the Committee he stated in a public announcement that he had become convinced that the Communist Party was a menace and that it was his duty to help the Committee. Had they browbeaten him into it? I didn't know. I didn't ask. He and I never spoke of it again.

I requested a postponement to which the Committee acceded, since I was in the midst of producing a new play, *Good as Gold*, by John Patrick. My nights were miserable. What did I know? *Who* did I know who might be subversive? What would they ask? What would I answer? The fact is that I didn't know much. By now I knew there had been a cell in the Group Theatre; many of the actors I knew had been called before the Committee. Marc Blitzstein was a radical, but we never talked about overthrowing the government. Almost everyone I knew had been sympathetic to the Russian Revolution at the time, idealistically glad that a people had overthrown their oppressors. But politics had always been incidental to me. Would McCarthy and his cohorts believe that I kept my nose to the theatrical grindstone to the exclusion of everything else—love, for instance, which certainly would have come before politics if there had been world enough and time? I had watched the McCarthy hearings on TV with the fascination of someone watching a deadly snake: evidence was twisted, lies were told as truth, facts destroyed. I hoped that I would behave as well as Lillian Hellman, even though I could not express myself with her memorable words. I hoped.

Then suddenly, for no reason I ever knew, I received a wire saying that my appearance was indefinitely postponed. It was a great relief. Yet, without realizing it, I had grown used to the idea of the challenge. Perversely, I was disappointed as well as relieved. But that kind of disappointment is bearable. It is the kind one feels when one is off the hook. It passes.

Good as Gold passed, too—quickly. Sometimes the opening night flowers last longer than the play. At the same time I was elected to the Board of the Lincoln Center Theatre project. After Mrs. Vivian Beaumont gave money to build a theatre, she declared at a meeting of the Board that she hoped "none of those morbid plays by Tennessee Williams" would ever be done in her theatre. I resigned the next day. Ironically, the biggest success the Vivian Beaumont Theatre ever had was a revival of *A Streetcar Named Desire* in 1975.

In 1958, again two failures: *Comes the Day* by Speed Lamkin and *Shadow of a Gunman* by Sean O'Casey.

Out of town *Comes the Day* was considered "powerful and provocative with keen psychological insight and a brilliant cast." Besides Judith Anderson and Arthur O'Connell, there were George C. Scott, Larry Hagman and Michael Pollard, all in their first Broadway roles. Alan Pakula, now an important film director, was co-producer. But the New York critics disagreed with the out-of-town reviews.

I was working sixteen hours a day on these productions, and

the strain began to take its toll. Three successive osteopaths seemed unable to put me, like Humpty Dumpty, back together again. So I thanked God for Eastham, which was always restorative, a retreat where I could lick my wounds, watch the seasons change and participate in nature with the squirrels and chipmunks, who didn't give a damn about Broadway.

One woodchuck lived in a deep, comfortable hole, coming out only to eat. A frisky squirrel played near his home. I would watch them, fancying the squirrel asking the woodchuck, "How can you lead so dull a life? Why don't you come out more often?"

The woodchuck would reply, "Yes, it's dull, but it's safe. At least I'm alive."

To which, in my mind, the squirrel shot back, "How would you know?"

Such was my conflict. Frisky was probably right, but I decided to go the woodchuck's way and took a respite. Then in 1959 I was approached to head the Shakespeare Festival Theatre in Stratford, Connecticut. The job offered pleasant security, but I wasn't the woodchuck after all, and I couldn't see confining myself to the Bard. So I refused. Luckily, I then arranged to do *Sweet Bird of Youth*.

I must now tell an unusual story, one of my naiveté and misplaced trust. Sometime in 1957 I received a long letter from Peoria written by a young man named Richard Chandler, saying he was coming to New York and wished to work for me. I didn't answer the letter, but one day he turned up anyway. He would work for nothing, he said, until he proved himself useful. This sort of thing happens all the time in the theatre. Its glamour attracts people, particularly affluent ones, who are willing to do anything just to be a part of it. Free help was not to be scoffed at, so I let Chandler try. He proved to be very useful. Tall, good-looking, with slightly curly brown hair and blue eyes, he had an eminently presentable Ivy League appearance. He was well educated, well read and an excellent typist. He was also extremely dedicated. Gradually, he became my right hand, and I began to pay him a small salary. Indeed, he was so helpful that I felt bad about not being able to pay him more. But Richard was one of the affluent ones: it developed that he had an enormously wealthy aunt with homes in London, Majorca and Paris whose fortune he was due to inherit. One day he showed me a picture of her in an old *Time* magazine: she was one of a group of ladies surrounding Elsa Maxwell. My concern was assuaged. As time passed, we became good friends, and I came to trust and depend on Richard. He worked for me for twelve years.

During those years he sometimes wrote me notes like this one: "I want to work with you as long as I can, and I want to fight on your side as long as I am able. I don't know what the future will whisper to me, but I know that no matter where I am or what I am doing, you'll always be my chief." Such affirmations of faith and affection were a wonderful support during a period when I felt alone, tired and hard-pressed sometimes for belief in myself.

Richard eventually became one of the family, so to speak—another younger brother. We dined together usually twice a week and went to the theatre together. In time I listed him on my stationery as my partner. He worked days, he worked nights, along with me. He was always on call. In fact, the only problem I had with him was that he was careless about paying bills and overzealous about opening my mail at the office. During the two years of the Actors Studio Theatre he served as general secretary. Following that, when a musical I produced, *Chu Chem*, failed out of town, he wrote a play, *The Freaking Out of Stephanie Blake*. It was good enough to be put into rehearsal in 1967. I cast Jean Arthur as Stephanie Blake; she was very right for the part and assured me that her withdrawals were a thing of the past. Unfortunately, they weren't. The first preview went fairly well. Jean's film stardom was remembered, and audiences were eager to see her. At the second preview, a full house matinee, I was sitting on the aisle in the last row. Jean came out, removed her hat, got on her knees and told the audience she couldn't go on, she felt sick. Before she finished I found myself screaming, "You will go on. You *will* play the play!" She was stunned, but she did the performance. And that was that. She left and called a doctor who said she was unable to continue. So much for *Stephanie Blake*, on which I lost more money than I care to think about.

Meanwhile, Richard's aunt had died. Soon after the play folded, Richard informed me that his Peoria lawyer was coming East to arrange a transfer of a hundred thousand dollars from the legacy and also to sign papers giving me an annuity for life. I was touched that Richard wanted to make me comfortable. He knew, being close to me, how concerned I was about money. With more shows failing than succeeding, I was worried about my future.

Part of his immediate money Richard wanted to distribute to needy playwrights and poets; we had discussed this, and I was to help him choose them. As I sat at my desk making a list, he came up behind me and suddenly I felt a sharp crack on my head. It stunned me, and my head bled badly. The poster of *One Touch of Venus* had fallen, Richard said, hitting me with a sharp edge. He got me quickly to a doctor, who made ten stitches. When I recovered, I was puzzled about how the poster could have fallen with such force, but I believed him and put the matter aside. The lawyer didn't turn up, but a few weeks later he was due again and I was to meet him at lunch. We ate and waited for him. There was a heavy fall of snow, almost a blizzard, and Richard explained that the man was delayed at a bank downtown. At my request he kept phoning (I thought), but at three o'clock we were still waiting, now sitting at the bar having a drink. Suddenly I felt so ill I could scarcely move. I asked Richard to take me to my apartment and call my doctor. While I went to bed, Richard called, or so he claimed, but was unable to get an answer. Fortunately, my maid was there and I sent her out to get medicine, since Richard said he felt ill too. Thinking we had eaten something bad, I made him take the medicine too, over his protests. A friend, Charlotte Abramson, came in later to keep a date for dinner with me. After a few hours I staggered into the living room saying, "You know, I feel just as though I had been given a Mickey Finn." At the time my remark was in jest. Now I believe that that was precisely what had happened.

A few weeks later I arrived at my office one morning to find no Richard but a note saying he had left town forever and would I forgive him. Forgive him for what? I got the number of the Peoria lawyer from Information and called. The lawyer knew

Chandler, but he himself hadn't been to New York for many years. There was no legacy. The mansion back home in Peoria that Richard had described was in reality a lower-middle-class dwelling. For some time Richard had been in charge of my bookkeeping. When I opened my mail, I found a bank statement with forged checks made out to him. For many weary days I reconstructed what monies had been sent to me that I knew nothing about. He had closed out one office account and established another one, into which he would put all checks sent to me. When canceled checks came through, he would then pay sums of money to himself, forging my name. When there were not sufficient profits to keep this scheme going, he quit.

The total amount he had taken was very large. My lawyer and I went to the district attorney with the proof. Chandler meanwhile returned to New York, but I never saw him again. Called to court, he acknowledged the theft. He was left free, being ordered to report weekly to a probation officer and return to me most of anything he made.

I had fed the mouth that bit me: he had lived high in a duplex garden apartment filled with books, records and pictures; he had taken trips abroad—and I had paid for all of it. The wealthy aunt was a fiction of his abnormal imagination; I was his "wealthy aunt." This was no ordinary con job. The man worked, and worked hard, for twelve years. His case was a terrible mixture of ability and distorted ambition.

How could I have been so vulnerable? It was a difficult period, and he was very supportive. And very convincing—for twelve years. And obviously I trust people too easily. I had never been conned; I did not know it could happen to me. Trust had always been a strength to me, not a weakness. I was more vulnerable, wide open, than I realized.

It took me a very long time to recover. The popular song is mistaken—time does not heal everything.

During those Chandler years there had been other ups and downs. In 1960 I had produced *The Long Dream* adapted by Ketti Frings from a novel by Richard Wright. It had to do with the clash of blacks and whites in a Southern town. It was not a poor play, but it was imperfectly realized on the stage. The scenes were not sufficiently lived in. The black belt should have been full of blacks, the police fearful to come among them. Most of the basic conflict developed from this, but it was not dramatized in the production. Consequently, the play seemed like a tract from which the daily life had been removed. I faulted myself for not being aware of this sooner. The same year fortunately had Tennessee's *Period of Adjustment*.

Throughout 1961 I searched for material. Tom Jones and Harvey Schmidt were working on something for me that they called *Ratfink*. But in the meantime, I *had* to have a success. I flew to London, Berlin, Rome, meeting agents and producers. In East Berlin I saw several productions of the Berliner Ensemble and had tea with Helene Weigel, Brecht's wife, in the actors' canteen, where we talked about *Mother Courage*, which I had decided I must put on: I would give it its first American production.

In 1962 I saw a single matinee performance of *Brecht on Brecht* presented at the Theatre de Lys as a showcase by the American National Theatre and Academy and Lucille Lortel. It had an impressive cast of six: Lotte Lenya, Anne Jackson, Viveca Lindfors, Dane Clark, George Voskovec and Michael Wager. I thought the production had an excellent chance of success, and took it over. I was right. We enjoyed a long run in New York and on tour. A plus for a change.

The same year, in Rome, I met Max Frisch, author of a new play entitled *Andorra*, which I had heard about. I understood not a word of German, but I was impressed by the excited response of audiences in Münich and Frankfort. Max, who spoke English well, explained the story to me. Roger Stevens, always willing to take a chance, joined me, and we had it translated by George Tabori and put it into production. It lasted one week. Maybe we should have had it translated before we decided to produce it. Or maybe we shouldn't have had it translated!

I couldn't stop. I started on *Mother Courage*, co-produced and directed by Jerome Robbins, starring Anne Bancroft. My first choice for the part had been Anna Magnani, with whom I had several discussions in Rome and in New York. She finally decided she was unable to play eight performances a week for a year and be away from her son. "My dear Cheryl," she wrote, "I have decided today, after much thought, not to accept your offer, but I am telling you with great and sincere displeasure. Please don't be cross with me."

Mother Courage is the kind of play that actors and director should be permitted to spend months on, improvising, filling out the characters with life, since in the script they are like line drawings that need to be fleshed out. Days could well be spent exploring the characters' behavior as they tramped the desolate war-torn countries. How did they find food, if any? Clothing? Where did they sleep? Was there any energy left for sex, any desire to stay clean, any feelings of comradeship or every-man-for-himself, any awareness of their degradation? But there was no time for this. Five weeks were permitted for rehearsal, that's all. They were not enough. The daily papers were critical, the magazines much better.

Newsweek reported that Anne Bancroft was "a toweringly heroic she-animal." *Time* said it was an "intellectual firestorm," showing "the indomitable life force in human beings that survives history."

One amusing bit in my production notes to Robbins states, "Gene Wilder is so insecure that he needs confidence now more than anything." This he has acquired with his excellent performances in the films *Blazing Saddles* and *Frankenstein*.

It ran for fifty-two performances.

I didn't really appreciate the irony of seeing *Andorra* and *Mother Courage* included in the Year's Ten Best Plays.

With all these failures, Eastham, my home and refuge, became a liability. Backing and filling, one day saying I must sell it, the next saying I couldn't, I would walk from room to room looking at all my treasures. When prospective purchasers came, I would raise the price, unable to face the loss. I borrowed money. I kept hoping the *next* production would save my home for me.

Then on February 5, 1969, fate intervened. It was late evening when the phone rang in New York: Eastham was burning!

I couldn't believe it. The house was closed, the heat and water shut off. Frantic, I phoned Westport, where my friend Ruth Norman was living. She dashed to the house, and with friends managed to save some smoke-covered books and charred furniture. The next day I was driven up to see it. I could hardly bear to look at the black skeleton. Now I had no home, no refuge. And no explanation. Neither firemen, police nor insurance agents ever determined the origin of the fire. I still walk through the old place in dreams, and I have never entirely recovered from the canker of uncertainty as to how it could have happened.

For a year I had no heart to continue. I coasted, couldn't seem to get up any steam. I played around with a few ideas, but mostly I was "do-less," a woodchuck again. Then in 1970 something came along that I found irresistible. Tom Jones's wife Elinor Jones brought me *Colette*, which was a digest of portions of the book *Earthly Paradise*. I said I would do it only if I could get Zoe Caldwell, who seemed to me an ideal Colette (she even looks somewhat like her), and Mildred Dunnock, who seemed just right to play her mother. I got them both to read the script aloud with some other actors. Zoe was tempted but not completely sold, so I went through the book, extracting additional material that I thought would enrich the roles. There was not much in the material that covered her love affair with Maurice Goudeket and her marriage to him, but an out-of-print magazine contained a story by Colette that I had never seen before about a woman's attraction to a handsome young man. We extracted some of the dialogue, which gave us a love scene. Meanwhile, I had interested Mary John in becoming co-producer. When we had another reading with the new material, which Elinor had worked into her script, Zoe was hooked. Gerald Freedman directed with great invention, and Tom and Harvey Schmidt wrote some delectable songs.

The reviews were all a producer prays for. For the first time the carriage trade of Rolls and Cadillacs filled the street on the Lower East Side where we played—the inhabitants leaned from their tenement windows in wide-eyed wonder. It was gratifying to have Maurice Chevalier come backstage after seeing a performance to tell us how much he had enjoyed it, that he thought Zoe was perfection as Colette and that we had achieved an authentic French style.

But-but-but! The sellout business lasted for only four months, when Zoe left to fulfill an engagement in London. I couldn't find an adequate replacement. The many stars I tried to persuade were intimidated by Zoe's wonderful notices. (In London such substitutions are frequent. Perhaps the stars there are more confident of their ability.) The result was that the backers were repaid only partially, and I was on the ropes again.

During the run I had endured a serious operation. I was glad just to be alive, and grateful not to be destitute. The Eastham tragedy had had its brighter side: the house and furniture were heavily insured, and the five and a half acres of land were by then worth more than the original cost of the property, including the house. When the insurance was settled and the land sold, I had a healthy sum. It sat safely in a bank. Should I save it for my old age or find another refuge? After Eastham's demise I had spent many weekends with various friends in various places—on soft beds and on hard beds, with dinners at four and dinners at ten, and although I was grateful, I didn't want to spend the rest of my life as a weekend guest. On a visit to Bridgehampton on Long Island, I saw a reconstructed stable for sale. It had large window doors overlooking a lovely pond, which rambled like a river to the sea, where cows stood hock deep chewing their cuds of marsh grass. Overnight I bought it. It has delighted me ever since. The rolling breakers close by put me to sleep at night, the white swans move in state on the blue water, the geese cackle at dawn, reminding me of a ladies' Wednesday matinee.

But I could never give up New York. As Marianne Moore said in her poem about the city, its attraction is its "accessibility to experience." Frequently I stand at my sixteenth floor window gazing out over the lighted, thrusting skyscrapers, thinking that here anything is possible. From the windows I was once able to see the East River with the Fifty-ninth Street Bridge, glamorous at night with vari-colored lights. And on the west I was able to see the spires of St. Patrick's with the sun setting behind the

Hudson, looking, as St. John Gogarty once said, "like a bishop's bottom, rosy and round and hot." But over the years about fifty skyscrapers have obscured the views. Fortunately they are far enough removed to serve as a glittering theatre backdrop. I guess after fifty years in the theatre it is never far from my mind.

After *Colette* I produced only two more shows before 1975, *The Web and the Rock,* an adaptation of Thomas Wolfe's book, and *Love Suicide at Schofield Barracks* by Romulus Linney. Neither of them worked. It disturbs me to think that when I saw both of them, the first during a successful run at a small theatre in Washington, the second at Herbert Berghoff's Studio, I liked them and the audiences liked them. I have been unable to figure out clearly what sea change occurred when I presented them.

In order to keep eating, I taught a course in 1974 at Hunter College entitled "First Script to First Night," for students with a mania for producing. And I worked with a group of actors at Lee Strasberg's Institute. But I really don't care for teaching. It may be safe, but it is not as exciting as finding a play, working with an author, choosing a director, designer and a company of actors. And well, yes, reading rapturous reviews, however infrequent.

Epilogue

An epilogue seems obligatory for a book that opened with a prologue, but it does not mean that my theatrical activities have come to an end. In 1975 I saw a lovely production of *Yentl* by Isaac Bashevis Singer and Leah Napolin at the Chelsea Theatre in Brooklyn. Based on Singer's story "Yentl, the Yeshiva Boy," it told the bittersweet story of a girl too intelligent and independent to accept the traditional restrictions Orthodoxy imposed on women. Perhaps its theme touched a personal chord in me. In any case, I was so taken with *Yentl* that I joined the Chelsea and the producer Moe Septee in bringing it to Broadway, where it enjoyed a healthy run. It was a pleasure to work with the talented young Chelsea directors and to become a member of their Board. Allan Walker of *Newsday* wrote of them, "The moving forces of Chelsea are among the most adventurous and innovative people in the theatre." You might think that by now I would look on adventurous and innovative people with a jaundiced eye, but, as ever, I cannot resist. With Marilyn Stasio of *Cue* magazine, I "thank heaven for a theatre that still harbors a few sublime lunatics like the Chelsea. . . . What madness . . . how bold, how really eloquent the madness."

I have other irons in the fire. I dream of doing an *Othello* based on notes by Meyerhold, who also dreamed of doing it before he was imprisoned. I would cast Brock Peters as Othello and Frank Langello as Iago. Most Iagos I have seen play for slyness and evil, which makes Othello a fool to trust Iago. I see Iago played with deceptive openness and false charm.

Looking back, do I have regrets? Of course. Three in particular: my inability to discern some distinguished plays—those fateful "errors." Most of all, the collapse of the Actors Studio Theatre, to which so many talents were dedicated. Least of all, that I was never asked to have my caricature drawn to adorn the walls of Sardi's, where I have eaten—when I could afford it—since 1932.

Was I ever completely satisfied with a production? No, not entirely, but I tried to pursue excellence. Certainly I had a lot of failures. I also had flops. A failure is different from a flop: one can be proud of a failure. A flop is a failure undertaken for poor reasons—because, for instance, you think it will make money, even though you aren't really enthusiastic about it.

These days I debate with myself: should I go on? I wonder. Fifty years is a long time—a life time—to work at only one profession, and an evanescent one at that. What do I have to prove out there alone in the jungle? Why not sit back and enjoy life?

But it isn't a question of proving, not now. It's the teasing of dreams, the dream production of *Othello,* the dream production of—but I must keep my secrets.

People frequently ask me if the theatre is getting better or worse. I don't know the answer. Investors are harder and harder to come by, and although Broadway seems healthier this season, it is in the glowing color not in the blood. Producers and investors prefer plays with one set and few characters—to cut costs. That is suicide for creativity. Off-Broadway, which was once the breeding ground for special plays and new talents, is nearly dead; costs have risen about six hundred percent. Off-Broadway is now simply baby Broadway. No longer is it easy to do something there that is wild or original, just for the fun and arrogance and promise of it. Thus does economics affect playwriting. That is pitiful, for plays and playwrights are the backbone of the theatre.

I do know that as long as people are curious about human behavior there will certainly be a theatre: playwrights will write plays and audiences will attend them. It is true that there are fewer plays each season, but since the mid-twenties, when O'Neill began, we have had more plays that try to reveal us to ourselves, plays that are not meretricious parlor games for lazy minds. The ones that are successful run much longer than before and are even being made into movies for a wider public. Yes, even Hollywood has learned that there are more adults in the United States than they had suspected, and nearly all of our finest plays have been filmed without as much white-washing as there used to be. Today there are a large number of people who prefer to be people, not ostriches.

I believe that the advances made by science have increased people's curiosity, not diminished it. We have new social and economic mores, and many cherished prejudices and taboos now look false. As science probes for new truths, we become aware that society cannot remain the same. The theatre's task, as I see it, is to explore and illuminate these changes in personal terms.

To me the scientist and the artist are not opposed. Each is a discoverer. They constantly question and search. As Alfred North Whitehead said, "The major advances in civilization are processes which all but wreck the societies in which they occur." This cannot, and does not, deter the scientist or the writer. They seek new truths regardless of consequences. As the scientist experiments with fungus to find out more about how human beings breed, so the writer probes to find the answer to the mystery of even the most commonplace character, the subterranean motivations that make him both unique and universal.

Both science and art, then, educate us. Can we take it? I wonder. Only healthy people can stand to be shook up; I'm not certain how healthy our society is. What scientists tell us is often frightening: they have made us aware of a universe in which there are at least one hundred million galaxies, each containing one million or more planetary systems. And what about the fearsome new expression that has recently been added to one of the oldest dictionaries, the Catholic Vatican dictionary? It is the Latin for "atom bomb": *globus atomicus de displodens.* Yes, it makes us tremble, but it is something we have to face, examine and deal with.

Carl Van Doren once told me that after a lecture he delivered on the subject of One World, a woman jumped to her feet in anger and cried out, "Do you realize, sir, that you are endangering our *soverginity?*" As you can see, she was personally frightened, very personally, by this new concept.

Similarly, people complain that many of our playwrights emphasize the morbidity and violence of life. I've made my position clear: I think our writers truthfully reflect the general social uneasiness of our times and try to interpret it for our greater understanding. For me, the theatre is great when it leaves us stretched in every dimension—not just intrigued and charmed, but moved out of and beyond ourselves to a deeper understanding.

When playwrights have nothing to say, that is when the theatre will die. It is up to them to stir change—expand, explore, illuminate, attack the ethics and values of our society. Shaw and Ibsen tried to do this. Who now is bold enough to challenge us?

I wish we had more plays with characters we might emulate —not the goody-goody heroes and heroines of fairy tales, but men and women who struggle courageously for their beliefs against great odds. Whether they succeed or fail is not the point. The point is that they fight. They make us proud to be human. Gerard Manley Hopkins wrote some thrilling lines about human beings:

> Flesh fade, and mortal trash
> Fall to the residuary worm; world's wildfire, leave but ash:
> In a flash, at a trumpet crash,
> I am all at once what Christ is, since he was what I am, and
> This Jack, joke, poor potsherd, patch, matchwood, immortal
> diamond,
> Is immortal diamond.

Writers, pick up the gauntlet!

As for producers, our teeth have been pulled in the last thirty years by the power of the unions. We exert influence only by the force or persuasiveness of our personalities. It is true that before there were unions producers often took unfair advantage of the people they employed in the various crafts. But today I think the unions are frequently unfair to us. We all have a common dilemma, the skyrocketing cost of productions, of operating, of ticket prices that go up to make the first two feasible. Is anything or anybody going to change this? Is it impossible for all of us to discuss the problem and try to find a plan that would be to our mutual advantage?

In spite of all obstacles, younger dreamers frequently ask my advice. How can I become a producer? they ask. If they cannot be induced to engage in a more sensible profession; if they are not deterred by the failure of their best efforts or by panic over how to pay the rent and eat; if they are able to endure, without recriminations, scrubby betrayals by neurotic talents; if they can accept the power of those Cyclops critics; if they can persuade wealthy widows and smart moneymen who see no profit in their cherished dream to invest anyway; and if they have an overwhelming desire to entertain, to instruct, and to enjoy an unpredictable life doing so; then I have only one piece of advice to offer—Try.

Appendix

PRODUCTIONS

THE GROUP THEATRE

1931	*The House of Connelly* by Paul Green
	1931 by Claire and Paul Sifton
1932	*Night over Taos* by Maxwell Anderson
	Success Story by John Howard Lawson
1933	*Big Night* by Dawn Powell
	Men in White by Sidney Kingsley
1934	*Gentlewoman* by John Howard Lawson
	Gold Eagle Guy by Melvin Levy
1935	*Awake and Sing* by Clifford Odets
	Waiting for Lefty by Clifford Odets
	Till the Day I Die by Clifford Odets
	Weep for the Virgins by Nelisse Childs
	Paradise Lost by Clifford Odets
1936	*The Case of Clyde Griffiths* by Theodore Dreiser
	Johnny Johnson by Paul Green and Kurt Weill

INDEPENDENT

1937	*Yankee Fable* by Lewis Meltzer with Ina Claire (closed in Boston)
1938	*All the Living* by Hardie Albright
1939	*Family Portrait* by Leonore Coffee and William Cowen with Judith Anderson
1940	*Another Sun* by Dorothy Thompson with Celeste Holm

THE MAPLEWOOD THEATRE

1940   *Enter Madame* with Helen Menken
The School for Scandal with Ethel Barrymore
Criminal at Large with Florence Reed
Ah, Wilderness! with Sinclair Lewis
The Second Mrs. Tanqueray with Tallulah Bankhead
No Time for Comedy with Francis Lederer
Biography with Ina Claire
The Guardsman with Miriam Hopkins
Margin for Error with Sheldon Leonard
Ladies in Retirement with Flora Robson
The Royal Family with Edna Ferber and Louis Calhern
The Emperor Jones with Paul Robeson
The Male Animal—the New York cast with Elliott Nugent
Elmer the Great with Joe E. Brown
The Milky Way with Jack Haley
The Time of Your Life—the New York cast with Eddie Dowling
Smart Spot Varieties with Henny Youngman and Paul and Grace Hartman
The Big Story—a try-out
Private Lives with Ruth Chatterton
Beverly Hills—a try-out
Richelieu with Walter Hampden
Dante the Magician (Dante)

1941   *Twelfth Night* with Helen Hayes and Maurice Evans
Charlie's Aunt with José Ferrer
George Washington Slept Here with Charles Butterworth
Meet the Wife with Mary Boland
Mr. and Mrs. North with Peggy Conklin
Two for the Show with Paul and Grace Hartman
Her Cardboard Lover with Tallulah Bankhead
Old Acquaintance with Jane Cowl and Peggy Wood
Native Son with Canada Lee
The Man Who Came to Dinner with Clifton Webb
Johnny Belinda with Louise and Jean Platt
The Hot Mikado with Bill Robinson
Golden Boy with Sylvia Sidney and Luther Adler
Anna Christie with Ingrid Bergman
Autumn Crocus with Madge Kennedy and Francis Lederer
A Kiss for Cinderella with Luise Rainer and Dennis King
The Beautiful People—the New York cast

Our Betters with Ricardo Montalban and Elsa Maxwell
1942 *Reflected Glory* with Gloria Swanson
Escape Me Never with Elisabeth Bergner
Black Narcissus with Cornelia Otis Skinner
The Little Foxes with Tallulah Bankhead
Watch on the Rhine with Mady Christians
Pal Joey with Vivienne Segal
Porgy and Bess

INDEPENDENT

1942 *Porgy and Bess* by George and Ira Gershwin and DuBose
Heyward
The Flowers of Virtue by Marc Connelly
A Kiss for Cinderella by James Barrie with Luise Rainer
1943 *One Touch of Venus* by S. J. Perelman, Ogden Nash and Kurt
Weill with Mary Martin
1944 *The Perfect Marriage* by Samson Raphaelson with Miriam
Hopkins and Victor Jory
1945 *The Tempest* by Shakespeare with Vera Zorina and Canada
Lee

AMERICAN REPERTORY THEATRE

1946 *Henry VIII* by Shakespeare
What Every Woman Knows by James Barrie
John Gabriel Borkman by Henrik Ibsen
Androcles and the Lion by George Bernard Shaw
1947 *Alice in Wonderland* adapted by Eva Le Gallienne
Yellow Jack by Sidney Howard

INDEPENDENT

1947 *Brigadoon* by Alan Jay Lerner and Frederick Loewe
Galileo by Berthold Brecht with Charles Laughton [For
ANTA]
1948 *Skipper Next to God* by Jan de Hartog with John Garfield [For
ANTA]
A Temporary Island by Halsted Welles with Vera Zorina [For
ANTA]
Love Life by Alan Jay Lerner and Kurt Weill with Nanette
Fabray and Ray Middleton
Ballet Ballads by John La Touche and Jerome Moross [For
ANTA]

1949   *Regina* by Marc Blitzstein with Jane Pickens
        The Closing Door by Alexander Knox

1950   *Tower Beyond Tragedy* by Robinson Jeffers with Judith Anderson [For ANTA]

1951   *Peer Gynt* by Henrik Ibsen with John Garfield [For ANTA]
        The Rose Tattoo by Tennessee Williams with Maureen Stapleton and Eli Wallach
        Flahooley by Fred Saide, Yip Harburg and Sammy Fain with Barbara Cook, Ernest Truex and Yma Sumac
        Paint Your Wagon by Alan Jay Lerner and Frederick Loewe with James Barton and Olga San Juan

1953   *Camino Real* by Tennessee Williams with Eli Wallach
        Oh Men! Oh Women! by Edward Chodorov with Franchot Tone

1954   *Trouble in Tahiti* by Leonard Bernstein
        The Thirteen Clocks by James Thurber (1 bill; summer stock)

1955   *The Honeys* by Roald Dahl with Jessica Tandy, Hume Cronyn and Dorothy Stickney
        Reuben Reuben by Marc Blitzstein with Eddie Albert

1956   *Mr. Johnson* by Joyce Cary, adapted by Norman Rosten
        Girls of Summer by N. Richard Nash with Shelley Winters

1957   *Good as Gold* by John Patrick with Roddy MacDowell

1958   *Comes the Day* by Speed Lamkin with Judith Anderson
        Shadow of a Gunman by Sean O'Casey with Susan Strasberg

1959   *The Rivalry* by Norman Corwin with Richard Boone
        Sweet Bird of Youth by Tennessee Williams with Geraldine Page and Paul Newman

1960   *The Long Dream* by Ketti Frings
        Kukla Burr and Ollie
        Period of Adjustment by Tennessee Williams

1962   *Brecht on Brecht* by Berthold Brecht with Lotte Lenya, Anne Jackson, Viveca Lindfors, Dane Clark, George Voskovec, Michael Wager

1963   *Andorra* by Max Frisch with Hugh Griffith and Horst Buchholz
        Mother Courage by Berthold Brecht with Anne Bancroft
        Jennie by Arnold Schulman, Arthur Schwartz and Howard Dietz with Mary Martin

ACTORS STUDIO THEATRE

1963   *Strange Interlude* by Eugene O'Neill with Geraldine Page and Franchot Tone

Marathon 33 by June Havoc with Julie Harris

1964 *Dynamite Tonight* by Arnold Weinstein and Bill Bolcom with Barbara Harris and Gene Wilder

Baby Want a Kiss by James Costigan with Paul Newman and Joanne Woodward

Blues for Mr. Charlie by James Baldwin with Rip Torn and Diana Sands

The Three Sisters by Anton Chekhov with Kim Stanley, Geraldine Page, Shirley Knight, Barbara Baxley and Kevin McCarthy

INDEPENDENT

1966 *Chu Chem* by Ted Allen and Mitch Leigh with Molly Picon and Menasha Skulnik

1967 *The Freaking Out of Stephanie Blake* by Richard Chandler with Jean Arthur

Scandal Point by John Patrick

1969 *Celebration* by Tom Jones and Harvey Schmidt

1970 *Colette* by Elinor Jones with Zoe Caldwell and Mildred Dunnock

1971 *The Web and the Rock* by Tom Wolfe, adapted by Dolores Sutton

1972 *Love Suicide at Schofield Barracks* by Romulus Linney

CHELSEA THEATRE

1975 *Yentl* by Isaac Bashevis Singer and Leah Napolin with Tovah Feldshuh